当代国际商务文化阅读丛书

Readings for Modern International Business Culture

强烈的第一印象

——『商务礼仪』篇

A Powerful First Impression

Business Etiquette

【英汉对照】

吴斐 编著

武汉大学出版社
WUHAN UNIVERSITY PRESS

图书在版编目(CIP)数据

强烈的第一印象:"商务礼仪"篇:英汉对照/吴斐编著.—武汉:武汉大学出版社,2016.5

当代国际商务文化阅读丛书

书名原文:A Powerful First Impression:Business Etiquette

ISBN 978-7-307-13996-1

Ⅰ.强…　Ⅱ.吴…　Ⅲ.商务—礼仪—英、汉　Ⅳ.F718

中国版本图书馆 CIP 数据核字(2014)第 181987 号

封面图片为上海富昱特授权使用(ⓒ IMAGEMORE Co., Ltd.)

责任编辑:郭园园　金　军　　责任校对:鄢春梅　　版式设计:韩闻锦

出版发行:**武汉大学出版社**　(430072　武昌　珞珈山)

(电子邮件:cbs22@whu.edu.cn 网址:www.wdp.com.cn)

印刷:武汉中远印务有限公司

开本:880×1230　1/32　印张:10.875　字数:238 千字

版次:2016 年 5 月第 1 版　　2016 年 5 月第 1 次印刷

ISBN 978-7-307-13996-1　　定价:28.00 元

前　言

人类社会进入 21 世纪后，国家间的商务往来更加频繁，商务交际手段随着互联网的诞生和电子信息的进步日新月异，国际化企业的文化和理念千差万别，商务话题的表达和沟通能力无疑是人们所遇到的最大障碍。 在我们熟知的生活英语、学术英语之外，商务英语不仅是我国目前从事或即将从事涉外商务人员英语实际应用能力不可多得的辅助工具，更是商务工作人员在这个国际化的高科技时代商务竞争能力、外贸业务素质和英语水平的重要体现。《当代国际商务文化阅读》(英汉对照)丛书以从事国际商务活动所必需的语言技能为经，以各种商务活动的具体情景做纬，将商务精神和商务元素巧妙融合，展示时尚而又经典的商务文化世界流行风，为广大读者提供一套语言规范、内容新颖、涉及面广、趣味性强、具有实用价值、富于时代精神的读物，既注意解决人们在国际商务环境中因遇到不熟悉的专业词汇而无法与外国合作者就工作问题交流沟通的难题，又着力解决人们学外语单纯地学语言而缺乏商务专业知识的弊端。

《当代国际商务文化阅读》(英汉对照)丛书由 10 个单行本组成:《拥抱新欢亚马逊(Embracing Amazon Service)——电子商务篇(E-Commerce)》、《华尔街梦魇 (Nightmare on Wall Street)——商界风云篇（The Business Circles）》、《路易斯·波森的朋克摇滚（The Punk Rock of Louis Posen）——商界精英篇（Business Elites）》、《希波克拉底誓言（Hippocratic Oath）——商务交际篇（Business Communication）》、《强烈的第一印象（A Powerful First Impression）——商务礼仪篇（Business Etiquette）》、《企业帝国继承权之争（Corporate Empires' Grappling with Succession）——商务文化篇（Business Culture）》、《紫色血液（The Purple Blood）——商务心理篇（Business Psychology）》、《多米诺骨牌效应（The Domino Effects）——商务知识篇（Business Knowledge）》、《公开的赌注（Public Stakes）——商务演讲篇（Business Speeches）》、《伊斯特林悖论（The Easterlin Paradox）——感悟财富篇（Comprehension of Wealth）》。这套丛书的编写旨在帮助读者在国际商务环境下，能够读懂英文的商务信息和商务新闻，并能对某一商务话题的知识有全面透彻的了解，领悟当代时尚商务文化成长的环境和思维方式，提高在全球化高科技时代的商务竞争能力、外贸业务素质和英语交际水平。丛书中的阅读材料力求做到题材广泛，内容精辟，语言规范，遵循趣味性、知识性和时效性原则，培养读者在商务环境下的英语竞争能力和综合应用能力。丛书融时代性与经典性为一体，内容经得起时间考验，文字经得起反复咀嚼，保证其可读性。读者在阅读过程中接收大量的语言输入，为合理组织和娴熟运用英语语言表达自己的思想打下牢固的基础。丛书的单行本包括以一个主题为中心的30篇文章，每篇文章包括题记、英语原文、汉语译文、生词脚注和知识链接。"题记"用丰富生动的语言点评文章的精髓，对文章的内容起到提炼和画龙点睛的作用。"英语原文"主要摘自当代国际主流报纸杂志，具有语言规范、内容新颖、涉及面广、趣味性和时代感等特点。"汉语译文"力求准确流畅，既关注译文的文化语境及其内涵，也重视译文的外延和现当代标志性语言符号。"生词脚注"的难度把握在大学英语六级和研究生英语词汇程度，以帮助读者及时扫清阅读障碍。"知识链接"根据文章内容，或精解一个专业术语、或阐释一种新的商务理念、或介绍叱咤商界的企业或公司，以帮助读者培养游弋商海、运筹帷幄的能力，具备洞悉中西文化的国际视野。

《强烈的第一印象》(A Powerful First Impression)——"商务礼仪"篇(Business Etiquette)给读者展示了一个璀璨斑斓的商务礼仪世界，包括商务交际礼仪，商务办公礼仪，商务着装礼仪，电子邮件礼仪，商务聚餐礼仪，商务电话礼仪，商务旅行礼仪，求职面试礼仪等。商务交际礼仪在交往越来越密切、越来越频繁的高度商业化时代，犹如一面移动的广告牌，不仅营造出企业家的踏实和自信，也对商务伙伴形成了强烈的第一印象。而在以男性为主导的国际经济舞台上，职场女性的行为举止恰似一道亮丽的风景，她们融汇了法国女性饮誉五洲的优雅、美国女性震撼政坛的魅力、英国女性享受生活的经典、亚洲女性热爱家庭的风范。商务办公礼仪为商务人士打造出细意浓情的人性化管理和服务礼仪，既帮助商务人员塑造了良好的个人形象，也折射出企业的文化水平和企业的管理境界。商务着装礼仪展现了企业领袖和员工的风度和仪态，向他人积极地传递着事业心、人品、能力等信息。商务男士的职业着装对时尚的追求从一季到下一季的变化并不明显，而商务女士的职业着装则需要符合女性的行业和行业内的职位和头衔，以及女性优雅得体的商务公关能力。电子邮件礼仪——netiquette（network etiquette）带来了 3G 时代互联网革命的成果和商务交往的动态变迁，越来越多的人在商业洽谈和日常沟通中对电子邮件趋之若鹜。商务聚餐礼仪可以归结为常识加上善意，尽情享受进餐和朋友们带来的愉悦，同时心无旁骛地与他人自由交换商务信息，顺理成章地达成交易。商务电话礼仪在某种意义上是企业的生命线，它使企业的生命绚丽多彩，充满探索的欲望和好奇的动力，朝着通向成功的道路展开并延伸。商务旅行礼仪讲述着世界各国的社会规范和礼仪准则，敦促频繁地穿梭于海外的商务人士遵守不同国家的不同习惯和风俗、同一种行为在不同国家表达的不同文化。求职面试礼仪帮助求职者将自身良好的气质和渊博的学识等静态因素转变成动态的竞争力，在物欲横流、竞争日益激烈的世界中坚守自己的道德底线，成功获得梦寐以求的职位。

本书的主要阅读文章包括：商务交际礼仪，商务办公礼仪，商务着装礼仪，电子邮件礼仪，商务聚餐礼仪，商务电话礼仪，商务旅行礼仪，求职面试礼仪以及各国商务礼仪和它们的文化背景。

商务礼仪在商务活动过程中，以尊重、友好和真诚的姿态，指导、协调着商务活动中人际关系的行为方式和活动形式，约束着人们日常商务活动的方方面面。阅读风靡全球的商务礼仪，让我们鉴赏企业和商务人士焕发出的自信的光环和气场，突破和化解社交困境，建立持久的个人魅力和竞争优势，为企业搭建走向成功的阶梯，享受世界流行文化创造的快乐、荣誉、价值和成就感！

作　者

2016 年 1 月

目　录

目　录

题 记

在八仙过海、各显其能的商界打拼，良好的第一印象对未来的发展起到了举足轻重的作用。商务人士的举手投足、穿着打扮、行为方式和相貌外表构成了一种特殊的气场，这些肢体语言营造出企业家的踏实和自信。将谈话视作网球比赛，提高双方交流的频率，积极表达欣赏不仅给他人一种支持和力量，也是调剂人际关系的灵丹妙药。说话单调的企业家令人沮丧，说话太平静的企业家给人反复无常的感觉，语速太快的企业家冲淡了信息，因此，掌控说话的方式是初次见面取得成功的关键。简而言之，在交往越来越密切、越来越频繁的高度商业化时代，企业领袖和员工的风度和仪态就是公司的一面移动广告牌，他们对商务伙伴形成了强烈的第一印象。

A Powerful First Impression

Learn the art of presence and small talk from communications experts who swear you can do it even if you don't think you can.

If it's true that time is money, then it's small wonder business owners find they can never truly clock out. Wherever they go and whomever they meet, entrepreneurs are walking billboards for their companies.

In a tough economy, where advertising budgets are cut to the bone①, that kind of person-to-person marketing is more important than ever. But if you're a billboard, how can you be sure you're communicating the right message? How do you get people to notice you without offending, boring or confusing them?

Body language

Lillian Bjorseth, a communications consultant and author of *Breakthrough Networking*, says people decide many things about you within 10 seconds of seeing you—usually before you even open your mouth. That's why entrepreneurs should always be conscious of their aura②, she says.

---

① be cut to the bone 大幅度地减少某事物

② aura [ˈɔːrə] *n.* 特殊气氛

强烈的第一印象

如果想从沟通专家那里学习仪态和聊天的艺术，即使你认为你做不到，他们也能保证一定让你学会。

如果时间确实是金钱，那么企业家发现他们从未下班休息过就一点也不奇怪了。无论身在何处，与何人见面，企业家们都是公司的移动广告牌。

在困难的经济形势下，广告预算已经削减到底限，这种人与人之间的营销比以往任何时候都更加重要。但是，如果你一旦成为广告牌，又怎样确定你传递的是正确信息呢？你怎样吸引人们的注意力而又不使他们感到厌恶、无聊或迷惑呢？

肢体语言

沟通顾问及《突破网络》的作者莉莲·布爵森斯认为，人们在见到你的最初10秒钟内就可以判断出关于你的很多事情，而且经常是在你开口说话之前。她表示，这就是为什么企业家应该始终意识到自己的光环。

她说：“你的穿着打扮、行为方式和相貌外表造成了你周围的气场。这一切共同构建出一种印象。你可以穿非常昂贵的西装，但

"The aura is the area around you that you create by what you wear, how you act, how you look," she says. "It all goes together to make one impression. You could wear a very expensive suit, but if you stand slumped over with your head down, you won't give a confident aura."

Though every person's aura is complex and unique, Bjorseth says entrepreneurs can focus on a few simple, non-verbal priorities to appear confident and in control. First, don't slip into a room "all smiles." Instead, "claim your space" in the room by planting your feet six inches to eight inches apart, one slightly ahead of the other—a stance that will make you feel grounded and confident.

After you've established eye contact, Bjorseth says a smile will create an upbeat, positive environment. Maintain eye contact 85 percent of the time during a conversation, she recommends. Doing so will make you seem trustworthy *and* it will demonstrate that you're interested in what the other person has to say.

To avoid a fumbling① introduction, Bjorseth says every entrepreneur should have in mind a "verbal business card"—a quick, 30-word summary of who you are and what you can do. Focus on benefits for the other person rather than job titles or even company names, she recommends. "You want to make sure people remember you as opposed to others who do the same thing you do."

Conversation

When it's time to move beyond the handshake stage, simple conversational skills are the key to a successful first meeting, says Rosalie Maggio, bestselling author of *How to Say It* and *The Art of Talking to*

---

① fumbling[ˈfʌmbliŋ] *adj*. 盲目的

如果你站在那儿耷拉着头无精打采，就难以营造自信的光环。”

虽然每个人的光环复杂而独特，但莉莲认为，企业家可以优先关注少数简单、非语言的行为，以显示自信并控制场面。首先，不要“满脸堆笑”地进入房间。同时，双脚保持6~8英寸的距离，一只脚伸到另外一只脚前面一点的地方，在房间里“索要你的空间”。这是一种让你感到踏实和自信的姿态。

莉莲认为，在建立目光接触之后，微笑能够创造一种乐观、积极的环境。她建议人们在交谈中保持85%的目光接触时间。这样做会使你看起来值得信赖，并表明你对他人说的事情感兴趣。

莉莲认为，为了避免初次见面的尴尬，每个企业家都应该时刻记住“口头名片”，即一份简短约三十字的总结，说明你是谁及你能做什么。她建议，企业家要关注他人的利益，而不是职务名称，甚至是公司的名字。“混在做同样事情的人群中，要确保人们能够记住你。”

交谈

畅销书《怎么说》和《与人会话的艺术》的作者罗莎莉·马乔认为，握手环节结束之后，简单的会话技巧是初次见面取得成功的关键。

她说：“提前做好准备，并尝试忘掉自己。过于强调自我意识只会搬起石头砸自己的脚，这是最快的方式。要记住，其实交谈的是别人的事情——这才是最有可能取得积极的第一印象的方法。”

Anyone .

"Prepare in advance, then just try to forget yourself," she says. "Being too self-conscious is the quickest way to shoot yourself in the foot. Remember that it's about the other person—that's the best possible way to make a positive first impression."

To help shift focus to the other person, Maggio says a bit of small talk is appropriate in almost every setting. When meeting someone new, the conversation should resemble a tennis match, with each participant taking a quick swing before sending it back to the other person. Too many Americans confuse their sports metaphors, treating a conversation "more like golf, where you just keep hitting your own ball over and over again... If you've talked for more than a minute, it's too long."

From formal pitches to impromptu[1] meetings at a trade show, no two conversations will ever be the same. But Maggio says one element is critical no matter what the setting: the ability to show appreciation.

"In every conversation, include at leastone appreciative remark," she says. "Praise the other person's business acumen, charity work, or even her taste in shoes. As long as the appreciation is brief, sincere, and specific, the feeling will be remembered long after the words are forgotten."

Voice

Beyond body language and conversational skills, the actual tone of your voice is an important part of the impression you create, says Sandra McKnight, owner of Voice Power Studios in Santa Fe, N.M.

"In face-to-face conversation, the other person first sees you, then hears the tone of your voice, and only then listens to your words. It can

---

① impromptu [imˈprɔmptjuː] *adj*. 临时的

马乔认为，为了把焦点转移到他人身上，几乎在任何场合下都可以找机会聊天。与陌生人见面时，谈话应该像一场网球比赛，每个参与者快速地来回移动，然后将球打回给对方。太多的美国人搞错了运动的引申含义，认为会话“更像高尔夫球赛，只不过是一次又一次地击自己的球……如果你谈话的时间超过一分钟，就有点太长了”。

在交易会上，无论是正式场合还是临时会面，两种交谈方式从来都不会相同。但是马乔认为，无论是哪种场合，都存在一个至关重要的元素——表达欣赏的能力。

她说：“在每次会话的过程中，至少要包含表示欣赏的言辞。称赞对方的商业头脑、慈善工作，甚至是夸奖对方鞋子的品位。只要这种欣赏是短暂的、真诚的和具体的，即使人们会忘记那些话，这种感觉却会长久地保留在心中。”

表达

新墨西哥州圣特菲声音功率工作室的老板桑德拉·麦克奈特指出，除了肢体语言和会话技巧，声音的实际语调也是给人留下印象的重要组成部分。

“面对面交谈时，对方首先看到你这个人，然后听到你的声调，只有在这之后才会听到你说的话。如果你没有掌控说话的方式，很容易产生消极的印象。”

说话单调的企业家令人沮丧，而说话太平静的企业家给人反复

create a negative impression very easily if you're not in control of the way you speak."

Entrepreneurs who speak in monotone will be perceived as uninspiring, while those who speak too quietly will come across as uncertain. But the most common problem, McKnight says, is speed-talking, which dilutes the message and makes the speaker sound anxious.

"Bright people have a tendency to talk fast because their minds move fast," she says. "But it's not about data dumping. It's about communicating so that you're understood."

To ensure that you're speaking at the right pace, McKnight suggests reading aloud from a book for 60 seconds. When time is up, go back and count the words in the selection you just read. The ideal speaking pace, she says, is about 145 words per minute—but don't forget that you probably speak even faster than you read.

The keys to creating a positive first impression aren't secrets that are hidden away and accessible only through visits to an oracle or a high-priced seminar. Body language, conversation and voice are three of the most important aspects of a first impression. The bad news is too many people think they lack skill in these areas. The good news is that most anyone can practice each of them and master their first impression.

(910 words)

无常的感觉。麦克奈特指出，最常见的问题是说话语速太快，语速冲淡了信息，使说话人听起来带有焦虑感。

她说："聪明的人有一种倾向，他们由于思维敏捷而语速很快。但这不是数据倾泻。这是交流信息，以便你可以被他人理解。"

为了保证说话时的语速正常，麦克奈特建议花 60 秒的时间大声朗读一本书。时间一到，回头数一数你刚刚选读的字数。她说，理想的说话语速大概是每分钟 145 个单词，但请记住，你说话很有可能比阅读更快。

留下积极的第一印象的关键并不是被隐匿的秘密，也不是拜访哲人或参加高价研讨班就可以掌握的技巧。肢体语言、交谈和表达是留下第一印象的三个最重要的方面。不幸的是，太多的人认为他们缺乏这些方面的能力。幸运的是，大多数人都可以逐一练习这三种技能，掌握他们的第一印象。

知识链接

First impression 第一印象。在与陌生人交往的过程中，所得到的有关对方的最初印象称为第一印象。第一印象在日常生活中非常普遍，它主要是根据对方的表情、姿态、身体、仪表和服装等形成的看法和感觉，往往成为今后交往的依据。

题　记

石油王国沙特阿拉伯是一片幸福的沙漠，它的石油储量和产量均居世界首位，使其成为世界上最富裕的国家之一。时光在绿色的枣椰树下流逝，随着清真寺宣礼塔传出的召唤声荏苒，经济的全球化悄然推开了沙特阿拉伯对外商贸的大门。但是，尽管人们在咖啡厅和会客室对国家的未来明智而踊跃地高谈阔论，沙特阿拉伯的社会和习俗并没有和经济同步前进，它仍然是一个保守的穆斯林社会。那些根深蒂固的沙特商务礼仪，伴随着时光的流逝和历史的演进，在长期的潜移默化中深入人心：永远对他人表示尊重，千万、千万不要对官员发脾气，避免在工作场所与女性单独相处是基本的商务规范，不可过多谈论有关政治与宗教等问题。古老的阿拉伯伊斯兰文化传统及其伦理道德价值观念在沙特华丽的商务礼仪中得到了最充分的体现和发挥。

Times Change in Saudi Arabia

How quickly, and slowly, times change in Saudi Arabia. A few years ago the Islamic extremist insurgency[1] had many expatriate[2] families fleeing for the safety and creature comforts of neighbouring Bahrain and Dubai. Embassies barred non-essential travel to the oil-rich kingdom as bombings and kidnappings targeting foreigners turned the dream of tax-free salaries into a macabre[3] nightmare.

Now, business is booming again—and the memories of those darker days have receded. A six-year bull run in the energy markets has left the world's biggest oil exporter with hundreds of billions of dollars in surplus revenues. A commitment to building infrastructure and reforming the economy has also opened the doors for foreign companies to do business in the Gulf market with the most untapped potential, from construction, engineering and finance all the way through to retail.

But the businessmen—and it is still usually men—travelling to the capital, Riyadh, the more liberal trading centre of Jeddah or oil

---

① insurgency [inˈsɜːdʒənsi] *n.* 叛乱

② expatriate [eksˈpætrieit] *n.* 脱离国籍的人

③ macabre [məˈkɑːbr(ə)] *adj.* 令人毛骨悚然的

时光在沙特阿拉伯流逝

时光缓慢地流淌，又转瞬即逝，沙特阿拉伯悄然发生着变化。几年前，穆斯林极端分子的暴动迫使许多家庭逃离本土，移居到安全和衣食无忧的邻国巴林和迪拜。各国使馆禁止本国公民前往这个盛产石油的王国进行非必要的旅游，因为狂轰滥炸和把外国人作为绑架目标的行径使无税收的美梦变成了令人毛骨悚然的梦魇。

现在，商业重新恢复了繁荣，那些不堪回首的日子在记忆中慢慢消退。能源市场六年的牛市行情使这个世界上最大的原油输出国获得了数千亿美元的额外收入。建设基础设施和重整经济的承诺也为外国公司打开了商贸的大门，业务包括建筑、工程、金融、零售等所有最具潜力、尚未开发的海湾市场。

但是，越是靠近沙特阿拉伯西部港市吉达的自由贸易中心或东部省份艾尔·霍巴等原油卫星城，前往首都利雅得做生意的商人（通常还是男性）越是应该记住，沙特阿拉伯的社会和习俗并没有和经济同步前进。它仍然是一个保守的穆斯林社会，尽管人们在咖啡厅和会客室对国家的未来明智而踊跃地高谈阔论。

大英帝国即将衰退之时，枯槁憔悴的外籍人士来到这个气候灼热的海湾。他们的旅行指南和这批日暮西山的群体均列出了一长串

conurbation[①] of Al-Khobar in the eastern province, should also remember that Saudi society and customs have not necessarily moved on at the same clip as the economy. It is still a very conservative Muslim society—despite a healthy dose of debate about the country's future heard across the coffee shops and parlours[②].

Guidebooks and the declining breed of wizened old expatriates who came out to the scorching climes of the Gulf when the British Empire was only starting its decline will lay out a long list of "dos and don'ts". This guide is deemed essential for the confused foreigner to make his way through the etiquette minefield of this society that remains rooted firmly in the desert life of the Bedouin: never show the soles of one's feet; never use your left (toilet) hand to eat or shake hands; and don't ask after the health of your contact's wife.

While abiding by these old customs cannot hurt, nor is breaking them such a crime these days, there are few faux pas that a little common courtesy and politeness will not fix.

"Always show respect, especially to elders—it's best to be over polite in English as that is the closest to correspond with Arabic's flowery etiquette," says a European businessman with years of experience in the kingdom. "That doesn't mean you can't be tough when negotiating-just always be polite."

There are also some red lines.

Travellers should still be aware of tight security in the kingdom to control the lingering threat of extremist attacks.

Be careful when photographing. One hapless executive got himself

---

① conurbation [ˌkɔnəˈbeiʃən] *n.* 具有许多卫星城的大城市

② parlour [ˈpɑːlə] *n.* 会客室

的“注意事项”。人们认为这个手册对那些困惑的外国人很有必要，帮助他们顺利通过这个社会的礼仪雷区，这些礼仪在贝都因人的沙漠生活方式中根深蒂固，如从不露出脚底；从不用左手吃饭或握手（入厕时使用左手）；从不问候对方妻子的健康情况。

尽管遵守这些古老的风俗不会让你受伤，现在破坏它们也不算犯罪，但如果不会处理一些常见的礼仪和礼貌也会相当失礼。

一位在阿拉伯王国具有多年生活经验的欧洲商人认为，“永远对他人表示尊重，特别是对长者。最好是用相当礼貌的英文，因为这种方式几乎最符合阿拉伯人的华丽礼仪。这并不意味谈判时你不可以强硬，只是要常常注意礼貌”。

下面是一道道不可逾越的红色警戒线。

旅行者还应该知道，为了控制极端分子持续的威胁和攻击，沙特阿拉伯王国戒备森严。

拍照时要小心。一个倒霉的高管在带着相机和地图找住处时遇到了麻烦。他不幸与安全部队发生了争执，这场事故引起了一场愤怒的冲突，他也极不情愿地被送进监狱关了两天。

然而，拍照在这里还不是最糟糕的过错，最糟糕的莫过于对官场放肆的反应。所以黄金法则是：千万、千万不要对官员发脾气。

笃信宗教的警察在祷告期间带穆斯林信徒闯入清真寺、强制沙特阿拉伯人实行性别隔离，这种现象极为罕见。众所周知，这些美德的守护者已经影响了沙特阿拉伯国际会议的潮流，他们采取了一些更为自由的规范：女士可以揭开面纱，自由地和男士交往，而不

into trouble while searching for accommodation with a camera and maps. An unfortunate incident with the security forces led to an angry confrontation and an uncomfortable two-day stint① in jail.

Still, the photography probably was not the worst offence here—it was the intemperate② reaction to officialdom. The golden rule: never, ever lose your temper with officials.

It is rare to come across the religious police, who drive Muslims into mosques at prayer times and enforce Saudi society's gender segregation. These guardians of virtue have been known to descend upon international conferences in the kingdom, which have adopted some more liberal codes: women—unveiled—mixing freely with men, rather than participating from a separate room. Conferences provide the easiest avenue for single businesswomen to enter the kingdom, but invitations from companies can also work. The government has permitted single women to stay in hotels alone, while some women travellers stay at furnished apartments attached to hotels—but the rules continue to make it difficult for women to travel without a male guardian.

Similarly, western businessmen travelling to the kingdom with their wives should adopt a cautious and polite attitude if challenged by the religious police. Non-Muslim women should wear the voluminous③ abaya to cover the entire body, while keeping to hand a headscarf to wear in public—though many Saudis no longer expect foreigners to cover their hair. Last, to err on the safe side, westerners should avoid being alone with a woman in the workplace.

---

① stint [stint] *n.* 限制

② intemperate [inˈtempəreit] *adj.* 无节制的;放纵的

③ voluminous [vəˈljuːminəs] *adj.* 大量的;庞大的

是在一个隔离的房间里参加会议。会议为未婚女商人提供进入王国的最便捷的路径，来自公司的邀请也同样奏效。政府允许未婚女士单独待在旅馆，而有些女性旅行者则住在附属于旅馆的带家具的公寓中，但是，女士还是必须在男士监护人的陪伴下才可以外出旅行，要突破这些规则非常困难。

同样，携妻同行的西方商人在进入王国时，若不受笃信宗教的警察欢迎，就应该在他们面前表现出谨慎和礼貌。非穆斯林教徒的女性应该穿宽大的长袍遮住整个身体，同时手边放一条头巾，以备在公开场合佩戴，尽管许多阿拉伯人不再认为外国人需要遮盖他们的头发。最后，为稳妥起见，西方人应该避免在工作场所与女性单独相处。

如果把性别政治放在一边，大多数来访的商人在寻求达成协议或建立新的联系之时，往往会发现大量不可抗拒的魅力。长期在此居住的沙特人敦促游客花尽可能多的时间与他们潜在的商业合作伙伴打交道。

边喝咖啡边随意交谈是打破沉默的有效方式。摇晃一下甜甜的、豆蔻炮制的咖啡或姜汁咖啡（一种用咖啡外壳制作的饮料）的小杯子，表示你已经喝得差不多了，借此显示你的文化常识。午餐和晚餐的宴会通常以传统的烤羊肉和大米为主。在丰盛、隆重的餐桌中央的主菜端上来之前，会上很多道菜肴，所以，请掌握好吃的节奏。

私下交谈的内容会很广泛，并常常涉及政治。最好不要评议当

Gender politics aside, most visiting businessmen will find plenty of charm as they seek to close a deal or make new contacts. Longstanding Saudi residents urge visitors to spend as long as possible with their potential business partners.

Plenty of small talk over coffee is a great way to break the ice. You can show off your cultural nous by shaking the small cups of sweet, cardamom-infused coffee or qishr—a drink hewn from the coffee husks—to signal that you've had enough. Lunch and dinner usually revolves around a traditional feast of roast lamb and rice. And many courses can arrive before the rich, heavy centrepiece arrives—so pace yourself.

In private, conversations can be expansive, often covering politics. It may be best to refrain from commenting on the local political situation, but mocking US presidents—a common thread in the Saudi conversation these days—is probably OK.

"The interface between religion and politics isn't something Saudis like to talk about with strangers, but if conversation moves to the case for change and how things moved on and where is it going and general conversations—there isn't a problem with that," says one seasoned diplomat. "It's all down to presentation—nice polite conversation and interest in society works—but going for the throat and asking difficult questions isn't a good thing."

(890 words)

地的政治局势，但是嘲弄美国总统，这是如今阿拉伯人交谈中的常见话题，应该没有问题。

一位经验丰富的外交官认为，“阿拉伯人不喜欢和陌生人交换对宗教和政治的看法。但是，如果谈话涉及变革、事情如何发展、发展到什么地步以及一般的交谈时，就不会有问题。这一切要归结于表达方式，即细致入微的礼貌交谈和对社会工作的兴趣。但切中要害和询问棘手的问题并不是什么好事情”。

知识链接

Business appointments in Saudi Arabia 沙特阿拉伯的商务预约。在沙特阿拉伯做生意，像其他阿拉伯国家一样，会见松散不守时，但会见须事先预约。即使是约定的时间去拜会，最好仍需在日程上留一点余地，因为对方晚到15~30分钟是常有的事。沙特阿拉伯的公司依类别而定，上班时间千差万别，夜间上班的公司也很多，最好约对方到咖啡店单独谈判。在洽谈业务时，沙特阿拉伯的商务人员常被来往人员打断。阿拉伯人认为这是“家庭”的延伸，不认为是失礼。遇到这种情况，一是耐心等待，二是预约到外面单独洽谈。

The Bedouin 贝都因人。贝都因人原住阿拉伯半岛，后来随着游牧业的发展逐渐扩散到西亚、北非许多国家，绝大部分为穆斯林沙漠游牧民族，一般生活在沙漠、荒原、丘陵和农区边缘地带，靠饲养骆驼为生，其中生活在沙特阿拉伯的人数最多。他们使用当地的阿拉伯方言及阿拉伯文，信仰伊斯兰教。现在许多贝都因部落已经放弃游牧生活进入都市生活或半游牧生活。

题　记

当人们乐此不疲地谈论着法国女性饮誉五洲的优雅，美国女性震撼政坛的魅力，英国女性享受生活的经典，亚洲女性热爱家庭的风范时，职场女性恰似一道亮丽的风景，丰富了人们茶余饭后的谈资。在以男性为主导的国际经济舞台上，她们的行为举止格外引人注目。但是，与职场女性打交道还需小心翼翼，绝对不可恪守约定俗成的思维方式和与生俱来的偏见。不要企图与女性主管单独相处，不要认定女性会因为家中有孩子就把事业看得不那么重要，不要假设女性主管只是撑场面的女人，不要使美丽的职场女性产生边缘化的感觉，不要在工作场所谈论女性的年龄，不要从女性的角度赞扬女性主管的成就，不要打探女性主管的隐私。女性主管是职场的一支伟大力量，她们中的很多人都是行业的佼佼者；女性主管是一本意犹未尽的书，需要细细品尝，耐心咀嚼。

Things NEVER to Say to Women Executives

Sometimes, a term of endearment can be anything but endearing.

"I had this manager who started referring to me as 'honey,'" recalls May Snowden, former chief diversity officer for both Starbucks and Eastman Kodak Co., who is now president and CEO of Snowden & Associates, Inc. "It was when I took my first director position. I was in a male-dominated job in the telecommunications industry and I did not want to embarrass him in front of his peers, so I invited him to my office and indicated that 'I won't call you sweetie if you won't call me honey.' We had that little conversation and he stopped. He was really embarrassed, and because he calls his wife, his daughters and other women 'honey', he did not even think about it."

"We all come to the table with biases and histories and upbringings in life that give us a perspective that may have 20, 30 years behind it," says Sherry Nolan, vice president of diversity and organizational capabilities at Pepsi Bottling Group. "The truth of the matter is that we all come to the table with different perspectives, and what we'd rather have is folks saying, 'Hey, how do I address that? ' or 'How would you like me to think about this? ' or 'What should I call you? ' We use this notion

绝对不能对女性主管说的话

有时候，除了“亲爱的”这一称谓，爱称能够表示任何东西。

星巴克和伊斯门柯达公司的前任开发总监、现任斯诺登事务所董事长和首席执行官梅斯诺登回忆说：“我遇到过这样一位经理，初次相逢他就叫我‘亲爱的’。那是我第一次担任主管职务的时候。我在一个男性占主导地位的电信行业工作，我不想在他同行面前给他难堪，所以我把他叫到我的办公室，向他表明了我的态度，‘如果你叫我亲爱的，我就称你甜心。’我们几乎没有怎么交谈，但他不再这么称呼我了。他确实感到很难堪，因为他对妻子、女儿及其他女性都用‘亲爱的’这个称谓，甚至没有考虑这是否合适。”

百事瓶装集团开发与组织部副总裁雪莉·诺兰认为：“我们带着与生俱来的偏见、经历和教养赴任，这些习性使我们恪守20年前或30年前就已经形成的思维方式。事实的真相是我们所有人在赴任时就存在不同的思维方式，我们愿意做的事就是人们常说的‘嗨，我该怎么解决这个问题呢？’或者‘你希望我对此有什么样的看法？’或者‘我该如何称呼你？’初次这么说我们会有点犹豫不决，或者感觉说得不太对劲，但是说的次数越多，人们就会对各种各样的说法越来越习以为常，更加频繁地使用这些话语进行交流。”

that we may stumble① a little bit or not get it right the first time, but with more practice, the more authentic dialog we'll have with diversity in our organization, the more productive and engaged our people will be."

So to make sure there aren't some unconscious biases informing that harmless comment you are about to make to the woman in the next office, take a look atsome things you should never say to a woman executive or coworker.

Any kind of sexual comment

At a previous job, a supervisor approached me and jokingly said, "I'll give you a dollar for five minutes alone in the copy room." I was shocked, embarrassed and utterly offended. Unfortunately, I didn't feel at liberty to speak up, so I simply walked away.

"It's pure ignorance," says Karen Brown, chief diversity officer for Rockwell Collins, one of Diversity Inc's 25 Noteworthy Companies. "The best way to deal with these things is to consider it as a perfect awareness opportunity to teach that individual something that they never would have had the chance to learn before then."

Brown says offensive comments like these are a problem for more than just the employee on the receiving end. "You're going to create an environment where people struggle and therefore lack the freedom to be innovative and comfortable," she says. "When you remove those barriers and create a culture that allows people to flourish, you get better engagement, better retention and better results."

"You don't really want that promotion. You'll never see your kids."

---

① stumble [ˈstʌmbl] *vi.* 踌躇

所以，为了确保你不会因为某种潜意识的偏见对隔壁办公室的女士做出看似无害的评价，请看看下面你绝对不能对女性主管或女同事说的几件事。

不要发表任何性别评论

从事上一份工作时，一位主管走近我，开玩笑地说："如果跟你单独在影印室待 5 分钟我就给你 1 美元。"我感到非常震惊和尴尬，深受伤害。 不幸的是，我还不能随意地一吐为快，所以我只有选择走开。

在多元化公司中排名前 25 的罗克韦尔柯林斯公司的首席多元总监凯伦·布朗认为，"这是纯粹的无知。 处理这些事情的最好方式是将其视作一次完美的认识机会，教给这些人此前从没有机会了解的东西"。

布朗指出，像这样的攻击性言论不仅仅关系到员工受窝囊气的问题。 她说："你将会造成一种你争我夺的环境，并因此失去自由创新和享受舒适的机会。 当你消除这些障碍、建立起令人积极向上的文化之后，就可以聘用更好的员工，保持公司的活力，并获得更好的结果。"

"你并不是真的想要提升。 那样你就再也看不到你的孩子们了。"

布朗指出，"有一种先入为主的观点，即女性不可能一周工作 40 个小时以上，尤其是已经成家的女性"。

不要认定女性会因为家中有孩子就把事业看得不那么重要。 她

"There is that preconceived notion that a woman cannot work more than the 40 hours per week, especially if she has a family," says Brown.

Don't assume that a woman's career isn't as important to her because she has children at home. Her children may be what's driving her to excel to her highest potential.

Brown adds, "She may in fact want that promotion just as much as her male counterpart, but she's balancing family life and at the same time balancing leading a team."

"You'll get the job because you're a woman" or "You must be the token① woman."

Suggesting to a female coworker or executive that she is where she is because of gender is nothing short of disrespectful. It demeans② that woman's experience in the field and expertise as a leader. It also indicates, to a woman from an underrepresented group, that she was selected not only because she is a female but also because she is Black, Latina or Asian.

"I had a journalist ask me, 'Don't you think you got this job because you're a Hispanic woman?'" recalls Ana Mollinedo Mims, managing director of The Hunting Ridge Group. "I said, 'Did you read my bio③ before you came to interview me? Did you look at my résumé? Chances are that being Latina could have been the weighing factor that tipped me over all the other candidates.' And he looked at me and said, 'Are you OK with that?' I said, 'Absolutely. I don't care what gets me in the door.

① token [ˈtəukən] *adj.* 象征的

② demean [diˈmiːn] *vt.* 贬低……身份

③ bio [ˈbaiəu] *n.* 个人简历(biography 的缩写)

的孩子也许正是激励她努力超越、发挥最大潜能的动力。

布朗补充说："事实上，她可能与男性同事一样渴望升迁，但她还要同时在家庭和领导团队之间做到平衡。"

"因为你是女性，所以你会得到这份工作。"或"你一定是个撑场面的女人。"

对女同事或女主管表示，因为她的性别才使她拥有目前的职位，这只不过是无理取闹。这种说法贬低了那位女性在这个领域的经验和作为领导的专长。对一个来自未被充分代表的群体，它同样表明女性获选不仅因为她是女性，还因为她是黑人、拉丁人或者亚洲人。

猎岭团队的常务董事安娜·曼纽尔·敏思回忆道："有个记者曾问我，'你是否认为你得到这份工作是因为你是西班牙裔女性？'我说，'你来采访我之前看过我的个人简历吗？你仔细读过我的简历吗？身为拉丁人可能确实是令我超越其他候选人的重要因素'。他看着我又说：'你对此感觉还好吗？'我说，'非常好！我并不在意是什么让我进了这个门。因为是那些能让我待在这个门里的因素让我升到了这个位置。'"

"你很有魅力或很漂亮、很美丽"等等。

虽然不管男性还是女性都非常乐意接受别人对自己外貌的称赞，但是对女同事或女主管说这样的话会使她们产生边缘化的感觉，似乎她的外表比她的能力或者她所说的话更为重要。

布朗认为，"对接收者来说，正是这种感觉没有引起听者的关

Because what's going to keep me in the door is what I bring to the table.'"

"You're very attractive or pretty, or beautiful, etc."

Although women as well as men may enjoy a compliment on their looks, saying this to a female coworker or executive can leave the coworker feeling marginalized-as if her looks are more important than her skills or what she has to say.

"It is that feeling to the receiver that the listener isn't paying attention to what she has to say, and therefore, it doesn't matter how crisp, robust and powerful her message is; the impact to the listener is diminished because they're focused on the external beauty," says Brown.

"You look great for your age" or "Do you use Botox?"

Let's face it: This country is addicted to the notion of the fountain of youth. With new age-defying procedures and potions being touted① at every turn, there's a significant amount of pressure on women (and even men these days) to keep a youthful appearance. Especially inappropriate in the workplace, a woman's age should never be discussed unless she brings it up first. And if you suspect her great look is the result of a surgical procedure, keep it to yourself, unless your coworker volunteers that information to you.

"You do that so well ... for a girl."

Even if said in a joking way, the phrase implies that women are inferior to men, and the recipient may not receive it with the best of humor. "The reference is not appropriate. That's basically a demeaning term," says Snowden. "It indicates you're less than the fellows because you

① tout [taut] *vt.* 兜售

注，即她究竟要说什么，所以，不管她的信息是多么有活力、多么稳健和多么强大都无关紧要，因为他们关注的是外在美，对听者的影响逐渐减弱”。

“对你这个年纪的人来说，你保养得太好了”或者“你使用肉毒杆菌吗？”

让我们面对现实吧：这个国家正沉溺于青春之泉的观念中。随着抗衰老手术和药剂受到热捧，女性（甚至包括当今的男性）面临保持年轻外貌的巨大压力。绝对不要谈论女性的年龄，在工作场所尤其不合适，除非她自己先提出这个话题。如果你怀疑她完美的外表是整容的结果，自己知道就好，除非你的同事自愿向你透露这种信息。

“对一个女孩子来说，你做得非常好……”

哪怕是以开玩笑的方式说出来，这样的话也暗示了女性不如男性，听者并不会接受，认为它特别幽默。斯诺登认为，“这种参照不太恰当，从根本上说是贬低她人身份的语言。它暗示你不如同事，因为你是女性。任何暗示你‘不如……’的谈话都是不合适的”。

“你的预产期是什么时候？”

如果你不能完全确定某个女性已经怀孕了，千万不要，再说一遍，千万不要问这个问题。到目前为止，这可能是一个对没有怀孕的女性说的最侮辱人的话语，这个问题会让你言辞欠妥，终生树敌。

are a woman. Any conversation that implies you are 'less than' is inappropriate."

"When are you due?"

If you are not absolutely certain that a woman is expecting, do not, I repeat, do not ask this question. By far one of the most insulting things you could possibly say to a woman who is not pregnant, this question could leave you with your foot in your mouth and an enemy for life.

"I think it's inappropriate to say anything unless you get into a conversation about family," advises Snowden. "For example, I may say something about my family, children or something and then may ask them if they have children. They may say, 'No, I don't have children, but I'm expecting,' or they may not say anything about them expecting. I think it's very dangerous to get into personal kinds of things like that without someone letting you know its OK first."

(1,157 words)

斯诺登建议说，“我认为，除非你们谈到家庭这个话题，否则不宜谈论任何这方面的事。例如，我可能会说一些自家的事，孩子什么的，然后也许问他们是否有小孩。他们可能说：‘没有，我还没有孩子，不过我已经怀孕了’，当然她们也可能不会提及自己怀孕的事。我认为，在别人没有首先向你表示同意之前，讨论此类私人的事情真是如履薄冰。”

知识链接

Gender Discrimination 性别歧视。性别歧视指一种性别成员对另一种性别成员的不平等对待。尤其是男性对女性的不平等对待。两性之间的不平等，造成社会的性别歧视。

题 记

礼节是人际关系的“润滑剂”，能够有效地减少人与人之间的摩擦，最大限度地避免人际冲突，使商务场合的人际交往成为令人身心愉快的享受。事实上，良好的礼仪或礼节可以在一般应酬、工作环境和社交场合中发挥作用，帮助商务人士学会与人打交道：不要在公司内部以职位或身份区分不同的人，秘书和清洁工都会对个人的职业生涯起到很大的帮助或造成障碍；拜访他人时，注意提前到达；与他人交往时，积极向他人介绍自己；记下他人的信息，记住你了解的信息，创建“联系人数据库”；与同事和下属建立良好的关系。如果你以无可挑剔地礼貌对待贵宾，却对柜台办事员颐指气使，即使是公司最高层也会开始怀疑你的动机。简言之，良好的人际关系不仅仅是建立在共同进餐的刀叉之上，它更需要关注人与人之间的相互礼仪。

More than Just Eating with the Right Fork

Business etiquette is made up of significantly more important things than knowing which fork to use at lunch with a client. Unfortunately, in the perception of others, the devil is in the details. People may feel that if you can't be trusted not to embarrass yourself in business and social situations, you may lack the self-control necessary to be good at what you do. Etiquette is about presenting yourself with the kind of polish that shows you can be taken seriously. Etiquette is also about being comfortable around people and making them comfortable around you!

People are a key factor in your own and your business' success. Many potentially worthwhile and profitable alliances have been lost because of an unintentional breach of manners.

Dan McLeod, president of Positive Management Leadership Programs, a union avoidance company, says, "Show me a boss who treats his or her employees abrasively, and I'll show you an environment ripe for labor problems and obviously poor customers relations. Disrespectful and discourteous treatment of employees is passed along from the top."

Most behavior that is perceived as disrespectful, discourteous① or

① discourteous [dis'kəːtiəs] *adj*. 粗鲁的，无礼的

正确使用刀叉远远不够

与了解和客户共进午餐时如何正确使用刀叉相比，商务礼仪还有更为显著的重要组成部分。不幸的是，在他人看来，很多折磨人的问题都隐藏在细节之中。人们可能认为，如果你在商务和社交场合为了使自己回避尴尬而不能给人信赖感，那么你可能对自己擅长做的工作缺乏自我控制能力。礼仪是以一种优雅的方式展示自己，并表示你应该受到礼遇。礼仪就是要与周围的人舒适相处，并使周围的人感到舒适！

员工是你自己和企业成功的关键因素。由于无意间违反了礼仪，许多具有潜在价值和利润丰厚的联盟已经败走麦城。

一家联合规避公司的“积极管理领导计划”主席丹·麦克劳德认为，“如果让我知道了老板粗暴地对待他或她的员工，我会让你们见识一下为劳工问题和明显糟糕的客户关系导致的环境。无礼和粗鲁地对待员工是从上至下传递的问题。

大多数被视为不尊重人、不礼貌或者伤害感情的行为都是无意之间造成的，践行良好的礼仪或礼节原本可以回避这些问题。我们发现，与人打交道最消极的经历往往出于无心，保持开放的心态和

abrasive① is unintentional, and could have been avoided by practicing good manners or etiquette. We've always found that most negative experiences with someone were unintentional and easily repaired by keeping an open mind and maintaining open, honest communication. Basic knowledge and practice of etiquette is a valuable advantage, because in a lot of situations, a second chance may not be possible or practical.

There are many written and unwritten rules and guidelines for etiquette, and it certainly behooves② a business person to learn them. The caveat③ is that there is no possible way to know all of them!

These guidelines have some difficult-to-navigate nuances, depending on the company, the local culture, and the requirements of the situation. Possibilities to commit a faux pas are limitless, and chances are, sooner or later, you'll make a mistake. But you can minimize them, recover quickly, and avoid causing a bad impression by being generally considerate and attentive to the concerns of others, and by adhering to the basic rules of etiquette.

The most important thing to remember is to be courteous and thoughtful to the people around you, regardless of the situation. Consider other people's feelings, stick to your convictions as diplomatically as possible. Address conflict as situation-related, rather than person-related. Apologize when you step on toes. You can't go too far wrong if you stick with the basics you learned in Kindergarten. Not that those basics are easy

---

① abrasive [əˈbreisiv] *adj.* 使人厌烦的；粗鲁的

② behoove [biˈhuːv] *vt.* 理所当然；对……有此必要

③ caveat [ˈkæviæt] *n.*警告，附加说明

公开、真诚地沟通，可以轻松地修复负面影响。礼仪的基本知识和习惯是一种宝贵的优势，因为在很多情况下，重新纠正错误是不可能和行不通的。

有许多书面或口头的礼仪规则和指导方针，商务人士当然有必要了解他们。提醒一下，不可能了解所有的礼仪规则！

这些指导方针有一些很难把握的细微差别，这取决于公司、地方文化和形势的要求。失礼的可能性是无限的，或迟或早你有可能犯错。但是你可以将错误降到最低，并迅速加以改正。一般说来，要无微不至地关心他人，坚持基本的礼仪规则，以避免引起不良印象。

不管遇到什么情况，切记：最重要的事是对周围的人保持礼貌和体贴入微。考虑他人的感受，尽可能在与人打交道时坚持自己的信念。根据相关情况解决冲突，而不是针对个人。踩到脚趾时需要道歉。如果坚持你在幼儿园学到的基本知识，你就不会错得太多。参加讲究实际的商务会议时，这些基本知识并不是很容易被人记起！

这听起来过分简单化，但这些都是我们在领导者身上看到的最令人羡慕的品质，都是我们想方设法努力在孩子们身上培养的特质。如果你总是这样表现，你就不会介意你的配偶、孩子或祖父母对你的关注，你可能做得不错。避免提高嗓音，令人惊讶的是，降低嗓音会给人印象深刻，使你获得更多的关注。不要向在场或不在

to remember when you're in a hard-nosed business meeting!

This sounds simplistic, but the qualities we admire most when we see them in people in leadership positions, those are the very traits we work so hard to engender in our children. If you always behave so that you would not mind your spouse, kids, or grandparents watching you, you're probably doing fine. Avoid raising your voice, surprisingly, it can be much more effective at getting attention when lower it, using harsh or derogatory language toward anyone present or absent, or interrupting. You may not get as much "airtime" in meetings at first, but what you do say will be much more effective because it carries the weight of credibility and respectability.

The following are guidelines and tips that we've found helpful for dealing with people in general, in work environments, and in social situations.

Talk and visit with people. Don't differentiate by position or standing within the company. Secretaries and janitorial staff actually have tremendous power to help or hinder your career. Next time you need a document prepared or a conference room arranged for a presentation, watch how many people are involved with that process and make it a point to meet them and show your appreciation.

Make it a point to arrive ten or fifteen minutes early and visit with people that work near you. When you're visiting another site, linger over a cup of coffee and introduce yourself to people nearby. If you arrive early for a meeting, introduce yourself to the other participants. At social occasions, use the circumstances of the event itself as an icebreaker. After introducing yourself, ask how they know the host or how they like the

场的任何人使用严厉或贬损的语言，或者直接打断他们的讲话。初次出席会议时，你可能得不到太多的“发言时间”，但是希望你无论说什么都能产生较为强烈的效果，因为它承载着极有价值的信誉和尊重。

以下是相关的指南和小贴士，我们认为，这些礼貌原则可以在一般应酬、工作环境和社交场合中发挥作用，帮助大家学会与人打交道。

与人交谈和访问。 不要在公司内部以职位或身份区分不同的人。实际上，秘书和清洁工都会对你的职业生涯起到很大的帮助或造成障碍。下次你需要准备一个文档或安排会议室的演示时，看看有多少人参与了这一过程，一定要特意与他们见面，表达你的感激。

拜访在你附近工作的人时，注意提前 10 分钟或 15 分钟到达。访问其他地方时，你可以一边悠闲地品尝咖啡，一边向周围的人介绍自己。如果你提前到达会场，应向其他与会者介绍自己。在社交场合中，根据具体场合做一个打破沉默的人。介绍完自己后，询问他们如何认识主人的，或他们觉得蟹酱的味道怎样。稍微谈点自己的事，如你的爱好、孩子或宠物。只需让人们敞开心扉并了解你这个人就足够了。

记下别人的信息。 有几款为推销员设计的“联系人管理”应用软件，但在商务交易中，几乎每个人都是推销员，他们具有这样或

crab dip. Talk a little about yourself—your hobbies, kids, or pets; just enough to get people to open up about theirs and get to know you as a person.

Keep notes on people. There are several "contact management" software applications that are designed for salespeople, but in business, nearly everyone is a salesperson in some capacity or another. They help you create a "people database" with names, addresses, phone numbers, birthdays, spouse and children's names; whatever depth of information is appropriate for your situation.

It's a good idea to remember what you know about people; and to be thoughtful. Send cards or letters for birthdays or congratulations of promotions or other events; send flowers for engagements, weddings or in condolence for the death of a loved one or family member. People will remember your kindness, probably much longer than you will!

Impressing the boss isn't enough. A study by Manchester Partners International, says even in this tight job market, 40% of new management hires fail in their first jobs. The key reason for their failure is their inability to build good relationships with peers and subordinates.

Social rank or class is a cornerstone of social interaction in many cultures. The corporate climate in the United States is no exception. People tend to feel uneasy until they've seen an "organizational chart" or figured out who reports to whom. They feel that it is more important to show respect and practice etiquette around superiors than around peers or subordinates.

The current social and economic climate is one of rapid advancement

那样的能力。他们帮你创建"联系人数据库"：包括姓名、地址、电话号码、生日、配偶和子女的名字，以及任何对你有用的深度信息。

记住你了解的信息并对人体贴入微是个好想法。发送贺卡或信件祝贺他人的生日、升职庆祝或其他活动；在约会、婚礼、哀悼已逝亲人或家庭成员的追悼会上送花。人们会记住你的好意，很可能比你期望的要长久得多！

光给老板留下印象还不够。"曼彻斯特国际合作伙伴"的一份研究指出，即使在这种紧缩的就业市场，40％的新管理层仍然在首次就职中败下阵来。他们失败的关键原因是他们没能与同事和下属建立良好的关系。

在许多文化的社会交往中，社会等级或阶级是一座基石。美国的企业环境也不例外。人们只有看到"组织结构图"或了解谁向谁报告之后，才会感到轻松自如。他们认为，对上司表示尊重和注重礼仪比对同事或下属更重要。

当前的社会和经济环境是技术快速发展的原因之一，它很有可能使令人讨厌的推销员成为重要的客户，或使行政助理成为经理。兼并和收购增加了这种"阶级混合"，造成前竞争对手一夜之间成为同事。

如果你根据不同的"公司身份"区别对待他们，就有可能使事情变得很尴尬。如果你对每个人都表现出尊重和礼貌，无论他们是

through technology, which makes it very possible for a pesky① salesman to become an important client, or an administrative assistant to become a manager. Mergers and acquisitions add to this "class mixing," causing a former competitor to become a coworker overnight.

This can make things awkward if you treat people differently depending on their "corporate standing." If you show respect and courtesy to everyone, regardless of position or company, you avoid discomfort or damaging your chances in any unexpected turn of events.

Having a consistent demeanor improves your credibility. Even the people at the top will begin to suspect your motives if you treat VIPs with impeccable courtesy and snap at counter clerks.

The only thing you owe your boss above and beyond what you owe peers and subordinates is more information. Un obtrusively② be sure he or she knows what you're doing, is alerted as early as possible to issues that may arise, and is aware of outcomes and milestones.

Never surprise your boss. It goes without saying that you should speak well of him or her within and outside the company, and give him or her the benefit of the doubt, which you would do for anyone, of course!

(1,164 words)

---

① pesky [ˈpeski] *adj*. 烦人的；让人讨厌的

② obtrusively [əbˈtruːsivli] *adj*. 冒失地，莽撞地

什么职位或公司，你就可以避免任何始料不及的事情对你造成的伤害或破坏你的机会。

行为举止始终如一可以提高你的信誉。如果你以无可挑剔的礼貌对待贵宾，却对柜台办事员颐指气使，即使是公司最高层也会开始怀疑你的动机。

你唯一欠老板的是更多的信息，它超出了你对同事和下属的歉疚。谨慎的做法是让他或她知道你在干什么，尽早提醒他可能出现的问题，并使他意识到后果和重要性。

永远不要让你的老板感到惊讶。不用说，在公司内部和外面都要说他或她的好话，肯定他或她做出的成绩，当然，你对任何人都应该这么做。

知识链接

Eatingwith the Right Fork 正确使用刀叉。首先，刀叉的摆放方式要传达出“用餐中”或者“用餐结束”的信号。用餐中为八字形。用餐结束后，可将叉子的正面向上、刀子的刀刃侧向内与叉子并拢，平行放置于餐盘上。其次，一般通用的刀叉拿法是右手拿刀，左手拿叉。再次，刀叉的基本使用方法是“右手拿刀将其切开，然后左手用叉将食物叉起”。用叉子压住食物的左端，固定，顺着叉子的侧边用刀切下约一口大小的食物，叉子即可直接叉起食物送入口中。

题　记

在世人的眼中，德国人墨守成规和一成不变；但他们讲究秩序和沉稳勤劳的优秀品质，同样也令举世瞩目。实际上，在商务交际圈中，德国人也会无拘无束地与朋友聚会。德国商务餐桌礼仪既包容了普鲁士人的传统民族饮食文化，也涵盖了现代商务活动用餐礼仪中的精华。午餐和晚餐都被视为商务会议不可或缺的重要组成部分，就餐为与会者提供私人交流的机会，使他们在更加随意轻松的氛围里洽谈公事。主人付账时应避开宾客，在高级餐厅点上等的自酿葡萄酒，喝餐前汤时举起杯子一饮而尽，牙签和唇膏可以随意摆放在餐桌，用餐结束后千万不要把用完的餐巾扔到餐盘里。当然，你不必刻意复制德国人的餐桌礼仪。如果你在自己的国家就已经训练有素，在德国也会应对自如。

Business Dinners in Germany

It is traditional in Germany to eat the main meal of the day at lunchtime, between 11:30 AM and 1:30 PM.

In contrast to a long, several-course meal, a German lunch usually consists of an appetizer (usually soup), a main course, and a dessert.

When you are attending a business conference, both lunch and dinner are considered important components of the conference. Meals allow those attending to make personal contacts and to continue discussing business issues in a more casual atmosphere.

Contrary to earlier traditions that frowned upon women speaking with the waiter, tasting the wine, or paying the bill, all of these things are normal today. It is not only acceptable for a woman to ask for the bill, but also to enter a restaurant first, and—if acting as hostess—to try the wine before it is served. However, this last situation will usually not come into question at business luncheons because, in most cases, only non-alcoholic beverages are served.

The consumption of alcohol in Germany (even during the work day) may be more common than you are used to in your country, and when others drink, you may feel pressured to drink as well. Again, you don't

德国商务餐桌礼仪

在德国，人们习惯在上午 11:30 到下午 1:30 的午餐时间吃正餐。

与时间长、好几道主菜的用餐习惯不同，德国式午餐一般由一道开胃菜（通常以汤为主）、一道主菜和一道甜点组成。

但是在商务会议中，午餐和晚餐都被视为会议不可或缺的重要组成部分。就餐为与会者提供私人交流的机会，使他们在更加随意轻松的氛围里洽谈公事。

早期的传统认为女性不能与餐厅侍者讲话、不能喝酒、不能付账，现在的观念恰恰相反，这些都已经成为普遍现象。人们理所当然地认为，女性不仅可以付账，而且可以优先进入餐厅，若是女主人请客，还要在酒水上桌前事先品尝。然而，在商务午宴中，女性也不必担心喝酒的问题，因为大多数商务午宴只提供无酒精饮料。

德国人对酒精的消费（甚至在上班时间）可能比你自己国家的习惯更普遍。看到别人喝酒时，你也不由自主地被迫来上几口。不过，你也不必对此过于担心，在现代礼仪中，拒绝饮酒是能够被接受的。实际上，你甚至可以自己为大家点酒水饮料，这样就能避

need to worry-modern etiquette suggests that it is acceptable to refuse a drink. In fact, you can even offer to order drinks for others and refrain from drinking alcohol yourself.

Generally, the rule states that 10-15% of the bill's total should be left as a tip if you were satisfied with the service you received. If you weren't satisfied, you can simply not leave a tip, and others will not frown upon you. You may, on the other hand, want to leave more than the standard 10-15% tip if the restaurant staff really went out of their way to accommodate your needs. Also, when leaving, it is polite to thank the staff or your waiter / waitress with, "Danke schön." ("Thank you.") This lets you express your appreciation in addition to the tip that you leave behind.

When in Germany, should I conform my table manners to those of the Germans? For the most part, you do not have to make too much effort to mirror the Germans at the table. If you practice good table manners at home, they will suffice in Germany; it is not necessary to worry about how to hold your fork or where to place your napkin. But be careful—some behavior should be avoided. For example, in Southern Asia, it is normal to chew loudly when eating and to belch① after a good meal. If you were to do this in Germany, it could embarrass you as well as those sitting with you.

What are a few table manners that I should keep in mind in Germany?

- Before eating, wish everyone at the table "Guten Appetit." ("Enjoy your meal.")

---

① belch [beltʃ] *vi.* 打嗝

免沾酒了。

一般说来，如果你对用餐时享受的服务感到满意的话，习惯上要付小费，数额在总餐费的10%-15%。如果你对用餐服务感到不满意，也可以不给小费，别人也不会对此有什么看法。另一方面，作为对餐厅招待细心周到、无微不至服务的回报，你也可选择给他们超过标准的10%-15%的小费。当然，在用餐结束即将离开的时候，应该对为你提供服务的男女侍者们说声“Danke schön”（谢谢），以表示礼貌。除了留下的小费之外，这种方式也表明了你对用餐满意的赞许。

在德国应该遵守这些德国人的餐桌礼仪吗？在很大程度上，你不必刻意复制他们的餐桌礼仪。如果你在自己的国家就已经训练有素，在德国也会应对自如；你也不必担心怎么拿叉子或怎么放餐巾的问题。但还是小心为妙，因为有些行为是应该避免的。比如说，在南亚，进餐时大声咀嚼和盛宴后打嗝不会被视作无礼，但是在德国千万不要这样，这会使你和坐在你身边的人都感到十分尴尬。

在德国应该牢记哪些餐桌礼仪呢？

- 在开始用餐之前，祝福用餐的每一位宾客“Guten Appetit”（好口福）。
- 尽量只夹取适量的食物，保证自己可以全部吃完。德国人通常都“清空盘子”。
- 和其他人一起用餐时，双手放在桌上，不要放在桌下。

- Only take as much food as you plan on eating. The Germans usually "clean their plates".
- When you or others are eating, keep your hands on the table, not under it.
- Sit up straight, close to the table.
- Don't prop your head up with your hands.
- Don't bend your head over your food when you are eating or "shovel" your food in your mouth.
- Don't begin eating until everyone at the table has been served.
- Don't begin drinking until everyone has something to drink and a toast has been made.
- Look others in the eye when toasting.
- Do not get up to leave when you have finished eating, but wait for the others; if you came to dinner with others, then leave with them also.
- Do not belch or chew with your mouth open.
- When you are finished eating, places your knife and fork together and rest them on your plate.

Should a host pay the bill at the table with the guests present? No! It is much more polite to pay the bill at the bar in order to avoid misunderstandings or discussions about paying. This also allows the host to inconspicuously① pay, look over the bill, leave a tip, and order an aperitif② for everyone.

Is it acceptable to ask for the house wine in a good restaurant? Yes! A

---

① inconspicuously [ˌinkənˈspikjuəsli] *adv*. 难以觉察地

② aperitif [əˌperiˈtiːf] *n*. 餐前汤

- 坐姿要挺立，身体尽量靠近餐桌。
- 不要用手撑头。
- 用餐或狼吞虎咽时，不要把头埋在餐盘里。
- 所有人的食物上桌后再开始进餐。
- 所有人的酒水备齐、相互敬酒后再开始喝。
- 敬酒时一定要注视对方的眼睛。
- 用餐完毕不要急于起身离开，应等待他人结束用餐；如果有人和你一同赴宴，也尽量和他们一起离开。
- 不要张着嘴巴大声咀嚼和打嗝。
- 用餐结束后，把刀叉一并放在餐盘中。

主人应当着宾客的面付账吗？ 决不！ 在柜台付款要礼貌得多，以避免付账时的误解和议价。这样主人可以不露声色地付款，检查菜单，给付小费，并且为每位宾客点一道开胃酒。

在高级餐厅点其自酿的葡萄酒是否合适？ 非常合适！ 上等的自酿葡萄酒是餐厅的金字招牌。 你也可以放心，在德国、法国和意大利这样的酒都，葡萄酒的质量绝不会差。 当你的预算不足以支付极其昂贵的酒时，可以让餐厅侍者向你推荐一款价廉物美的酒。 在向餐厅侍者报出你可接受的价格时应表现出自信和镇定，不要不好意思询问。

喝汤时举起杯子一饮而尽是礼貌的行为吗？ 是的！ 但是，需要掌握点小技巧，握住汤杯的其中一个杯把，稍事倾斜，然后把汤喝完。 要记住，只有用带把的汤杯这么做才算礼貌，汤碗的话就千

good house wine is a good advertisement for a restaurant. Also, you can be sure that a wine from wine countries such as Germany, France, and Italy will never be of bad quality. When your budget doesn't allow an extremely expensive wine, ask the waiter to recommend a low cost, quality wine. By naming the amount that you are willing to spend, you show that you are confident in the situation and not embarrassed to ask.

When I order soup, is it polite to tip up my soup cup and drink the last bit of soup? Yes! However, in order to do this tactfully①, take hold of one of the soup cup handles, tip, and drink. Keep in mind that this is only polite when your soup comes served in a CUP, not a bowl!

Is it appropriate to use toothpicks or put on lipstick at the table? Yes! These are not the most tactful things to do at the table, but if they have to be done, then go ahead. Lipstick can be put on discretely almost anywhere, but is it really necessary to put it on at the table? If you really want to freshen up your make-up, be sure to go to the bathroom.

When I attend a social event, should I wait to take off my sport coat or jacket until I am asked to do so by the host? Yes! Good hosts and hostesses should react quickly when they notice that the room temperature is rising and offer to take your coat for you.

Is it true that I should not lay my paper napkin in my plate when I am finished eating? Yes! In Germany it is customary to fold your napkin after eating and place it to the left side of your plate. The Germans have a very strict recycling system, and this helps ensure that the napkin ends up in the correct recycling bin. Cloth napkins should also be folded and laid

---

① tactfully [ˈtæktfuli] *adv.* 巧妙地;机智地

万不要这样做!

在餐桌上摆放牙签和唇膏合适吗? 合适! 把这些东西摆上餐桌并没有什么特别的讲究,想用就放心大胆地用。唇膏可以直接放在任何地方,难道真的有必要把它放在餐桌上吗? 如果你实在需要补妆,就去洗手间吧。

参加社交活动时,是否应当等主人主动要求时再脱掉运动衫或夹克衫呢? 是的! 细心的男主人和女主人一旦注意到房间的温度升高,就会马上帮你脱掉外套。

用餐结束后是不是不应该把用完的餐巾纸扔到餐盘里? 是的! 在德国,人们进餐后习惯把用完的纸巾叠好放到餐盘的左侧。德国有非常严格的垃圾回收系统,这样做可以确保纸巾回收,并放至正确的垃圾桶中。餐巾布也应该叠好,放在餐盘的左侧,千万别把它丢在餐盘上!

如果我在用餐时想说几句话或者致祝酒词,击打酒杯以引起他人关注的做法可取吗? 不可取! 虽然你在德国的老电影里看到过这种特别的行为,但现在更适宜的做法是站起来,以微扬的语调提请大家的注意。那些在座的人自然而然会停止讲话,并对你表示关注。

知识链接

Daily diet for German 德国人的日常饮食。德国人最讲究、最丰盛的不是午

to the left side of your plate, never in the plate!

If I would like to say a few words at the table or to make a toast, is it appropriate to bang on the side of my glass to get people's attention? No! Although you typically see this in old German movies, today it is more appropriate to stand and ask for their attention in a slightly raised voice. Those seated at the table should automatically stop talking and pay attention.

(1,122 words)

餐、晚餐，而是早餐。在普通百姓家，不论其家境穷富，早餐的内容一般都大同小异：首先是饮料，包括咖啡、茶、各种果汁、牛奶等，主食为各种面包，以及与面包相配的奶油、干酪和果酱，外加香肠和火腿。德国的午餐和晚餐一般是猪排、牛排、烤肉、香肠、生鱼、土豆和汤类等。德国人的午餐一般多在单位餐厅或快餐馆解决，绝对是名副其实的快餐，如一个由土豆、沙拉生菜和几块肉组成的拼盘，外加一杯饮料。德国人的家庭晚餐通常是冷餐，一盘肉食的拼盘，鲜嫩可口的蔬菜，如小萝卜、西红柿、黄瓜，新鲜的水果，如葡萄、樱桃等，以及各种风味的干酪，当然，主食仍旧还是面包。

题 记

在当今日益增长的虚拟商业世界中，越来越多的潜在顾客开始通过电子邮件相互沟通。尽管与回电话、发送信息包相比，这种做法可以节省很多时间，但是当潜在顾客变成付费客户时，它也会带来一些挑战。应对的秘诀是要懂得如何有效地利用每一封往来的电子邮件，让潜在顾客变成最好的客户和备用资源。幸运的是，电子邮件礼仪的规则会对人们有所帮助：尽快回复潜在顾客，标注潜在顾客的原始信息，邮件内容尽可能简短但要详细，始终附加联系方式，文件附件要有礼貌，运用恰当的语法，以及按照电子邮件礼仪建立客户名单。伴随着3G时代的到来，整个互联网必将发生翻天覆地的变化，而占据重要地位的电子邮件应用和随之改变的电邮礼仪，也必将在3G时代带给人们深刻的互联网革命和生活变迁。

The Rules of E-Etiquette

In today's ever-increasing virtual business world, more and more prospects are making the initial contact with you by e-mail communication. While this may be a big time-saver when it comes to returning phone calls and sending information packets, it does pose some challenges for turning those prospects into paying clients. The secret knows how to use every e-mail correspondence effectively to convert prospects into your best customers and referral sources.

The reasons why many prospects favor e-mail correspondence these days are plentiful. First, they don't have to talk to a live person on the initial query. This makes them more relaxed and eager to find out information about you and your company. Also, they can request the information they need any time of day, not just during your business hours. This is especially appealing to those prospects in different time zones and countries. Finally, when prospects receive your reply via e-mail, they get the instant attention they desire without the interruptions that come with phone calls. Unfortunately, despite all these advantages to the prospects, you as the business professional need some special skills to effectively work with this kind of communication. The good news is that with proper e-etiquette, you can easily turn email correspondences into one of your most profitable client sources.

电子邮件的礼仪规范

在当今日益增长的虚拟商业世界中，越来越多的潜在顾客开始通过电子邮件与你取得联系。尽管与回电话、发送信息包相比，这种做法可以节省很多时间，但是当潜在顾客变成付费客户时，它也会带来一些挑战。应对的秘诀是要懂得如何有效地利用每一封往来的电子邮件，让潜在顾客变成你最好的客户和备用资源。

许多潜在顾客现在喜欢用电子邮件的原因有很多。首先，他们在初次咨询时不需要与真人交谈。这使他们感到更放松，渴望查询有关你和你公司的信息。此外，他们不只是在你的工作时间，而是在一天中的任何时候查询所需的信息。这尤其吸引那些不同时区和不同国家的潜在顾客。最后，当潜在顾客通过电子邮件收到回复之后，他们就得到了自己期待的即时关注，可以免受电话的打扰。不幸的是，尽管对潜在顾客有这么多好处，作为职业商务人士，你还需要掌握一些特殊的技巧，以便有效处理这种类型的通信。好消息是，运用恰当的电子邮件礼仪，你可以轻松地将电子邮件通信变成一个最有可能带来客户的资源。

The Rules of E-Etiquette

The most recent findings show that the average businessperson sends and receives about ninety e-mail messages per day. While these e-business correspondences are done at an incredible pace, you need to remember that the same rules of traditional correspondence etiquette apply. Your prospects choose to use e-mail because they are busy people who do not wish to have intrusions, who may not have time for idle chitchat[1], but who still need to know about your products and/or services. In order to turn these prospects into clients, follow these guidelines for effective e-mail communication.

Reply to your prospects as soon as possible

The very nature of e-mail is instant communication. Your prospects want to know what you can offer them right now. While you may not be able to respond to their inquiries the moment you receive them, you do need to respond in a timely manner. The same day is best-but definitely within 24 hours. When your prospects see that you are able to respond quickly with the information they need, it plants the seed for future speedy service and makes them more apt to do business with you.

Always reference your prospects' original message

More than likely, your prospects send multiple messages a day to various businesses. In order to make it easier for them to determine which request you are responding to, be sure to reference the original message in your reply. This can be done in a simple sentence stating, "Thank you for requesting information about (your company/product name)." Or,

---

① chitchat [ˈtʃittʃæt] *n.* 闲聊

电子邮件的礼仪规范

最近的研究显示，商务人士平均每天收发 90 封电子邮件。尽管这些电子商务通信的速度让人难以置信，但是你需要记住与传统信件礼仪相同的应用规则。你的潜在顾客之所以选择使用电子邮件，是因为他们公务繁忙，不希望被人打扰，没有时间闲聊，但是他们仍然需要了解你的产品或服务。为了将这些潜在顾客转变成客户，请遵循以下有效的电子邮件通信指南。

尽快回复潜在顾客

电子邮件的自然属性是即时交流。你的潜在顾客希望马上知道你能给他们提供什么。尽管你也许不能一收到邮件就回复他们的请求，但你必须及时回复。当天回复邮件最好，但是一定要在 24 小时之内。你的潜在顾客可以看到，你很快就回复了他们需要的信息，这就为未来的快捷服务做好了铺垫，使他们更愿意和你做生意。

标注潜在顾客的原始信息

你的潜在顾客很有可能在一天内给不同的公司发送多种信息。为了让他们更容易确认你回复的是哪个要求，一定要在回复中注明原始信息。可以用一个简单的句子表述："谢谢你对（你的公司/产品的名称）信息的咨询。"或者，根据电子邮件程序，它会自动注明你回复的信息。与公司的 IT 主管一道检查一下，查证你的邮箱是

depending on your e-mail program, it may automatically reference the message you are replying to. Check with your company's IT Director to find out if yours does. By making it as simple as possible for your prospects to know what your message is in reference to, you eliminate the possibility of them inadvertently① pressing the delete key before reading your message.

Be as brief but detailed as possible

Your prospects want information, but they don't want to be bogged② down with pages and pages of text. Your replies to them need to be brief, yet filled with just enough information to help them make a buying decision. Before sending your replies to your prospects, send it to yourself to see how it looks on the screen. Are there pages and pages of text that will intimidate③ your prospects? Are the paragraphs overwhelming? Does the formatting look awkward on the screen? Since this correspondence will be the prospects' first impression of you, be sure you are not conveying a negative or overbearing impression by bombarding④ your prospects with too much information. Say what you need to say, and then stop. You can supply additional information in your follow-up.

Always include additional contact information

Even though your prospects are contacting you via e-mail, you still need to give them other options for reaching you for further information.

---

① inadvertently [ˌinədˈvəːtəntli] *adv*. 不注意地

② bogged [bɔgd] *adj*. 陷于困境的

③ intimidate [inˈtimideit] *vt*. 吓唬

④ bombard [bɔmˈbɑːd] *vt*. 轰炸；炮击

否有自动标注功能。尽可能简单地让潜在顾客了解你的信息指的是什么，以避免他们在阅读邮件信息时无意中按删除键的可能性。

尽可能简短但要详细

你的潜在顾客需要信息，但是他们不想陷入一页一页的文本堆。你给他们的回复必须简短，只需填写帮助他们做出购买决定的信息即可。在给潜在顾客发送你的回复之前，先将邮件发送给自己，看看屏幕上的界面是什么样的，是不是吓退潜在顾客的一页一页文本？段落是不是太多了？屏幕上的格式是不是看起来不舒服？既然这次通信将是潜在顾客对你的第一印象，所以一定不能用太多信息轰炸你的潜在顾客，不可以传递负面或者傲慢的印象。说你必须说的，然后打住。你可以在后续邮件中补充附加信息。

始终附加联系方式

尽管潜在顾客通过电子邮件和你联系，但是，你仍然需要将你的其他联系方式发送给他们，以便他们获得进一步的信息。这通常包括你的电话、传真或者手机号等信息。大多数商务人士喜欢在信件上签名，可以将其程序化，自动插入每封邮件的末尾。更有效的方法是：签名要简短，采用公司的广告语，一行的长度保持在 60 到 70 个字符。如果必要，你的潜在顾客很乐意知道他们可以通过其他方式联系上你。

文件附件要有礼貌

根据潜在顾客需要的信息，有时候你需要发送附件。尽管这种

Always include your phone, fax and/or cell phone numbers, as well as mailing information in every correspondence. Most business people prefer to do this in their signature, which can be programmed to be automatically inserted at the end of every e-mail message. To be effective, keep your signature short, use your business slogan and keep the line length to sixty or seventy characters. Your prospects will appreciate knowing they can reach you by other means if necessary.

Be courteous with file attachments

Depending on the information your prospects want, there may be times when you need to send a file attachment. While these are big time-savers for information requests (no need to re-key information—just attach a file and send), you need to send your attachments judiciously① . Never send more than two attachments at a time. Attached files take longer for your prospects to receive and download, and they may not appreciate the increased time online. Additionally, some prospects are leery② of attached files because of possible viruses. If the information is not long, you may want to consider including it directly in the e-mail message by using a "cut and paste" method. Another option is to have the information posted online via your web site. This way you can simply direct your prospects to a web link and have them view exactly what they need.

Use proper grammar

If your prospects can't read or understand your message, there is a slim chance they will become clients. That's why you need to develop a

---

① judiciously [dʒuːˈdiʃəsli] *adv*. 明智而审慎地

② leery [ˈliəri] *adj*. 警惕的

做法在信息交流中非常省时（无需再强调重要信息，只需附上文件即可发送），但仍然需要明智而审慎地发送附件。一次不要发送两个以上的附件。接收和下载附件需要花费较长的时间，你的潜在顾客可能不喜欢延长在线时间。另外，有些顾客比较警惕，害怕附件可能染上病毒。如果信息不长，你可以考虑“剪切和粘贴”的方法，将信息直接放到邮件正文中。另外一种选择是让信息通过网站链接传送出去。你可以按这种方式直接简单地将网址链接发给潜在顾客，让他们只浏览自己需要的商品。

运用恰当的语法

如果潜在顾客无法阅读和理解你的邮件，他们成为客户的机会就很渺茫。这就是为什么你急需扩大词汇量和掌握适当的语法技能的原因。您需要知道如何构造句子，以精确地表达信息。因为电子邮件不是当面交流，还因为它快速且非正式，所以它缺乏语调变化、面部表情和肢体语言等常规交流线索。因此，遣词造句就成为沟通中更加关键的部分。在给潜在顾客发送电子邮件之前，需要再读一遍，确保要点已经解释清楚。毕竟，这是你与潜在顾客交流的唯一机会。你需要确保发送的信息清楚地回答了潜在顾客的问题，并给他们一个和你合作的理由。

按照电子邮件礼仪建立客户名单

毫无疑问，电子邮件是未来的交流方式。掌握电子邮件礼仪技巧的商务人士将在与潜在顾客有效交流的过程中获得最大的回报。

strong vocabulary and proper grammar skills. You need to know how to construct a sentence to accurately convey your message. Because e-mail communication is not in person, and because it is fast and informal, it lacks the common communication cues that come from voice inflection, facial expression and body language. Your choice of words, therefore, becomes an even more critical part of your communicating. Before sending your e-mail to your prospects, read it over to be sure you got your point across. After all, this may be your only chance to communicate with your prospects. You need to be sure your message clearly answers your prospects' questions and gives them a reason to want to do business with you.

Build your client list with e-etiquette

Make no doubt about it-e-mail communication is the way of the future. Those business people who have the e-etiquette skills to communicate with prospects effectively will be the ones who reap the most rewards.

Most important, always remember that no matter how your prospects contact you, the goal is to turn them into paying clients. Your e-mail correspondence prospects are no different. Instead of defeating your chances of converting these prime prospects by displaying sloppy e-etiquette skills, you need to do everything you can to convince them that your company is ahead of the times and can deliver the necessary products and/or services. By using these e-etiquette tips and some common sense, you will turn more prospects into clients, and gain more referrals in the process.

(1,202 words)

更重要的是，始终记住：不管你的潜在顾客如何与你联系，目标是让他们成为你的付费客户。通过电子邮件与你联系的潜在顾客也不例外。你需要竭尽全力，说服潜在的顾客，说明你的公司走在时代的前列，能够提供必要的产品和服务，而不是展示草率的电邮礼仪技巧，失去获得这些主要的潜在顾客的机会。通过利用这些电子邮件礼仪小贴士和一些常识，你会将更多的潜在顾客转变为客户，并在这个过程中获得更多的资源。

知识链接

Electronic mail 电子邮件。电子邮件(简称 E-mail，标志：@，昵称："伊妹儿")是一种用电子手段提供信息交换的通信方式。它可以是文字、图像、声音等各种方式，也是互联网应用最广的服务：通过网络的电子邮件系统，用户可以用非常低廉的价格(不管发送到哪里，都只需负担电话费和网费即可)，以非常快速的方式(几秒钟之内可以发送到世界上任何你指定的目的地)，与世界上任何一个角落的网络用户联系。

题 记

作为互联网服务最早、最广泛应用之一的电子邮件，是世界上发展最快的通信媒介，稳坐最受欢迎的通信工具次席，仅次于电话。但是，电子邮件里也会出现很多灰色地带，即便是明辨是非的高管，他们在人力资源会议上能保持清醒，但却因为不注意细节或是其他不经意的疏漏而栽跟头。合理利用电子邮件礼仪，可以帮助人们走出困境：发送邮件时始终填写详细的标题栏；允许对方有充裕的回复时间；了解给发件人回信的合适时间；适当使用“回复”按钮；适当设置电子邮件回复功能；请求在信息列表中加入联系人的权限。电子邮件是继电视之后最成功的传播新宠，随着现代移动数据网络的普及，可以预见，历尽沧桑的电子邮件仍有着蓬勃的生命力，电子邮件礼仪也会随之家喻户晓、妇孺皆知。

Make Sure your Message Gets across

E-mail correspondence is the fastest growing communication medium in the world.Every year, more than 7 trillion e-mail messages traveled the wires in the U.S. alone, up from a mere 4 trillion. Additionally, the most recent findings report that the average businessperson sends and receives a total of about ninety e-mail messages daily. And if you think your e-mail box is full now, just wait, when e-mail usage is expected to exceed 5 billion messages per day!

While e-mail is certainly powerful and popular, it's not always the most effective way to get your ideas across. Between the limitations of ASCII text, odd line breaks inserted by mail servers, clients who use bizarre① terms, spamming② , never-get-to-the-point authors, tedious③ e-mail lists and hard-to-decipher④ unsubscribe routines, it's amazing anything gets communicated electronically at all.

---

① bizarre [biˈzɑː] *adj*. 奇异的

② spamming [spæmiŋ] *n*. 垃圾邮件

③ tedious [ˈtiːdiəs] *adj*. 单调乏味的

④ decipher [diˈsaifə] vt. 译解;破译

确保信息畅通

电子邮件通信是世界上发展最快的通信媒介。单就美国来看，它已由每年4万亿封邮件信息往来，增加到7万多亿。而且，最近的调查发现，每位商务人士平均每天收发邮件信息的总数约为90封。如果你认为自己的邮箱现在已经爆满的话，等着瞧吧，据估计，电子邮件的使用量每天会超过50亿！

虽然电子邮件确实具有强大的功能，而且也广受欢迎，但它并不总是表达观点的最有效途径。令人惊奇的是，尽管ASCII文本、邮件服务器嵌入的奇怪换行符、使用怪异语言的客户、垃圾邮件、从不着边际的作者、单调的邮件列表，以及难以破译的注销规则之间仍然存在着局限性，但所有用来交流的手段已经全部电子化了。

为了有效地使用电子邮件，并且确保他人能够读懂和理解邮件信息，应该遵循一些简单的电子邮件交流规范。通过合理利用电子邮件礼仪，你可以把邮件通信转变为自己使用最频繁的通信工具。

In order to use e-mail effectively and ensure that others read and understand your messages, follow some simple email communication guidelines. By utilizing proper e-etiquette, you can turn e-mail correspondences into your most coherent communication tool.

1. Always include a detailed subject line.

Because e-mail messages arrive without going through a screening process or gatekeeper, many people use the subject line to determine which messages get read and which get instantly deleted. So even though your message may be important for the recipient, if you make the subject line vague or leave it blank, there's a good chance the message will never get read. When you create your subject line, be sure it adequately reflects the message's content. Trying to trick recipients with "sensational" subject lines will only make them wary of future correspondences from you. In the process, keep your subject line brief, as most e-mail programs will only display the first seven to ten words. The more concise and truthful your subject line is, the greater the chance your recipient will read your message.

2. Allow ample time for a response.

Nearly everyone regards e-mail as "instant communication." As such, they expect an immediate response to every message. Unfortunately, immediate responses are not always feasible. Depending on your recipient's workload, log-on habits and time restraints, responding to your message may take several days. The general rule is to allow at least three days for an e-mail response. If you don't receive a reply, resend the original message and insert "2" into the subject line. So if your original message subject

1. 始终填写详细的标题栏。

由于电子邮件信息的传递没有筛选过程或是人为观察，很多人根据标题栏来判断哪些信息该读、哪些信息可以立即删掉。所以，即使你的信息对于收件人来说非常重要，但如果标题栏太模糊或是空白的话，那这条信息永远不被阅读的可能性就非常大。创建标题栏的时候，一定要确保它能够充分反映信息的内容。试图用“耸人听闻”的标题栏来戏弄收件人只会让他们提防你以后的邮件。在创建过程中，应保证标题栏的简洁，因为大多数邮件程序只会显示前7到10个字。标题栏越是简洁真诚，收件人阅读邮件的可能性就越大。

2. 允许充裕的回复时间。

几乎所有人都把电子邮件视为“即时通信”。在这种情况下，他们希望能够收到每条信息的即时回复。但不幸的是，即时回复并不总是可实现的。根据收件人的工作量、查收邮件习惯和时间限制，你有可能需要几天后才能收到回复的邮件。一般规则是至少三天内回复。如果没有收到回信，可以重发原始邮件，并在标题栏插入“2”字。所以，如果原始邮件标题栏是“你需要的产品信息”，重发邮件的标题栏改为“你需要的产品信息-2”。如果第二次尝试仍然没有得到回复，则考虑给收件人打电话，提醒他或她查看你的邮件信息。

line reads, "product information you requested," the resent subject line would read, "Product information you requested-2." If your second attempt doesn't get a response, consider calling your recipient and alerting him or her to your message.

3.Know when to and when not to reply to a sender.

One challenge with e-mail is that everyone wants to have the last word. As a result, an e-mail trail can continue on for days, with each additional message not adding anything to the subject's importance. Consider this typical e-mail exchange:

Person 1: "Let's meet at 3 p.m. in the conference room."

Person 2: "That works for my schedule, too. See you then."

Person 1: "Great. Looking forward to it."

Person 2: "Me, too. Talk with you later."

Person 1: "Okay. See you at three."

And on and on the exchange continues simply because neither person can resist the temptation to reply. Such correspondences not only waste time, but they also take up bandwidth① space on the server and add to people's frustrations as their e-mail boxes are continually full. If your intended reply does not add anything to the original message's objective, don't send it.

On the other hand, know when you definitely should send a response. If someone e-mails you a document to review, for example, a simple acknowledgment stating you received it and are reviewing it is sufficient.

---

① bandwidth [ˈbændwidθ] *n.* 频带宽度

3. 了解给发件人回信的合适时间。

使用电子邮件的一个挑战是每个人都想说最后一句话。结果是一封邮件来回持续好几天，而每次附上的内容并没有增加任何与主题相关的重要信息。看看下面这条典型的邮件交流记录：

人物 1：“我们下午 3 点在会议室见。”

人物 2：“正好与我安排的时间吻合。到时见。”

人物 1：“太好了。期待与你会面。”

人物 2：“我也是。下午再聊。”

人物 1：“好的。3 点见。”

只是因为难以抵制回复邮件的诱惑，双方便有了这种你来我往的持续交流。这种信件不仅浪费时间，而且占用了大量宽带服务器的空间，随着收件箱越来越满，人们的烦恼也越来越多。如果你打算回复的邮件对原信息的主题没有添加任何新的东西，就不要再回邮件。

另一方面，一定要清楚什么时候回复邮件最为合适。如果有人给你发了封文件让你审核，比如说，一份简单的确认陈述，就需要你说明已经收到了这份文件，并正在审核之中。不要让他们心神不定地等待，一旦收到重要的信息，应给出简短的确认，类似于从网上零售商那儿收到订单确认一样。

Don't force people to wait in limbo, unsure of the status of their request. Give a brief confirmation when you receive important messages, similar to the order acknowledgments you receive from online retailers.

4. Use your "reply" button properly.

All e-mail programs have a "reply" and a "reply to all" option. Using the wrong one could cause you undue embarrassment. Clicking the "reply" button sends your message to the original sender only. In contrast, the "reply to all" button sends your message to the original sender and to all the other addressees listed in the original message's To, CC (carbon copy), and BCC (blind carbon copy) fields. Unless you want all these people to read your reply message, it's wise to simply use the "reply" button. Additionally, since the addresses in the BCC field are not revealed to you, there's no way of knowing precisely whom your "reply to all" message will be sent to. When in doubt, use the "reply" option only.

5. Set up your e-mail reply feature appropriately.

When you set up your e-mail program's reply preferences, you have many options to choose from. To make replies easy for you and your recipient, make sure your new message is set to appear as the first block of text above the original message. Making your reply message appear below the original message can confuse your recipient, as he or she may not scroll① all the way down and may think you did not add any new information. Also, if the original message is lengthy, start a new e-mail message rather than replying. All the additional text could slow the e-mail

① scroll [skrəul] *vi.* 拖滚动条

4. 适当使用“回复”按钮。

所有的电子邮件程序中都有“回复”和“回复所有人”选择。选择错误会给你带来不必要的尴尬。点击“回复”按钮将会把你的信息只传给原始发件人。相反，“回复所有人”按钮则不仅会把你的信息传给原始发件人，还会传给其他所有在原始信息副本和复写副本中存在地址的人。除非你想让所有这些人都阅读你的回复信息，否则就应该明智地选择只使用“回复”按钮。此外，由于复写副本中的地址并没有显示给你，你就没法精确地知道自己的“回复所有人”信息将会发给谁。不能肯定时，仅可使用“回复”选项。

5. 适当设置电子邮件回复功能。

设置电子邮件程序的回复选项时，有很多可供选择的选项。为了让回复对你和收件人更容易，要确保你的新信息作为首显字符块置于原始信息之上。回复信息在原始信息之下也许会使收件人混淆不清，因为他或她有可能不会把滚动条一直往下拉，并且有可能认为你并没有添加什么新信息。而且，如果原始信息很长的话，最好新建邮件信息，不要回复。所有的附加文本都会降低邮件的传输速度。最后，如果你要回答一系列的问题，每条回答前应该重述原来的问题。不要试图回到原邮件，输入你的回答，因为这种方法很难使对方筛选出所需要的信息。

transmission. Finally, if you are replying to a series of questions, restate the question before each answer. Resist the temptation to go back into the original message and type your answers there, as this approach makes it difficult for the other party to sift out the requested information.

6. Ask permission to add people to your message list.

Because of the sheer number of e-mail messages people receive daily, always ask permission before you automatically put someone on your daily message list. While you may enjoy receiving jokes, photos and silly cartoons throughout the day, others may not appreciate such items taking up space on their server. Additionally, you won't always know what kind of technology the other party has, so your 250KB photo may take your recipient over an hour to download if the technology is outdated.

E-mail communication is definitely coming of age. Ranked as the second most popular tool next to the telephone, there s little doubt that e-mail will one day take the lead. Before that can happen, though, people everywhere need to master the rules of e-mail etiquette in order to get their messages across accurately and coherently.

(1,088 words)

6. 请求在信息列表中加入联系人的权限。

由于人们每天会收到大量的电子邮件信息，在自动将某人加入日常信息列表前始终要征得他人的同意。虽然你可能喜欢整天收到笑话、照片和愚蠢的漫画，但别人也许不喜欢让这些东西占用他们的服务器空间。此外，你也并不总是知道另一方使用什么类型的技术，所以，如果技术过时的话，有可能 250KB 的照片就会让收件人花一个多小时下载。

电子邮件通信的时代确实已经来临。作为仅次于电话、高居最受欢迎的通信工具次席的电子邮件，毫无疑问终有一天会居于领先地位。但是，在这一幕发生之前，为了让自己的信息更准确而连贯地发出，人们都需要掌握电子邮件的礼仪规范。

知识链接

ASCII 美国信息互换标准代码(American Standard Code for Information Interchange)。它是基于拉丁字母的一套电脑编码系统，主要用于显示现代英语和其他西欧语言。

题 记

互联网革命使人们不知不觉地减少了口语交流，而电子邮件的横空出世又增加了文本的使用频率，提供了可靠和便捷的全天候高效交流方式。时尚的新名词——netiquette (network etiquette)网络礼仪的出现，吸引越来越多的人在商业洽谈和日常沟通中对电子邮件趋之若鹜。效率原则、职业原则和免责原则是我们需要掌握电子邮件礼仪的三个理由。效率原则指通过简明扼要的电子邮件获取良好的沟通效果；职业原则希望使用合适的邮件语言传递职业形象；免责原则强调员工的电子邮件风险意识，避免公司陷入代价高昂的法律诉讼。电子邮件礼仪引领着电子邮件的规范化或专业化，丰富了电子邮件的有效内容和组织管理，通过用户友好功能，构造并修改客户程序和基于网络的电子邮件服务的连接结构，使人们能够更好地使用电子邮件承载的信息。

The Primary Means of Business Communications

In the fast moving global economy, e-mail offers the certainty and convenience of being able to communicate effectively at any hour of the day or night. However, it is this ease and accessibility that allows e-mail to be used in odd or unprofessional ways.

The Internet revolution has had the unintended effect of decreasing the use of oral communication and increasing the importance of text—particularly e-mails—as the primary means of business communications.

Why has e-mail become so popular? Why use e-mails instead of phone calls? It is harder to control the conduct of phone calls than e-mail, their length, subject matter, depth of content, and the availability of other participants. Phone calls leave scant records, are impractical for reaching large numbers of people instantly and often consume more time and mental effort than is needed to send an e-mail.

Our discussion proceeds as follows: Why good e-mail practices are needed, good e-mail practices, writing effective content, and organizing e-mails.

There are three reasons why we need e-mail etiquette: efficiency, professionalism, and protection from liability. Efficiency means e-mails that

商务沟通的主要手段

在全球经济迅速发展的进程中，电子邮件提供了可靠和便捷的全天候高效交流方式。 但是，这种既灵活又便利的特点也让电邮的使用变得不规范或不专业。

互联网革命使人们不知不觉地减少了口语交流，增加了文本的使用频率，而电子邮件的运用尤为突出，它已经成为商业洽谈的首选方式。

为什么现在电子邮件会如此受欢迎？ 为什么人们更愿意发电子邮件而不是打电话？ 相对于发电子邮件而言，打电话是一种更难以掌控的沟通方式，你既无法控制它的长度、话题、内容的深度，又很难再邀请其他人参与对话。 打电话不会留下文字记录，无法将信息及时传递给很多人，与发送电邮相比，常常需要耗费更多的时间和精力。

我们的论述从以下几点展开：为什么需要规范的电邮训练，什么是规范的电邮训练，写出有效的内容和电邮的组织管理。

效率原则、职业原则和免责原则是我们需要掌握电子邮件礼仪

get to the point produce better results, professionalism prefers proper language conveys a professional image, and protection from liability maintains employee awareness of e-mail risks can protect your firm from costly lawsuits.

Tara Bradford, an outsourcing client liaison① manager at an InternationalStaff.net contract facility in South India, provides the following tips on how to use e-mail effectively.

Use informative subject lines.

Personalize messages.

Be clear and concise.

Use proper grammar and punctuation.

Know when to send an e-mail.

Use signatures.

Spell check and review your e-mails before sending.

Bradford said that liability control should drive organizations to train all staff in proper e-mail etiquette. In addition, liability can also be controlled by the use of pre-approved responses to frequently asked questions (FAQs) and by the use of quality assurance measures.

It is possible to provide quality assurance checks on all outgoing e-mails, particularly in customer service and support centers. On the other hand, you could try a lesser approach, say with new staff having all their e-mails checked before they are sent out, and more experienced staff having reduced percentages reviewed.

Chris Mitchell of Microsoft said that many people do not scroll down

---

① liaison [liˈeizən] *n.* 联络

的三个理由。效率原则指通过简明扼要的电子邮件获取良好的沟通效果；职业原则希望使用合适的邮件语言传递职业形象；免责原则强调员工的电子邮件风险意识，避免公司陷入代价高昂的法律诉讼。

塔娜·布莱德福特是“国际职员网”外包项目管理公司南印度分公司的客户经理，她给我们提供了几条如何高效使用电子邮件的小贴士：

使用信息翔实的主题栏。

信息个性化。

内容清晰并简明扼要。

语法恰当，标点正确。

邮件发送适时。

使用签名。

发送前检查拼写，复审全文。

布莱德福特认为，责任控制促使公司训练全体员工掌握恰当的电子邮件礼仪。此外，利用“常见问题解答”（FAQs）等措施，预先核准和保证电子邮件的质量，也可以控制法律责任。

为所有的外发邮件、特别是客户服务和支持中心的电子邮件提供质量保证检查是可能的手段。另一方面，可以对新员工尝试一种辅助方式，如在他们发送邮件之前，让人将全部邮件检查一遍，而对更有经验的员工，则可减少检查量。

in the e-mails they receive. To communicate effectively with non-scrollers, put essential information at the beginning. In long, complex e-mails, he often provides summaries at the beginning. If readers need additional details, they can scroll down into the body of the text.

E-mail is thought based. E-mails sometimes do not contain the entire thought, which might be spread out over several e-mails. When an e-mail has been passed back and forth, readers might have to scroll down to the bottom to catch the original exchange or question that prompted subsequent replies.

To be effective, Chris says that it helps to restate the central idea or original query at the beginning of an e-mail that has gone back and forth. This is particularly important when communicating with people who use free e-mail services that truncate① replies, making it impossible to consult the original exchange.

In e-mails that have questions in multiple locations, Microsoft's Mitchell will highlight those questions with a colored font in his reply, with his responses given beneath each question. For the 15 percent of American men who are colorblind, alternate approaches should be used such as uppercase② letters, bold font, or italics. Since bold or italic fonts might not be transmitted or preserved in some e-mail systems, uppercase letters might be the best option for highlighting questions.

For internal communications, Mitchell says it is not necessary to always produce highly organized and precisely worded e-mails. However,

---

① truncate [trʌŋˈkeit] *vt.* 缩短；把……截短

② uppercase [ˈʌpəˈkeis] *adj.* 大写字母的

微软公司的克里斯·米歇尔认为，很多人收电邮时没有向下拖滚动条。为了和这些不拖滚动条的人有效沟通，要把重要信息放在开头。对冗长而复杂的邮件，他常常在开头概括一下主要内容。如果读者需要了解其他细节，他们可以拖动滚动条，进入文本的主体部分。

电子邮件的功能是传文达意。有时，电子邮件并不能囊括发件人的所有想法，这些想法可能要通过几封邮件才能表达清楚。一封邮件往返多次之后，阅读者一定要将滚动条拖到邮件底部，核实引出后续回复的原始交流信息或问题。

克里斯认为，对于已经往返多次的邮件，高效的办法是在邮件开头重申主要的想法或最初的询问。这个方法在与使用免费电邮服务的人沟通时尤为重要，因为免费电邮会删除回复，使读者无法看到最初的交流记录。

对于多处存在疑问的电子邮件，微软公司的米歇尔会在回复中用彩色字体将这些问题标出，并将答复写在每个问题的下方。由于15%的美国人患有色盲，可以用大写字母、黑体字或斜体字等方法替换。因为有些电子邮件系统无法传输黑体字或斜体字，所以大写字母对所要强调的问题也许是最佳选择。

米歇尔认为，对公司内部的交流来说，没有必要总是强求结构严谨和言辞准确的电子邮件。但是，这并不意味着内部交流就可以完全抛弃礼仪，特别是涉及专业礼貌时更是如此。

etiquette is not totally abandoned in internal communications, particularly when it comes to professional courtesy.

The subject line of e-mails might often be the only part of an e-mail that many people will read. You can summarize the action item of your e-mail in the subject line, e.g., "Tues. meeting canceled."

To avoid having your e-mail blocked by spam filters, refrain from using words in your subject line that are common in the subject lines of spam. Words such as "free" or "Viagra"[1] in your subject line invites trouble.

Mitchell receives between 50 and 100 e-mails per day, plus another 300 from list services. Some are automatically routed to folders within his Outlook e-mail client program, where they might remain unread unless needed. He budgets time every morning for e-mails and prioritizes e-mails to read and respond to, thereby preventing his entire day from being consumed by e-mail.

Chris uses Conversation View in Outlook to group related e-mails together and create threaded discussions. Threading techniques borrowed from online bulletin boards can be used to organize e-mails and allow complex discussions to be tracked and managed efficiently. The organization of information is called syndetics[2], with structures for organizing information called syndetic structures. An index or catalog is a syndetic structure.

In the future, we can expect to see more user-friendly capabilities for

---

① viagra [vaiˈægrə] *n.* 伟哥(一种药物名称)

② syndetic [sinˈdetik] *adj.* 连接的

电子邮件的标题栏通常是很多人会读到的唯一部分。你可以在标题栏中总结电子邮件的任务项，如“周二会议取消”。

为避免垃圾邮件过滤器阻止你发送的电子邮件，绝不可在标题栏中使用垃圾邮件标题栏中常用的字眼。标题栏中出现“免费”、“伟哥”等字眼会给你带来麻烦。

米歇尔每天都会收到50到100封邮件，再加上列表服务发送的另外300封邮件。有些是自动路由到Outlook软件电邮客户端程序文件夹内的邮件，需要时才被调出来阅读。他每天早上都会安排好时间处理邮件，确定邮件的轻重缓急，然后阅读和回复电子邮件，从而防止整天耗在电子邮件中难以自拔。

克里斯常常使用微软Outlook中的“会话视野”功能，将相关的电子邮件编组，创建在线讨论。线程技术借用在线公告栏，可以用来组织电子邮件，有效跟踪和管理复杂的讨论。信息的组织称之为连接技术，为组织信息的结构称之为连接结构。索引和目录就是一种连接结构。

将来，我们可以期待看到更多的用户友好功能，构造并修改电子邮件客户程序和基于网络的电子邮件服务的连接结构。这种连接结构可以模仿网络公告栏的线性特点，根据讨论的线索和次级线索决定邮件的排列顺序和讨论展开的顺序。这将使我们能够更好地使用电子邮件承载的信息。

constructing and modifying syndetic structures in e-mail client programs andweb-based e-mail services. Syndetic structures can imitate the threading features used by online bulletin boards where discussion threads and subthreads determine the order in which postings are arranged and discussions branch out. This will enable us to make better use of the information contained in e-mails.

(888 words)

知识链接

Spam 垃圾电子邮件。垃圾邮件指未经用户许可就强行发送到用户邮箱中的任何电子邮件。垃圾邮件一般具有批量发送的特征。内容包括赚钱信息、成人广告、商业或个人网站广告、电子杂志、连环信等。垃圾邮件可以分为良性和恶性的。良性垃圾邮件是各种宣传广告等对收件人影响不大的信息邮件。恶性垃圾邮件是指具有破坏性的电子邮件。垃圾邮件可以说是互联网带给人类最具争议性的副产品，它的泛滥已经使整个互联网不堪重负。

题 记

被誉为信息社会、电子世界的“圣人”、“先驱”和“先知”的马歇尔·麦克卢汉不仅是20世纪名副其实的传播学大师、最富有原创性的传播学理论家，他对商业关系网的深邃理解也不乏天才启示录式的思想：“我们塑造了工具，此后工具又塑造了我们。”商业人际关系网络是构筑贸易流通渠道、人与人之间进行信息交流的重要纽带，其结点是网络中的人或机构，其联系是交流的方式和内容。建立良好的关系网依赖于人们能否遵循它的礼仪规范，这其中包括关系网的物理距离，即待在合适的地方、保持联系、上升到一个新的水平等；互动距离，即闲聊、商业名片等；社会距离，即跳上“品牌车”，“经营”活动等；心理距离，即给他人深刻的印象、了解你想要的结果等。请记住梅达尔·波士说过的一句话：“你的生存状态完全取决于你的人际关系”，从而把人际关系的积累作为自己职业生涯规划发展过程中的一项重要事情去准备。

Networking Business Etiquette

Everybody is doing it. At least, successful people are doing it. And " it" isn't even a dirty word. " It" is Networking. Successful business people network for a variety of reasons.

Career networking is an excellent tool for finding and landing your next great job opportunity. In fact, according to the Wall Street Journal, 94% of new job finders cited networking as their primary mode of job search.

Networking is also used to build relationships with potential and existing clients and vendors. Let's face it, people prefer to do business with and refer business to people they know and trust.

Think you don't have to network because you are not looking for a new job and are not in sales? Think again. A recent poll by Inc. com found that 48% of their readers believed that personal connections are the primary factor that most often leads to getting ahead in an organization. No matter how qualified you are, unless you have strong relationships with key players, your advancement opportunities are limited.

There's even more to networking—it's an excellent source of information and ideas about events, trends, opportunities and industry news. You can also find support for your proposals and the chance to help others.

编织商业关系网

每个人都在这样做，至少，成功人士正在这样做。“它”根本算不上一个肮脏的词汇。“它”是关系网。成功的商业人士出于五花八门的理由编织着关系网。

就业网络是一个极好的工具，它可以帮助你寻找和捕获下一个不错的就业机会。事实上，根据《华尔街日报》的调查，寻找新工作的人中有94％表示，关系网是他们的主要求职方式。

关系网也被用来与潜在的和现有的客户以及供应商建立关系。让我们面对这个事实，人们更喜欢与那些他们了解和信任的人做生意，并把生意交给他们打理。

试想一下，难道你会因为不找新工作或不做销售就不建立关系网吗？肯定不会。Inc. com 最近发起的一项投票结果表明，48％的读者认为，人际关系往往是致使你在一个组织中位于前列的主要因素。不管你是如何符合条件，除非你与关键人有密切的关系，否则晋升的机会非常渺茫。

关系网甚至意味着更多的资源：它为相关事件、发展趋势、机会和行业新闻提供良好的信息和思想来源。你也可以找到支持提案的人，有机会帮助他人。慈善募捐在很大程度上受个人和职业关系网络的驱动。

Charitable fundraising is also driven heavily by personal and professional networking.

So what exactly is networking? It's simply building enduring relationships that are mutually beneficial. Not so simple is the ability to stand out from the networking crowd as being polished, professional and endearing. This ability gives you an edge to make an outstanding impression and outclass your competition. It comes from understanding and applying business networking etiquette. The following are business networking etiquette tips.

Jump on the "Brand wagon"

Personal Branding is the message you send—and your audience receives—about you. Do you want to be known as a problem solver, a rain man, a philanthropist? Creative? Aggressive? Dynamic or Disciplined?

For your audience to receive your intended message, it must be genuine. Take your true skills and strengths, combine them with your passions and identify your unique promise of value to your clients, your employer, colleagues and other important contacts. This message becomes your personal branding statement.

When you are networking, one of the first things people will ask you is what you do. Take this opportunity to communicate your personal branding statement and make it shine. Avoid stating your job title; focus on the value you bring to your client. Be prepared to customize your branding statement to suit the situation, while still maintaining authenticity. For example, instead of saying you are a financial planner, share how your analytical skills and interest in helping others enables you to achieve high returns on your clients' portfolios, while managing risk so they can sleep at night.

因此，到底什么是关系网？ 它只不过是建立双方互利的持久关系罢了。 能够从众多圆滑、专业和讨人喜欢的关系网络人群中脱颖而出并非如此简单。 这种能力显示出你的一种优势，给人出色的印象并远胜于你的竞争对手。 它来自于对商业社交礼仪的理解和运用。 下面是编织商业关系网的小贴士。

跳上“品牌车”

个人品牌包含你的信息，你发出信息，而听众则接收信息。 你想被人看做是问题的解决者、社交笨拙之人，还是慈善家？ 创新？进取？ 充满活力还是墨守成规？

为了使听众收到你想要传达的信息，必须保证信息的真实性。拿出真正的技能和力量，并把它们与你的激情相结合，与客户、雇主、同事和其他重要的联系人分享你具有独特价值的承诺。 这种信息就是你的个人品牌陈述。

建立关系网时，人们首先问的问题之一就是你是做什么的。 借此沟通机会，亮出你的个人品牌陈述来增添亮点。 避免陈述职位头衔；重点讲述给客户带来的价值。 随时准备使品牌声明适应不同的情况，同时保持它的真实性。 举例来说，不要在大众面前炫耀你财务规划师的身份，应该与大家分享你的分析能力和乐于助人的兴趣，这可以使你从客户的投资组合中获得高额回报，你帮助他们管理风险的同时，他们也可以高枕无忧。

给他人深刻的印象

最初的印象历时最久。 人类是非常极端的视觉动物。 人们对你的印象超过半数均基于亲眼所见。 为了给人积极的视觉印象，确

Impress with Your Impression

First impressions are the most lasting.Humans are very visual beings. More than half the impression you make is based on what people see.To make a positive visual impression, make sure you are well visual and feel good about what you are wearing at all times.

Not only does your personal appearance speakabout you, it also speaks to you. If you feel that you are appropriately dressed for the occasion, you will feel more confident and able to handle whatever comes your way in any situation.If you don't feel good about your appearance, it can inhibit your confidence and you may find yourself avoiding speaking to people, leaving networking opportunities unrealized.

When you network, you are promoting your personal brand. Like any product, your packaging defines and differentiates who you are as a professional business person. Make sure your visual message matches your verbal message.

Know Your Desired Outcome

Before going to a networking meeting or event, ask yourself, "Why am I going?" Be specific, such as "I am going to speak to 10 new people today and get contact information for 4 of them." Target individuals and research them on Google, or through mutual acquaintances so you are prepared to make small talk intelligently.

Your reason for going should not be to sell anything.You are there to meet people and develop relationships with them. Another reason is to "give to the group".When you identify a group to attend regularly, ask the leaders how you can serve.Is there a committee opening? Is there some task you can perform to add to the success of the group?

保自己看上去不错，对自己的穿着要时时刻刻保持良好的感觉。

个人外表不仅帮你树立形象，而且助你和他人交流。如果你在某个场合感觉穿着得体，你会感到更有信心，在任何情况下无论发生什么事都可以从容应对。如果你对自己的外貌感觉不佳，就会抑制你的信心，并且会发现自己不愿意和他人交谈，让建立关系网的机会白白溜走。

建立关系网时，你是在宣传自己的个人品牌。你的包装就像任何产品一样，界定和区分你是一位什么样的专业商务人士。一定要确保你给人的视觉信息符合你的谈吐举止。

了解你想要的结果

参加联谊会或活动之前，先问问自己，“我为什么去”？可以再具体点，如“今天我打算结交10个新朋友，并且要拿到其中4人的联系方式”。然后锁定个人目标，并在谷歌上收集他们的信息，或者通过双方的熟人引荐，为你充满睿智地与他们闲聊做好准备。

参加聚会的理由不应当是推销任何商品。到这儿来是为了结识更多的人，和他们拉上关系。另外一个理由是“加入集体”。当你确定定期参加一群人的活动时，询问头儿如何为大家服务。执委会有空缺的职位吗？为了大家的成功，还有哪些你可以做的工作？

闲聊

闲聊的目的是打破僵局，并建立和谐的关系。没有和谐的关系，就没有发展关系的基础。引荐和握手之后即可开始闲聊。仔细观察，根据当时的环境发问，如“那个说话的人还真花了时间研究过听众”，或“你是做什么工作的”？

Small Talk

The purpose of small talk is to break the ice and build rapport①. Without rapport, there is no foundation to develop a relationship.Start with an introduction and a handshake. Follow with positive observations and questions about your immediate surroundings, such as "The speaker really took the time to research the audience." or " What kind of work do you do?"

When you are engaging in small talk, keep your body language relaxed and confident. Lean in to show interest, but respect individual personal space.

For eye contact, the rule of thumb is 60% . This means look your companion in the eye 60% of the time.When you are not looking directly into the eyes, rest your gaze on the eyebrows or mouth.Don't let your eyes stray too far away from the face.The goal is to achieve a good balance between a scary stare and evasive② eye darting③ .

It's easier to build rapport with someone if you remind them of themselves.Without being obvious, try to match pace and volume of speech as well as body language.

Spend 80% of your time listening and 20% talking.As Dale Carnegie wrote, " become genuinely interested in the other person and encourage them to talk about themselves."

"Work" the Event

When you are at a networking event, recognize that everyone is there

---

① rapport [ræˈpɔː] *n.* 和谐一致

② evasive [iˈveisiv] *adj.* 逃避的

③ darting [dɑːtiŋ] *n.* 投射

参与闲聊时，肢体语言呈放松和自信的状态。身体前倾，表现出兴趣，但要尊重个人的私人空间。

闲聊时原则上要保持60%的目光接触时间。这意味着在交谈过程中60%的时间要看着同伴的眼睛。如果没有直接盯着对方眼睛，也应该注视对方的眉毛或嘴巴。不要让你的眼睛太过于游离对方的脸庞。盯住目标是在害怕凝视和回避目光之间实现良好的平衡。

如果你提醒他们注意自己，就会更容易与人建立融洽的关系。尽量让语速和声音大小与肢体语言相匹配，不要有明显的差异。

80%的时间倾听，20%的时间说话。正如美国著名的人际关系学大师戴尔·卡内基写下的："真正对他人感兴趣，并鼓励他们谈论自己。"

"经营"活动

在建立关系网的活动中，要意识到这儿的每个人也都在拉关系。务必不要独占任何人的时间。最多与每个人交谈10分钟。如果要优雅地结束谈话，只需说"很高兴见到你，也许我们可以在不久后一起喝咖啡"，然后离开。

活动开始前吃点小点心，以便集中精力会见不同的人。手上不要有任何东西，这样可以自由地握手并做出各种手势。如果你喜欢喝酒，请用左手拿酒杯，以保持右手干燥，避免被沾满了汗的酒杯弄得又粘又湿。

商业名片

准备好商业名片。商业名片应该放在干净、随手可拿的地方。放在外套口袋里的超薄型名片夹最为理想。绝不要从后衣口袋里掏

to network too. Make sure you don't monopolize any one person's time. Aim to spend a maximum of 10 minutes with each person. To end a conversation graciously, simply say, "It was a pleasure meeting you, perhaps we could have coffee in the near future," and depart.

Enjoy a snack before the event so your attention will be focused on meeting people. Keep your hands free to shake hands and gesture. If you fancy a drink, carry it in your left hand so that your right hand is not wet and clammy① from the sweaty glass.

Business Cards

Be prepared. Have a clean supply of business cards easily accessible. A slim business card holder that fits in a jacket pocket is ideal. Never take cards from your back pocket. You should never dig in your purse, fumble or make people wait while you retrieve your card. Present your card in a manner that demonstrates it is worth something. Ensure that the type is facing up and towards the other person.

When receiving a business card, take the time to look at it and comment favourably on some aspect of it, or ask a question that shows your interest.

Places, please

Avoid standing at the bar. People may congregate there, but it's not an ideal spot to engage people in conversation. Instead, stand near the food or dessert table where people are lingering and eating. You'll find them more open to talking because people like to chat during meals and people are usually happy and receptive when they have ready access to food.

---

① clammy [ˈklæmi] *adj*. 黏糊糊的

出名片。绝不要在钱包里找名片，七上八下地到处乱摸，或者是找名片时让别人在一旁干等。递名片的方式要有风度，并显示名片的价值。确保名片的打印面朝上，正对他人。

收到名片时，花点时间看一下，在某些方面给予积极的评论，或者问个问题，以表示你的关注。

请待在合适的地方

不要站在吧台旁。大家可能在那儿聚会，但吧台并不是与人交谈的理想场所。相反可以站在食物或甜点桌的附近，大家都在那儿来来往往地边吃边聊。你会发现他们的谈话更放得开，因为人们喜欢在吃饭的时候聊天，人们可以随意品尝美味佳肴时，通常非常开心并易于接受他人。

保持联系

双方的接触可能从建立关系的活动开始，但这种关系的建立还需要时间来酝酿。重要的是在第一次见面后以适当的方式继续保持联系，并使出浑身解数力求成功。你可以通过电子邮件或私人便条做到这一点："很高兴见到你。大约下周我会给你打电话，或找个时间聚一下。"

保持联系的另一种方式是定期发送相关的、即将举行的活动的重要信息、文章或通知。这表明你理解他人的需求并乐意效劳。当你得知相关交易或促销活动时，也可以设置谷歌新闻快讯和发送祝贺短信。

上升到新的水平

建立和维持最重要的商业关系往往超出了传统的工作环境。这

Keep in Touch

Your connection may start at a networking event, but the relationship is built over time. It's important to follow up the first meeting in an appropriate fashion to keep the momentum and stay top of mind. You can achieve this by email or personal note, "It was a pleasure meeting you. I'll call you in the next week or so to set up some time to get together."

Another way to stay in touch is by periodically sending important information, articles or notification of a relevant, upcoming event. This demonstrates your understanding of a person's needs and your willingness to be of service. You can also set up a Google news alert and send congratulatory notes when you learn of pertinent① deals or promotions.

Take It to the Next Level

The most important business relationships are often created and maintained outside the traditional work environment. This means that you should be prepared to meet your networking circle at restaurants, sporting events, association meetings, fund-raisers, golf courses, seminars, workshops, conferences and conventions. Be committed to knowing and practicing the particular etiquette for these venues② as well.

Understanding and applying networking etiquette will empower you to build and nurture your own network. These lasting, mutually beneficial business relationships begin with projecting an outstanding impression, but are sustained through trust and the investment of time and effort to help others.

(1,445 words)

---

① pertinent [ˈpəːtinənt] *adj.* 恰当的

② venue [ˈvenjuː] *n.* 会场；发生地

意味着你应该准备在餐厅、体育赛事、行业协会会议、募捐集会、高尔夫球场、研讨会、讲习班、学术会议和大型会议期间建立社交圈。还要致力于了解和实践这些场合的特殊礼仪。

理解和应用社交礼仪将会使你在建立和培育关系网时能够出奇制胜。虽然这些长期、互利的商业关系始于突出的印象，但他们还需要信任、投资时间和努力帮助他人才能历久弥新。

知识链接

Dale Carnegie 戴尔·卡耐基(1888—1955)，是美国著名的人际关系学大师、西方现代人际关系教育的奠基人。卡内基开创的“人际关系训练班”遍布世界各地。他早期的著作《人性的光辉》、《语言的突破》、《美好的人生》、《人性的优点》曾被译成28种文字，其中《人性的弱点全集》一书，是继《圣经》之后世界出版史上的第二畅销书。

Google news alert 谷歌新闻快讯，是一种谷歌新闻资讯，只要拥有谷歌账号，即可登录统一管理订阅。符合指定主题的新闻文章在线刊载时，可以通过电子邮件发送谷歌快讯。谷歌快讯的一些常见用途如下：监控新闻报道的进展情况，追踪竞争对手或业界最新信息，了解名人或事件最新动态，掌握喜爱的体育代表队的近况。

题 记

现代的商业交往遍及全球，人们穿梭于不同的国家，与不同的客户、同事、顾客打交道。不同文化背景中的商务人士固守着本国文化中约定俗成的礼仪原则，而且许多是不成文的规则。亚洲的商务人士重视“面子”：在中国和日本，你应该用双手交出和接收名片；欧洲的商务人士守时善谈：与他们约会切忌迟到；美洲的商务人士热情直率：在墨西哥，拍拍别人的背很正常，但在中国这是决不允许的；非洲的商务人士具有浓郁的异域风情：在信仰穆斯林的国家，任何礼品都不能含有酒精；在中东，你甚至可以和男人卿卿我我，但决不能碰女人。这些不成文的复杂礼仪反映了一种文化的价值观，对它的敬畏已经成为企业文化、企业理念不可或缺的组成部分，正如爱尔兰小说家和讽刺作家劳伦斯·斯特恩所言：“自尊引导我们的品行，尊重他人支配我们的行为。”

Cultural Values in International Business Etiquette

Working in foreign countries means working with foreign cultures. International business etiquette allows people to build better and longer lasting business relationships. "To have respect for ourselves guides our morals; and to have deference for others governs our manners." Lawrence Sterne, Irish novelist & satirist.

Etiquette, or good manners, is an important part of our day to day lives. Whether we realise it or not we are always subconsciously adhering to rules of etiquette. Much of the time these are unwritten; for example giving up your seat to a lady or elderly person, queuing for a bus in an orderly fashion according to who arrived first or simply saying "please" or "thank you". All are examples of etiquette; complex unwritten rules that reflect a culture's values.

Etiquette accomplishes many tasks. However, the one noteworthy function that etiquette does perform is that it shows respect and deference to another. By doing so it maintains good interpersonal relationships. Ultimately, it could be argued, etiquette is about making sure that when people mix together there are rules of interaction in place that ensure their communication, transaction or whatever it may be goes smoothly.

We all now how we or others feel when a lack of etiquette is shown.

国际商务礼仪中的文化价值观

在国外工作意味着与异域文化打交道。国际商业礼仪帮助人们建立了更好、更长久持续的商业关系。爱尔兰小说家和讽刺作家劳伦斯·斯特恩说:“自尊引导我们的品行，尊重他人支配我们的行为。”

礼仪，或者良好的行为，是我们日常生活的重要组成部分。不论我们是否认识到这一点，潜意识里我们总会遵守某些礼仪原则。大多数时候，这些礼仪是不成文的，比如说给女士或老年人让座，按照先来先到的原则自觉排队等候公共汽车，或者只是简单地说一声“请”或“谢谢”。这些都是礼仪的例子，复杂的不成文规则反映了一种文化的价值观。

礼仪在很多场合大有作为。然而，礼仪确实还表现出一个值得注意的功能，即礼仪展示了对他人的尊重和敬意。通过这样的做法，礼仪维持着良好的人际关系。归根结底，人们认为礼仪就是交往时要确信，这些交际原则能保证他们的交流、交易或任何其他的事情都能顺利进行。

我们都知道，当自己或他人失礼时的感觉是怎样的。如果有人插队，为人开门却得不到感谢，或忘记与你握手，我们会很自然地

If someone jumps the queue, does not thank you for holding the door open for them or forgets to shake your hand, we naturally feel disrespected and perturbed① .

Keeping the above points in mind, now consider the complexities of working on the international stage. Modern business is global and demands people travel to foreign countries and mix with foreign clients, colleagues or customers. Each one of those cultures will also have their own etiquette rules, many of them unwritten. When two or more different cultures mix, it is easy for small etiquette mistakes to be made that could have negative consequences. Just as you may have felt annoyed when a foreign businessman did not shake your hands upon greeting you, imagine how your Chinese client must have felt when you wrote on his business card or your Indian colleague reacted when you flatly rejected an offer of a meal. Sometimes, not understanding the etiquette of another culture means you show a lack of manners and as Lawrence Sterne said, a lack of deference. This can and does lead to soured relationships, lost deals and in the end poor business results. Anyone working on the international stage needs to understand international business etiquette.

International business etiquette manifests in many shapes and sizes. Throughout the world people from different cultures have varying etiquette rules around areas such as personal space, communication, gift giving, food, business meetings and much more. For those wanting to make a good impression and understanding of international business etiquette is crucial. By way of introducing some of the key areas within international business

---

① perturb[pəˈtəːb] *vt.* 使不安

感受不到尊重，并且惶恐不安。

除了记住以上的观点之外，我们现在还应该考虑在国际舞台上打拼时的复杂环境。现代的商业交往遍及全球，人们穿梭于不同的国家，与不同的客户、同事、顾客打交道。其中的每一种文化也会有自己的礼仪原则，而且许多是不成文的规则。当两种或更多的不同文化交融时，犯点很小的礼仪错误也容易产生负面效果。正如你对外国商人与你见面时没有握手问候感到恼怒一样，可以想象，你在中国客户的名片上写字时他的感觉是什么，或你断然拒绝印度同事的进餐邀请时他的反应又是怎样。有时，不了解另一文化礼仪意味着你的失礼，正如劳伦斯·斯特恩指出的：缺乏尊重。这可能并确实会导致关系恶化，交易中断，最终造成经营不善的后果。任何一位在国际舞台上打拼的人都应该了解国际商业礼仪。

国际商业礼仪以不同的方式和程度展现在我们面前。世界上来自不同文化的人在私人空间、交际、礼品赠送、饮食、商务会议及其他很多方面都维持着各种各样的礼仪。对那些想留下良好印象、了解国际商业礼仪的人来说，这些礼仪至关重要。通过引入国际商务礼仪中的一些关键话题，我们一起来看看下面这些常见的礼仪。

商务名片礼仪：

交换商务名片时（即使是你主动交换），你是不是给出名片就把它给忘了呢？在许多国家，交换商务名片都有特定的礼仪。比如，在阿拉伯国家，你决不能用左手传递或接收商务名片。在中国和日本，你应该用双手交出和接收名片。另外，仔细地查看名片并给出肯定的评价通常是良好的礼节。在英国，可以把商务名片塞到口袋里，而在许多国家，你应该以更加敬重的方式来对待商务名

etiquette we shall look at the following common areas.

Business Card Etiquette:

When you exchange business cards (even if you exchange them) do you simply pass it over and forget about it? In many countries the business card has certain etiquette rules. For example in the Arab world you would never give or receive a business card with your left hand. In China and Japan you should try and use both hands to give and receive. In addition it is always good etiquette to examine the card and make a positive comment on it. Whereas in the UK it may be OK to sling① the business card into a pocket, in many countries you should always treat it with much more respect such as storing it in a business card holder.

The Etiquette of Personal Space:

How close do you stand to people? Is it impolite to touch somebody? What about gender differences? In theMiddle East you may get very touchy-feely with the men, yet one should never touch a woman. A slap on the back may be OK in Mexico but in China it is a serious no-no. Touch someone on the head in Thailand or Indonesia and you would have caused great insult. Without an appreciation of international business etiquette, these things would never be known.

The Etiquette of Gift Giving:

Many countries such as China and Japan have many etiquette rules surrounding the exchange of business gifts. International business etiquette allows you an insight into what to buy, how to give a gift, how to receive, whether to open in front of the giver and what gifts not to buy. Great

① sling[sliŋ] *vt.* 扔;投掷

片，比如说，把它放到商务名片夹中。

私人空间礼仪：

站立时贴近别人的距离保持多远才算合适？触碰别人是不礼貌吗？不同性别应有不同的对待吗？在中东，你甚至可以和男人卿卿我我，但决不能碰女人。在墨西哥，拍拍别人的背很正常，但在中国这是决不允许的。在泰国和印度尼西亚，碰人的头被认为是对人的极大侮辱。如果你对国际商业礼仪毫无感知，这些事情可能永远都不会知道。

礼品赠送礼仪：

中国和日本等许多国家在交换商务礼品方面有很多礼仪规范。国际商务礼仪使你清楚地了解购买什么礼品、如何赠送礼品、如何接收礼品、是否当着送礼者的面打开礼物以及不要购买哪些礼物。要避免购买的礼物枚不胜举，比如在信仰穆斯林的国家，任何礼品都不能含有酒精；在日本，任何礼品都不能带有数字四；在中国，不能送钟。

交际礼仪：

有些文化喜欢高谈阔论（美国和德国），有些文化喜欢轻言细语（印度和中国）；有些说话直截了当（荷兰和丹麦），还有些说话含蓄隐晦（英国和日本）；有些文化允许打断别人的谈话（巴西），而另一些文化却不能容忍这种行为发生（加拿大）；有些文化在讲话时生硬直率（希腊），而有些文化在讲话时讲究艺术（中东地区）。所有人都相信自己的交际方式无可挑剔，但是，一旦进入国际化的背景之中，这一切就不再适用。如果缺乏正确的国际商业礼仪，就很容易冒犯对方。

examples of gifts to avoid are anything alcoholic in Muslim countries, anything with four of anything in Japan and clocks in China.

The Etiquette of Communication:

Some cultures like to talk loudly (US andGermany), some softly (India and China); some speak directly (Holland and Denmark) others indirectly (UK and Japan); some tolerate interrupting others while speaking (Brazil) others not (Canada); some are very blunt (Greece) and some very flowery (Middle East). All will believe the way they are communicating is fine, but when transferred into an international context this no longer applies. Without the right international business etiquette it is easy to offend.

By way of conclusion we can state that etiquette helps maintain good relations with people. When dealing with people from a shared culture, everyone knows the rules and there is not much to think about. Those that lack etiquette are branded as uncouth① and rude. However, this is not the same when working on the international stage. Someone may very well come across as being rude through a lack of etiquette but this may be because in their culture that behavior is normal. As a result international business etiquette is a key skill for those wanting to be successful when working abroad. Through a great appreciation and understanding of others' cultures you build stronger and longer lasting business relationships.

(968 words)

---

① uncouth [ʌnˈkuːθ] *adj*. 粗俗的

总而言之，我们可以声称，礼仪有助于维系人际之间的良好关系。与来自文化共享的人士打交道时，如果人人对规则心知肚明，那么事事就会顺理成章。那些缺乏礼仪的人则需要背负粗俗和粗鲁的恶名。然而，在国际舞台上施展拳脚却很不相同。有人也许由于缺乏礼仪知识，在交往过程中粗鲁无礼，但之所以如此，是因为在他们的文化中，这种行为属于正常范畴。因此，对那些想在海外工作、渴望成功的人士来说，国际商务礼仪是一个关键技能。通过对他国文化的充分欣赏和深刻理解，你将建立起更稳固、更长久的业务关系。

知识链接

Lawrence Sterne 劳伦斯·斯特恩(1713—1768)是18世纪英国最伟大的小说家之一，也是整个世界文学史上一位罕见的天才。他出生在爱尔兰，毕业于剑桥大学，后来在英国约克地区担任牧师。期间，他涉及了农业、狩猎和政治，并尝试了写作。他的两部奇异的作品《项狄传》和《多情客游记》问世之后引起了极大的反响，其怪异、与众不同的趣味深受那些厌烦了陈旧庸俗小说读者的欢迎，使他由一个乡村牧师一跃成为名人。可惜斯特恩的身体一向不好，有肺出血的毛病，最后因一次流感引起的胸膜炎去世。

题　记

人人都在享受交谈带来的乐趣，但有时候，许多人却会面临交流困难的局面。如果在交谈中滔滔不绝、盛气凌人，听众会恨不得掐住你的喉咙让你停下来；如果在交谈中神情内敛、结结巴巴，听众会恨不得敲开你的脑袋，希望你能将自己的情感表达出来。交谈在人类社会生活的发展过程中，形成了各种各样的习惯和行为规范，需要每一位商务人士恪尽职守地坚持：不要劫持谈话，给别人说话的时间，邀请别人参与，随时提问，给别人回答问题的机会，尊重他人的观点，不要泼冷水，不要自称无所不知，不要造成个人意见分歧，以及谨慎对待高难度的交谈。尽管交谈中的礼貌细节不需要使用华丽的辞藻，或者说嘴巴像抹了蜜一样地奉承，但在繁文缛节的商务谈话礼仪中，也有许多或隐或现的礁石，必须小心地绕开它们。

Details in Polite Conversation

Everyone enjoys being in a conversation but at times, many face difficulties. There's chance that you're too dominating in the conversation that the rest in the group feels like strangling your throat until you shut up. Even if you don't realize it, others may. Secondly, maybe you're just too of an introvert① to keep the conversation going. Others feel like knocking your head and hoping that you would express some feelings out.

Social etiquette in conversation isn't about being posh② or speaking with a plum in your mouth. It's about simple good manners. What's most important is that you put the person you're talking to at ease and that they feel as though they had chance to say what they wanted to say and that you listened to them and responded to them sensitively. There are a few things to bear in mind about conversation etiquette.

1. Don't hijack the conversation

Conversations should be two-way processes where you find out about the other person and what they think on a topic, as well as telling them what you think. Looking at the other person's body language will give you

---

① introvert [ˈintrəuvəːt] *n.* 个性内向者

② posh [pɔʃ] *adj.* 华丽的

交谈中的礼貌细节

人人都在享受交谈带来的乐趣，但有时候，许多人却会面临交流困难的局面。这可能是你在交谈中过于主动，以致其他人恨不得掐住你的喉咙让你停下来。即使你没有注意到这一点，但是别人可能会注意到。此外，有可能你过于内敛，交谈无法进行下去，其他人恨不得敲开你的脑袋，希望你能将自己的情感表达出来。

交谈中的礼貌细节不需要使用华丽的辞藻，或者说嘴巴像抹了蜜一样地奉承，它只是简单的礼貌。最重要的是你要让跟你聊天的人感到轻松，让他们感觉有机会畅所欲言，而你在听他们谈话，并能够思维敏捷地随时回应。关于交谈礼仪的几件事一定要谙熟于心。

1.不要劫持谈话

交谈应该是双方互动的过程，在这个过程中，你会了解其他人，他们在一个话题上有什么想法，以及告诉他们你是怎么考虑的。注意观察其他人的肢体语言，它会给你暗示，告诉你已经讲得够多了。他们呼吸急促，目光呆滞，不停地扫视手表，这种现象通常是对你的提示：应该尽快结束谈话。

2.给别人说话的时间

并不是每个人都可以轻松地表达自己想要说的话。不要担心在

hints about when you've talked enough. Their eyes glazing over as they heave heavy sighs and glance at their watches is always a clue you should stop talking pretty soon!

2. Give people time to speak

Not everyone finds it easy to say what they want to say. Don't be afraid of a few silences in your conversations. A quick look at the face of the person you're talking to will let you know whether they're pausing to think of what to say next; if they've fallen asleep in boredom or if they're scoping the room looking for an escape route! Whatever it is, you probably ought to let them do it.

3. Invite others in

If you can see that someone is struggling for something to say—help them out. Phrase what you said differently if it needs a response and they seem not to understand. But don't be patronizing①.

4. Also ask questions

Make the questions easy to understand and respond to. That will give the person you're talking to a prompt and help them relax into talking to you.

5. Give people a chance to answer

Some people jump straight in with an answer; others like to ponder a question and give a considered response. Either of those options is fine, so make sure you leave time for an answer to be given. You only have to look at facial expressions and body language to know if they want you to step in and rescue them by speaking again.

---

① patronizing [ˈpætrənaiziŋ] *adj*. 以恩人态度自居的；屈尊俯就的

交谈中偶尔出现的沉默。谈话时快速地瞅一下对方的脸，让自己知道他们是否正停下来思考接下来说什么，他们是否感到无聊、昏昏欲睡，或者是否在绝望地环顾四周，想在房间里找一条路逃开。不管是什么，你或许应该给他们自由。

3.邀请别人参与

如果你发现有人试图说些什么，让他们说出来。如果需要回应，并且对方看上去不是很理解，就换种方式表达。但是不要摆出屈尊俯就的姿态。

4.还要提问

让问题易于理解和回答。这样可以给你的谈话对象以提示，帮助他们在与你交谈时心情放松。

5.给别人回答问题的机会

有些人喜欢直接说出答案，有些人喜欢先提出问题，然后给出经过深思熟虑的答案。这两种选择都无可非议，所以要确保给人回答问题的时间。你只需要观察面部表情和肢体语言，就可以知道他们是否希望你插话，以及是否希望接着往下讲。

6.尊重他人的观点

全世界的人是否都同意你的观点并不重要，不是吗？人们有权坚持自己的意见，而且你也不必单枪匹马地说服别人，让他们承认自己的错误。你不管怎样都不会成功，这对你有什么要紧的呢？除非有人因为坚持自己独特的见解会受到伤害，否则的话，就顺其自然吧。即使存在着危险的风险，也要考虑清楚你是否是告诉他这个问题的合适人选。

6. Respect other people's opinions

It doesn't really matter whether the world agrees with you, does it? People are entitled to their opinion and you don't have to launch a single-handed campaign to convince them of the error of their ways. You won't succeed anyway and why does it matter to you? Unless someone is likely to be harmed by holding a particular opinion, leave it well alone. Even if there is a risk of danger, think carefully about whether you're the right person to tell them about it.

7. Don't rain on someone's parade

That's partly linked to the last point, but basically, it means don't dampen someone's enthusiasm. You may see all sorts of pitfalls in their plans or what they're saying, but do you really have to be the person to tell them? Can't you let them find out these things for themselves? After all, the problems you fear may not actually arise.

8. Don't be a know-it-all

You may have a wealth of wisdom and knowledge to pass on to someone, but unless you do it in the right way, it won't be appreciated and it won't do any good. It's important not to be smug when passing on advice. Don't pretend you have all the answers—because you really don't. Also-don't make the other person feel stupid. It's bad manners and they won't listen to you anyway.

9. Don't make disagreement personal

It's fine to differ in opinions—even with friends and loved ones. That's just life and it doesn't hurt anyone. A difference of opinion doesn't have to cause a row and it can actually lead to an interesting conversation—if you approach it right.

7.不要泼冷水

这与上面的观点有部分联系，但从根本上来说，它指的是不要浇熄别人的热情。你可能注意到他们的计划或者说话中的各种纰漏，但你是否应该告诉他们问题所在呢？难道你不能让他们自己发现自己的问题吗？毕竟，你担心的问题并不一定会出现。

8.不要自称无所不知

你可能希望将自己丰富的智慧和知识传给他人，但是，除非你用正确的方式做这件事，否则别人不会感激你，也不会有任何好处。重要的是，建议被采纳后不要自鸣得意。不要装作你什么都懂，因为事实上你并非如此。还有，不要让别人觉得自己很傻。这种做法没有礼貌，而且他们再也不会听你的了。

9.不要造成个人意见分歧

即使与朋友和爱人存在意见分歧也是件好事。这就是生活，它并不会伤害任何人。意见相悖不一定引起争吵，事实上，如果方法正确，也可以促成一次有趣的交谈。

这就意味着不要让对方感觉你的想法跟他们的一样愚蠢；不要威吓或斥责别人，强行让他们同意你的观点，实际上这并不起任何作用；即使他们当时表态赞同你的意见，他们可能也是在撒谎而已！不要毁谤和侮辱他人，听取他人的意见，你会活得更轻松——甚至可以学些东西。

10.高难度的交谈绝不容易

缺乏机智会使交谈严重失礼。它使你与人群疏远，意味着你没有听他们的谈话。例如，如果你认为他们正在设置具有潜在威胁的

That means not making the other person feel stupid for thinking as they do; don't bully or berate① someone into agreeing with you—this actually won't work anyway; even if they say they now agree with you, they'll probably be lying! Don't resort to abuse and name calling-and listen to the other person's point of view; you'll have an easier life—and you may even learn something.

10. Difficult conversations were never meant to be easy

Lack of tact is a huge conversation faux pas②. It alienatespeople and means you just don't get listened to. Think whether you really need to have a difficult conversation with someone—if you think they are making a potentially harmful choice, for instance. Choose your battles on this and make sure you're the right person to have the conversation; are you close enough and trusted enough to advise this person?

It's simple good manners to choose carefully what you say to people. Make them glad they talked to you. Try to make people feel better for having talked to you. If you know a comment will be unwanted, don't make it unless it's absolutely necessary for someone's welfare. Those are the simple rules of social etiquette in conversation.

An important point.

Neglect communication skills and you limit your happiness and success. And by default you give others control over your life. The only way to be the master of your destiny is to take charge. Know what you really want and have the courage to stand up andbe counted.

(989 words)

---

① berate [biˈreit] *vt.* 严责

② faux pas [ˌfəuˈpɑː] *n.* 失礼

选择时，试想一下，你是否真的需要与某个人进行一场困难重重的谈话。根据这种状况选择较量的方式，确保你就是这场谈话的正确人选。你有足够的亲和力和足够的可信度给此人建议吗？

与人交谈时斟词酌句是个简单的礼节。要让他们与你交谈时感觉愉快。试着让人们与你交谈时感觉更好。如果你知道那些不愿被提及的评论，除非万不得已，为了他人的幸福请不要张扬。这些是交谈社交礼仪中的一些简单规则。

还有一个重要的问题。

如果忽视沟通技巧，你就会限制自己的幸福和成功，并且默许别人控制你的生活。成为自己命运主宰的唯一途径就是承担责任。一定要清楚，自己真正想要的是什么，鼓足勇气，挺直腰杆，努力实现自身的价值。

知识链接

Conversation in a concise and comprehensive way 言简意赅的交谈。古人曰："语约而事丰"，是指说得很少，但语言的内涵很丰富，这是一种能力和本领。在商务交际中，这就要求在用词的概括性、表现力上下工夫，还要学会准确地用词，只有这样，才能真正做到言简意赅。

题 记

毕业季求职是一件残酷的事情，特别是在工作机会稀少的当下。除毕业生外，很多遭遇过裁员、解雇或以前的工作不那么令人满意的人也加入了求职者大军。他们带着一种茫然而不知所措的浮躁情绪，摩拳擦掌，在一场又一场的求职面试中像推销“商品”一样推销着自己。然而，在这个物欲横流、竞争日益激烈的世界，人们还能在求职过程中坚守自己的道德底线吗？道德标准关系到我们的需求和欲望是否超越了自己思维，在求职面试的过程中应用“把事情做得更好”的道德原则就是重点关注你如何帮助公司。这种行为不能以牺牲其他的道德原则为代价，如“尊重他人”原则要求我们诚实，“不伤害”原则要求我们既不能说也不能做损害他人或自己的事。正如富兰克林所言：“失足，你可以马上恢复站立；失信，你也许永难挽回。”坚持道德前沿和核心的价值观是求职面试取得成功的最佳方式。

In Interviews, Honesty Is the Best Policy

Job hunting is a cutthroat business, especially these days when work is scarce. But it still pays to stick to your ethical principles.

It's graduation season, and this means it's time for job hunting Joining the pool of applicants will be a lot of people who have been downsized, fired, or who found their previous employment to be less than satisfying. Whether you're a newbie or a seasoned veteran of the job search, it's helpful to get advice about the all-important but nerve-wracking experience known as the job interview.

Most of the articles on this topic are written from either the psychological or legal perspective. But ethics also is, or should be-a component of job interviews, and taking ethics seriously is beneficial not just for the employer but also for the applicant. Here's a look at the specific ways ethical behavior before and during an interview can lead to getting the job you want.

The art of the job interview seems to be mainly about strategy: how to get from point A (unemployment, underemployment, or otherwise unsatisfying employment) to point B (a good job). But there are lots of ways

诚实是工作面试的最佳策略

求职是一件残酷的事情，特别是在工作机会稀少的当下。 但是，我们仍然应该坚持自己的道德准则。

毕业季到了，这意味着该是找工作的时间了。 很多遭遇过裁员、解雇或以前的工作不那么令人满意的人加入了求职者大军。 无论你是找工作的新手还是经验丰富的老手，有必要了解求职面试的建议，这些经验非常重要，但又极其令人头疼。

大多数关于这个主题的文章要么是从心理的角度、要么是从法律的角度来进行阐述。 但是，道德也是或应该是工作面试的一个组成部分，严肃对待道德问题不仅对雇主、而且对申请人也有益。 让我们来看一看道德行为的具体方式，他们如何在面试前和面试中引导你获得你想要的工作。

求职面试的艺术似乎主要在战略方面：如何从 A 点（失业，不充分就业，或其他方式的不令人满意的就业状况）到 B 点（一份好工作）。 但是，从 A 点到 B 点有许多方式，有些方式比另一些方式更符合道德。 你可以在简历上作假，夸大你的成就，或在你的强项方面误导未来的雇主。 投机取巧可能会获得工作机会，但这要付出

to get from A to B, and some are more ethical than others. You can lie on your résumé, exaggerate your accomplishments, or mislead a prospective employer about what you can do well. Taking the low road may lead to a job offer-but at what cost?

If you have to become someone other than yourself, what does this say about your integrity? And what will happen to you, professionally as well as personally, if it comes to light that you lied to get the job?

Even if you are committed to being truthful, however, it is still possible to miss the main point of a job interview and run the risk of being passed over. A job interview isn't about you. Or rather, it's not merely about you. It is about whether or not the company will benefit from hiring you. Ethics is about thinking beyond our own needs and desires, and applying the ethical principle of Make Things Better in the context of a job interview means concentrating on how you will help the company. This can't be at the expense of other ethical principles, such as Respect Others, which requires us to be truthful, and Do No Harm, which asks us not to say or do things that will make things worse for others or ourselves.

Ethics thus lies at the core of any job interview. With this in mind, here are five guidelines that you can use to ace your next interview by taking the high road.

1. FOCUS ON WHAT YOU WILL BRING TO THE COMPANY.

It never ceases to amaze me how many people respond to my own job offerings with an endless discussion of why the position will help them: "This job is perfect for me, because I need something that will offer me

什么样的代价呢？

如果你不得不成为另一个人而不是你自己，这种说法如何证实你的诚信呢？ 如果你骗取这份工作的事情曝光，从职业和个人的角度来看，会发生什么样的结局？

即使你力求做到诚实，但仍然有可能错过最重要的求职面试，并面临着被淘汰的风险。 求职面试不仅仅是你的事，或者更确切地说，它不只是你的事，它关系到公司是否能从雇用你这件事中受益。 道德标准关系到我们的需求和欲望是否超越了自己的思维。

在求职面试的过程中应用“把事情做得更好”的道德原则就是重点关注你如何帮助公司。 这种行为不能以牺牲其他的道德原则为代价，如“尊重他人”原则要求我们诚实，“不伤害”原则要求我们既不能说也不能做损害他人或自己的事，否则事情会变得更糟。

因此，道德是任何求职面试的核心。 基于这一点，下面列出了五个指南，你可以作为下次面试时手中的王牌——当然是光明正大地出牌。

1. 关注你能为公司带来什么。

许多人回应我自己给他们提供的职位时会无休止地讨论为什么这个职位对他们有帮助：“这份工作很适合我，因为我需要能够为我提供灵活性的东西。”这一点从未让我感到过惊讶。 但员工的首要职责是帮助公司，而不是干其他的事情。

2. 诚实。

只有极少数人是高明的说谎者，这是一件好事。 当面试官问你一些问题，而你不知道答案时，坦白承认比不懂装懂要好得多。 此

flexibility." An employee should be concerned, first and foremost, with helping the company, not the other way around.

2. BE HONEST.

Few of us are good liars, and this is a good thing. When an interviewer asks you something to which you don't know the answer, it's much better to admit it than to pretend otherwise. Also, misrepresenting yourself on your résumé in any way is a big mistake, not just because it will come back to haunt you since it may not, but simply because it's wrong.

3. WHEN IN DOUBT, DON'T.

The most fundamental ethical principle of all, Do No Harm, applies to how you treat yourself as well as others. Resist the impulse to say something that would make you look foolish, incompetent① , or naive② . If you're not sure about how something will be taken, leave it unsaid.

4. DON'T BADMOUTH YOUR PREVIOUS EMPLOYER.

Your prospective employer may ask you about previous jobs and why you left, or why you want to leave your current one. If a poor relationship with a boss or colleague was a contributing factor, it's better to say something like: "My supervisor and I didn't see eye to eye on a lot of projects," rather than "He was the biggest jerk I've ever worked for." Criticism at its best centers on what a person has done, not on who a

---

① incompetent [inˈkɔmpitənt] *adj.* 不称职的

② naive [nɑːˈiːv] *adj.* 幼稚的

外，在简历上以任何方式弄虚作假是大忌，不只是因为它的不真实会使你心神不安，而只是因为这种做法本身就不道德。

3．不确定时，不要做。

“不伤害”是所有道德原则中最基本的准则，这条原则适用于你如何看待自己和他人。不要冲动地说一些让你看起来愚蠢、不称职或者幼稚的话。如果你不知道事情该怎么解决，请保持沉默。

4．不在背后说前雇主的坏话。

未来的雇主可能会问你以前的工作，你为什么离开，或者你为什么要离开你目前的工作。如果主要原因是与老板或同事的关系不好，最好像这样说：“我的上司和我在很多项目上的看法迥异”，而不是说：“他是我在工作中碰到过的最大的混蛋。”批评最好是对事不对人。

人身攻击会让你显得很小气，这可能是你错失工作机会的一个原因。还要记住，行业圈子可能很小，相互之间的联系又很紧密，面试官完全有可能认识你的前老板或同事。你当然不想摊上一个小气、报复心强或言行不得体的坏名声。

5．审视内心。

最后的规则是最重要的。在你申请工作之前，不妨进行深刻的自我反省，找出什么才是你真正的追求。为了成功地完成公司的任务，你必须了解自己在生活中的任务是什么，为什么要在这家公司奉献大量的时间和精力。诚实这项原则不仅适用于你与未来雇主的相处，也适用于你对待自己的方式。

是的，这就是一个残酷的世界，与过去几年的任何时候相比，

person is.

Personal attacks make you look petty, and this could be a reason for you to be passed over for a position. Also bear in mind that professional circles can be small and tightly knit; it's entirely possible your interviewer knows your previous boss or colleagues. You don't want to acquire a reputation for being petty, vindictive, or tactless.

5. LOOK WITHIN.

This last rule is the most important. Before you even apply for a job, do some soul-searching, and find out what it is you're really looking for. To embrace a company's mission successfully you have to know what your own mission in life is, and why you want to devote considerable time and energy to that organization. Honesty applies not just to how you deal with your prospective employer; it also applies to how you deal with yourself.

Yes, it's a cutthroat world out there, and finding work is probably more difficult now than at any time in the past few years. But that's no reason to throw ethics out the window. In fact, I hope I've shown just the opposite-that keeping ethics front and center is the best way to be successful.

(917 words)

现在找工作可能更困难。但是，我们没有任何理由摒弃道德。事实上，我希望我已经证明了一种恰好相反的模式——坚持道德前沿和核心价值观是成功的最佳方式。

知识链接

Integrity 诚信。从哲学的意义上说，"诚信"既是一种世界观，又是一种社会价值观和道德观，它是指一个人的诚实性和信用程度。诚信既体现于一个人的个性、价值取向之中，又与企业的顾客商誉价值紧密相关。具有诚信的员工，会随时随地以诚信开展业务，遵守公司制度规定和社会道德规范，对工作具有较强的责任心。

题　记

快餐时代，我们已经习惯了批量化和程序化的消费：麦当劳里的薯条让人乐不思蜀，肯德基的鸡翅招来了大量拥趸，必胜客里的披萨让公众趋之若鹜。然而，快餐店风景的看客们可曾了解过最基本的进餐礼仪？是否知道常见的商务宴会有多少道菜？使用成套餐具、碟子和杯子的宴会上如何进餐？应该用什么方式传递食物？刀叉的摆放规则是怎样的？喝汤的方式有什么讲究？餐后还有哪些规矩和细则？规范进餐礼仪不是让进餐者提心吊胆。像所有的礼仪元素一样，进餐礼仪可以归结为常识加上善意。了解和掌握进餐礼仪给人自信，使人可以放松，尽情享受进餐和朋友们带来的愉悦，同时心无旁骛地与他人自由交换商务信息。在这个让人能够快速地填饱肚子、又能快速地消化掉的时代，只有进餐礼仪还会令人难以忘怀。

Dining Etiquette for the Fast-food Generation

Everyone needs an etiquette book on his or her shelf, one of those five-pound encyclopedias of everything related to manners. I think it should be a mandatory① gift to every graduate, right along with the PDA② and new briefcase. I received one when I finished high school and I still have it on my bookshelf. It's a little dog-eared, but the advice within isn't showing its age unlike its owner.

Why is this book so important? You'll be glad you have it when you're faced with an invitation to a formal event. It will teach you first how to properly respond to the invitation and then, how to eat that multi-course meal with dozens of utensils, plates and glasses. It can help you plan a wedding, teach you how to write a letter, even how to get along with your co-workers.

But in this fast-food era, many people have forgotten—or were never taught—the fundamentals of dining etiquette. Which way should I pass? Which fork is mine? What do I do with my napkin? What follows are the answers to the basic questions many people have about dining.

The first thing to do after being seated at a table is to immediately

---

① mandatory [ˈmændətəri] *adj.* 必要的,强制的

② PDA 掌上电脑,个人数字助理(Personal Digital Assistant)

快餐一代的进餐礼仪

人人需要一本礼仪书放在他或她的书架上，这是5英镑一本的百科全书中的一种，书中的内容全部与礼仪相关。我认为此书应是每个毕业生的必要礼物，与掌上电脑和公文包具有同等的地位。我高中毕业后收到了一份这样的礼物，到现在还放在我的书架上。虽然书页已经有点卷边了，但里面的建议却不像他的主人那样，依旧光彩照人。

为什么此书如此重要呢？当你收到一个正式场合的邀请时，你会觉得拥有这本书很开心。首先，它会告诉你如何恰当地回应邀请，然后了解在有多道菜、使用成套餐具、碟子和杯子的宴会上如何进餐。它也可以帮助你策划婚礼，教你如何写书信，甚至如何与同事相处。

但是在这个快餐时代，很多人已经忘记了——甚至从未学过——最基本的进餐礼仪。应该用什么方式传递食物？哪个叉子是我的？怎样用餐巾？很多人进餐时会遇到这些基本问题，下面就是答案。

在桌子旁坐下后的第一件事就是立即将餐巾铺在你的大腿上。展开的餐巾呈大三角形或长方形。决不要把餐巾当纸巾用，但如果你觉得进餐时需要擦鼻子，可以就近放一条餐巾。女士应该在进餐

place your napkin in your lap. Unfold it into either a large triangle or rectangle. Never use your napkin as a tissue, but have one close by if you think you'll need to wipe your nose during the meal. Ladies should blot their lipstick with a tissue before eating so that they don't soil the cloth napkin and glassware. Don't flip over your coffee cup or other glassware you won't be using. If a beverage is served during the meal that you don't want, simply hold your hand over the cup and say, "No thank you."

If you have to leave the table during the meal, say a soft "excuse me" to the people on either side of you, leave your napkin on your chair not the table and push the chair under the table as you leave.

As you look at your place setting, remember that solids are on the left and liquids are on the right. In other words, your bread plate is on the left side above your forks and your drinking glasses are on the right side above the knife and spoons. Use silverware from the outside in. The first fork you will need will probably be your salad fork, the one farthest on the left. The larger fork directly to its right is your dinner fork. On the far right side of your place setting will most likely be a soup spoon, and on its left, a teaspoon followed by the knife. If you see utensils placed horizontally across the top of your place setting, save those for dessert. Remember—once a utensil has been used for eating, it never again touches the tablecloth, only the china!

Your "real estate" at a table consists of, not only your place setting, but also the other items directly in front of you. It is your responsibility to take notice of those things and initiate their use. Roll baskets, butter, cream, salad dressings, sugar, salt and pepper—if they're within your reach, pick them up and start them around. Pass to the right and refrain from helping yourself first. Those items should make a complete pass around the table

前用纸巾擦掉口红，这样才不会弄脏棉质的餐巾和玻璃器皿。不要敲打你不用的咖啡杯或其他玻璃器皿。如果进餐过程中端来了饮料而你又不想喝，只需要将手放在杯子上，说句“不必了，谢谢”即可。

如果需要在餐间离桌，对你两边的人轻声说“失陪一下”，把餐巾放在椅子上，不要放在桌子上，离开时把椅子推到桌子下面。

再看一看餐具的摆放，记住，盛食物的餐具在左，装饮料的器皿在右。换句话说，面包盘在叉子的左上方，喝饮料的玻璃杯在刀和勺的右上方。用银器餐具时要从外向内。你需要使用的第一个叉子可能是沙拉叉，在左边的最远处。紧接在右边的大一点的叉子是餐叉，餐具右边的远处最有可能是汤勺，汤勺的左边是茶勺，然后是刀。如果你看到餐具顶前方有水平放置的器皿，要清楚那是留作吃甜点用的。记住，一旦器皿用来就餐，就绝不再接触桌布，只有瓷器才放在桌面上。

桌子上的“不动产”不仅包括餐位餐具，还包括直接摆放在你面前的其他食品。你有责任关注这些东西，并着手享用。如果装面包卷的篮子、黄油、奶油、沙拉酱、糖、盐和胡椒粉就在你手边，不妨拿起来递给周围的人。向右分发，不要自己先吃。这些东西应该围着桌子转一圈，然后才轮到你这里。如果你等不及，想先吃面包卷，可以对右侧的邻座打个招呼：“介意我自己先来吗？”他们一般都会同意。只要是递带柄的东西，如调料酱，注意将柄把交给对方，这样他可以轻松地抓住。盐和胡椒粉总是要配套，即使对方只需要其中之一。

before you get your turn. If you just can't stand not having first choice of the rolls, turn to your neighbor on your right and say, "Would you mind if I help myself first?" They'll always say yes. Whenever you pass something with a handle, such as dressings, pass it with the handle facing the other person so that they can grasp it easily. And always pass the salt and pepper as a set, even if only one was requested.

It's important that you place the butter first on the bread plate before buttering your bread. Break up your bread or rolls into one- or two-bite morsels for buttering and eating. Whatever you take up to your mouth to eat should be eaten in one or two consecutive bites. Your tablemates don't want to see the part that didn't quite fit in your mouth placed back on your bread plate!

To eat soup properly, draw the spoon away from you and quietly sip the soup from the side of the spoon. Tilt the bowl away from you to get to the last drops.When you're finished, place the spoon on the plate beneath the soup bowl. If there is no plate, rest the spoon in the bowl. Follow these same guidelines for any dessert served in a bowl.

Salads should be prepared so that they consist of bite-size pieces. But if the salad contains leaves that are too big to eat, use your salad fork to cut them into smaller pieces. And if that doesn't work, use your dinner knife. But only use the knife when all other methods have failed. Why? Because you'll also need that knife for the main course, and after you've used it for the salad, there's no place to put it so that it doesn't also disappear with the salad plate.

When eating the main course, pace your speed of eating to that of your tablemates so that you don't make them feel uncomfortable. In the United States, we eat "American Style". Here's how to do it. Cut your food

先把黄油放进面包盘，然后在面包上抹黄油，这一点很重要。把面包或面包卷掰成一到两口，抹上黄油再吃。不管往口里送什么食物，应该连续吃一到两口。同桌的人不希望看到进口的食物与嘴巴的大小不相称，又被你放回面包盘！

喝汤的方式要合适，把汤勺挪远一点，用汤勺的一侧静静地啜汤。将汤碗放倾斜，离你远点，最好一饮而尽。喝完汤后，汤勺放在汤碗下的盘子里。如果没有盘子，把汤勺就放在汤碗里。任何碗装甜点也可以遵从同样的规则。

如果要准备块状沙拉，最好切成一块一口的大小。但如果是有叶子的沙拉，太大了吃起来不方便，可以用沙拉叉把它们切成小块。如果还不行，就用餐刀。但只能在其他方法不成功时才用餐刀。为什么呢？因为你还需要用餐刀吃主菜，用餐刀切沙拉之后，没地方放餐刀，而它又不能和沙拉盘一起被拿走。

吃主菜的时候，进食的速度要与同桌的人一致，这样才不至于让他们感到不舒服。在美国，我们按“美式风格”进餐。我们是这样做的：切割食物时左手拿叉，右手持刀，一次切一块。然后把刀放在盘子上部的边沿，叉子换到右手。叉尖向上，把食物送进口中。不要握着拳头去叉食物或拿银制餐具。不管上面有没有食物，注意不要用银制餐具做手势或指点物品。

如果就餐时嘴里要吐东西，怎么送进口就怎么取出来。换句话说，用叉子送进口，就用叉子拿出来。如果手抓食物，就用手指拿出来。把餐巾放在嘴前，遮住移出物，然后放在盘子的一边。不要把它藏在盘子下面，因为盘子一撤走，它就留在桌布上了！也不

with the fork in your left hand and the knife in your right hand. Cut only one piece at a time. Then lay your knife down along the top edge of the plate and transfer the fork to your right hand. Bring the food up to your mouth with the tines on the fork facing upward. Don't stab your food or hold the silverware with your fists. And be careful not to gesture or point with your silverware, whether or not it has food on it.

If you must remove something from your mouth as you eat, take it out the way it went in. In other words, if it entered your mouth on a fork, remove it with your fork. If it was finger food, use your fingers to remove it. Hold your napkin in front of your mouth to mask the removal, and then place the item on the side of your plate. Don't try to hide it under the plate, because as soon as the plates are cleared it will be left behind on the tablecloth! Don't hide any paper trash you've accumulated during the meal under your plate either. Just place it on the edge of your bread plate.

At the conclusion of the meal, imagine your dinner plate as a clock and place your utensils in the 4:20 position. It's considered rude to push your plates away, stack them up or hand them to the server. Place your loosely-folded napkin on the table just as you stand to leave, not before.

Maneuvering through a meal doesn't have to be scary. Like all elements of etiquette, it boils down to common sense combined with kindness. Knowing the guidelines for dining etiquette gives you confidence so that you can relax and enjoy the meal and company. And in this fast-food age, it can also make you unforgettable!

(1,220 words)

要把就餐时用过的一大堆废纸巾藏在盘子下面。就把它放在面包盘的边上。

吃完后，把餐盘想象成时钟，餐具放在4:20的位置。把盘子推开不礼貌，把它们摞起来或者递给侍者。站起来离开的时候把随意折起的餐巾放在桌上，没站起来之前不要这样做。

讲究进餐礼仪不是让进餐者提心吊胆。像所有的礼仪元素一样，进餐礼仪可以归结为常识加上善意。了解进餐礼仪的规则给你自信，使你可以放松，享受进餐和朋友们带来的愉悦。在这个快餐的时代，进餐礼仪还会令你难以忘怀。

知识链接

Fast food 快餐，最早出现于西方世界，英语称为“quick meal”或“fast food”，它指预先做好的、能够迅速提供给顾客食用的饭食，如汉堡包等。快餐可以充当主食，具有大众化、节时、方便等特点，已经成为现代人的一种生活方式，并因此出现了“快餐文化”和“速食主义”等文化新概念。

题　记

礼貌可以是一个人内在修养和素质的外在表现；它又是一门适用的艺术，是人际交往中约定俗成的示人以尊重、友好的习惯做法。日复一日地恪守礼仪的责任心是任何一家管理完善的企业的重要组成部分，没有礼貌使公司之间产生严重的摩擦，并留下难以弥合的永久伤痕。对于那些从来没有费心关注母亲的人来说，也许可以换个角度，听一听现代管理学之父彼得·德鲁克的真情告白：“礼貌是一个组织的润滑油。它是一种自然法则，即两个活动的物体相互接触产生摩擦。人类与无生命体一样，相互之间也存在这种状况。礼貌就是说一声‘请’和‘谢谢’、熟悉一个人的名字和问候她的家庭这样简单的事情，它使两个人能在一起工作，无论他们是否喜欢对方。”敬畏礼貌，就能使人与人之间的关系更加和谐，社会生活更加美好。

Regarding Good Manners with Reverence

For those of you who never bothered to pay attention to your mother, perhaps you'll listen to Peter Drucker, the father of modern management, instead. Peter Drucker would applaud a recent initiative in Anaheim, Calif., aimed at training tourism industry workers to mind their manners around out-of-towners.

This cheeky thought has crept into my head a couple of times in the last few weeks as I've noticed a run of stories about etiquette or lack thereof in the workplace. Most recently, there was the case study posted on this Web site about a worker who had to deal with a boorish① boss.

And just a couple of weeks ago, I saw that officials in Anaheim, Calif.-home to Disneyland—were set to hold classes for cabbies, hotel employees, and other service workers in town to ensure they act as knowledgeable and enthusiastic hosts for tourists, while also minding their p's and q's. The hope is that the lessons they learn—to be professional and gracious—will be noticed not only by visitors but by their colleagues, too. "We teach them that they're part of a team, and that what they do rubs off on the team,"

---

① boorish [ˈbuəriʃ] *adj.* 粗鄙的

敬畏礼貌

对于你们当中那些从来没有费心关注母亲的人来说，也许可以换个角度，听一听现代管理学之父彼得·德鲁克的真情告白。彼得·德鲁克近期在加利福尼亚州的阿纳海姆市发起倡议，旨在提醒旅游行业的工作人员注意自己在外地人眼中的形象。

在过去的几周中，当我注意到工作场所发生的一连串关于尊重或缺乏礼仪的事件时，脑海里好几次浮现出这种鲁莽粗俗的场景。最近，网上贴出了一个案例研究，讲的是一个不得不与粗鲁的老板打交道的员工。

就在几周前，我看到加利福尼亚州阿纳海姆市（迪士尼总部所在地）的官员开始着手为出租车司机、酒店员工和城里其他从事服务性工作的员工开设培训课程，以确保他们以知识广泛、充满热情的东道主身份迎接观光客，同时提醒他们注意自己的一言一行。人们希望，游客和他们的同事也来关注他们所学的课程，这些课程使他们变身为职业和优雅的人士。亚利桑那州图森市米奇舍费尔联合公司监督此次培训。公司的主席米奇·舍费尔说，“我们告诉他们，他们是团队的一部分，他们的所作所为影响到整个团队。我们这个社会太不拘礼节了，人们越来越不讲礼貌。我们想重新找回基本的礼仪，包括待人接物的态度、衣着整洁、热情友好等所有重要

says Mickey Schaefer, president of Mickey Schaefer & Associates, the Tucson, Ariz., firm overseeing the training. "We've become such an informal society that we all tend to slip. We want to get back to the basics... Your attitude, your cleanliness, your friendliness all matter."

Drucker, who recalled watching his grandmother confront a young thug on a Vienna streetcar in the early 1930s and lecture him about the virtue of good manners, would certainly agree. "Manners are the lubricating oil of an organization," Drucker wrote. "It is a law of nature that two moving bodies in contact with each other create friction. This is as true for human beings as it is for inanimate objects. Manners—simple things like saying 'please' and 'thank you' and knowing a person's name or asking after her family—enable two people to work together whether they like each other or not."

As the last part of his comment makes clear, Drucker was never particularly sentimental about all this. He wasn't interested in fostering friendships; he was, as usual, trying to enhance performance.

"Warm feelings and pleasant words are meaningless, are indeed a false front for wretched attitudes, if there is no achievement in what is, after all, a work-focused and task-focused relationship," Drucker cautioned in The Effective Executive, his classic. "On the other hand, an occasional rough word will not disturb a relationship that produces results and accomplishments for all concerned."

Yet Drucker knew that, day in and day out, maintaining a sense of decorum is an important ingredient in any well-managed enterprise. "Bad manners," he said, "rub people raw; they do leave permanent scars."

的行为规范。”

德鲁克当然赞同恢复礼仪教育，他回忆了20世纪30年代亲眼所见的一幕。当时，他祖母在维也纳的有轨电车上碰到了一个年轻的暴徒，祖母用礼貌的美德教训了这名年轻人。德鲁克写道：“礼貌是一个组织的润滑油。它是一种自然法则，即两个活动的物体相互接触产生摩擦。人类与无生命体一样，相互之间也存在这种状况。礼貌就是说一声‘请’和‘谢谢’、熟悉一个人的名字和问候她的家庭这样简单的事情，它使两个人能在一起工作，无论他们是否喜欢对方。”

德鲁克在评论的最后一部分讲得很清楚，对这一切他从来没有特别地伤感。他对培养友谊不感兴趣。像往常一样，他正在试图提高公众的礼仪水平。

德鲁克在他的经典著作《卓有成效的管理者》中告诫说：“温暖的情感和令人愉悦的用词是毫无意义的，毕竟，如果在什么是以工作为重心和以任务为重心的关系上没有取得成效，这些不过是包装陋习的虚假外壳。另一方面，偶尔蹦出一个粗鲁的词汇也不会妨碍所有相关人士之间创造成果和成效的关系。

但德鲁克也知道，日复一日地恪守礼仪的责任心是任何一家管理完善的企业的重要组成部分。他说：“没有礼貌使人们相互之间产生严重的摩擦，并确实留下了永久的伤痕。”

这种要求甚至可能是字面上的。联合委员会是一家美国卫生保健行业的认证机构，它在上个月要求15 000家医院、疗养院、实验室，以及其他部门执行有关标准，这些标准清楚地说明了什么是“可接受的和不可接受的”个人行为，并建立“一个正式的程序”，

Maybe even literally. Last month, the Joint Commission, an accreditation① body for the U.S. health-care industry, ordered 15,000 hospitals, nursing homes, laboratories, and other facilities to implement standards that spell out what is considered "acceptable and unacceptable" personal conduct and to establish "a formal process" to manage things when the rules get broken.

"Health-care leaders and caregivers have known for years that intimidating and disruptive behaviors are a serious problem," the commission said. "Verbal outbursts, condescending② attitudes, refusing to take part in assigned duties, and physical threats all create breakdowns in the teamwork, communication, and collaboration necessary to deliver patient care."

It isn't just medical personnel that could stand a reminder of this. A study released last year, based on a survey of more than 54,000 employees from 179 organizations across Australia and New Zealand, found that one in five employees experiences an incident of bad manners at work once a month.

People who exclude co-workers from situations, interrupt them when they're speaking, make derogatory③ remarks, withhold information, and disparage④ others' ideas, can have "a large impact on employee engagement," Barbara Griffin, an organizational psychologist from the

---

① accreditation [əˌkrediˈteiʃən] *n.* 信赖

② condescending [kɔndiˈsendiŋ] *adj.* 故意屈尊的;有优越感的

③ derogatory [diˈrɔgətəri] *adj.* 不敬的

④ disparage [diˈspæridʒ] *vt.* 贬低

以在规则被打破时维持秩序。

该委员会声称："卫生保健部门的领导人和护理人员多年来已经意识到，恐吓和破坏行为是一个严重的问题。口头纠葛、居高临下的态度，拒绝承担分配的责任以及身体上的威胁等行为对团队工作、沟通和协作造成了破坏，所有这些都有必要给予耐心的关注。"

需要受到提醒的并不只是医护人员。去年发布的一项研究显示，根据对来自澳大利亚和新西兰的179个组织的54 000多名员工的调查，五分之一的员工每个月经历一次由于不当的礼貌方式引起的小冲突。

西悉尼大学的组织心理学家和本研究的合作者芭芭拉·格里芬在该成果发布时指出，那些拒绝接纳同事的礼貌、别人说话时喜欢插嘴、讲话刻薄、隐瞒信息、蔑视他人创意的人，可以对"员工敬业度造成巨大的冲击"。事实上，她注意到，这种气氛很可能会决定"你是否会留在一个组织里，积极评价自己的工作，或者多做点事。它也可能造成心理困扰，并影响身体健康"。

尽管这看上去是一种基本常识，但很多经理都未能把握住礼貌究竟有多么重要。德鲁克写道："聪明的人尤其是聪明的年轻人，通常不能理解这一点。如果分析表明，一个人的卓越工作一旦需要与他人合作就一次又一次地失败，这很可能就意味着礼貌缺失，即缺少礼仪。"

当然，这种行为不仅暗中破坏了公司的声誉，也影响了个人的形象。马歇尔·古德史密斯在他的畅销书《今天不比以往：成功人士如何获得更大成功》中指出，"人际技巧"，而不是聪颖或者技术天才（才能），常常对你在职业生涯中"能走多远产生重要影响"。

University of Western Sydney and the co-author of the study, said at the time it was released. In fact, she noted, this kind of atmosphere may well determine " whether you stay in an organization, speak positively about your job, or go that extra mile. It can also cause psychological distress and poor physical health."

As commonsensical as this may seem, many managers fail to grasp just how crucial civility is. "Bright people, especially young bright people, often do not understand this," Drucker wrote. " If analysis shows that someone's brilliant work fails again and again as soon as cooperation from others is required, it probably indicates a lack of courtesy-that is, a lack of manners."

This, of course, undermines not only the organization but the individual. In his acclaimed book What Got You Here Won't Get You There: How Successful People Become Even More Successful, executive coach and fellow BusinessWeek.com columnist Marshall Goldsmith points out that " people skills," more than smarts or technical talents, frequently " make the difference in how high you go" in your career. Among the challenges in interpersonal behavior Goldsmith says many of us must strive to overcome: speaking when angry, being overly negative, making excuses, claiming undeserved credit, not listening well, and " failing to express gratitude—the most basic form of bad manners."

And with that, there is but one thing left to say: Thank you for reading.

(890 words)

马歇尔·古德史密斯是高管教练和《经济周刊》网站的资深专栏作家。古德史密斯认为，面对人际关系行为的这些挑战，我们中的许多人都必须努力战胜之，包括生气时讲话、过度消极、找借口、索取不应得的荣誉、不认真倾听以及“未能表达感谢——没有礼貌的最基本形式”。

讲了这么多，还有一句话要说：感谢你的阅读。

知识链接

Peter Drucker 彼得·德鲁克(1909—2005)是当代著名的思想家、现代管理宗师。他传奇式的背景与经历、渊博的学识及睿智的才思，使其在政治、法律、社会学，尤其是管理学等多个领域都留下了精辟、独到的见解。1950—1995年间，《哈佛商业评论》曾先后发表了他的32篇论文，其中6篇成为当年最具影响力的论文而获麦卡锡奖。他的多部论著被译成20多种文字，广为流传，被全世界管理者、学者奉为必读经典。他文风清晰练达，对许多问题提出了自己的精辟见解。杰克·韦尔奇、比尔·盖茨等人都深受其思想的影响。在《卓有成效的管理者》(*The Effective Executive*)中，德鲁克告诉我们：管理者的成效往往是决定组织工作成效的最关键因素；并不是只有高级管理人员才是管理者，所有负责行动和决策而又有助于提高机构工作效能的人，都应该像管理者一样工作和思考。

题　记

也许你刚刚开始大学毕业后的第一份工作，也许你已经被裁员，也许你的公司已经被另一家公司吞并，也许你高枕无忧但又觊觎着本公司的其他岗位，甚或其他公司的岗位。人们总以为在自己的岗位上安然无恙，从未想到自己会成为“求职者”，但他们眼下也开始磨砺技能，“以防万一”。面试着装礼仪是面试成功的神秘武器，男士的西装、衬衫、领带和皮鞋可以给人真诚和有深度的感觉，女士的套裙装、白色或浅色衬衣、皮鞋、裤袜和随身携带的公文包可以提升整洁美观、稳重大方、协调高雅的形象。电话面试需要通过电话线让面试官“听到”你的才干，不管你与他们交谈时是在赶公共汽车还是在网上冲浪。正式面试则需要注重细节，既不受制于人，又不抢风头。面试涵养考察指标为你的未来职业增加了成功的砝码。

The Observation of the Self-restraint Index

You may be entering your first job out of college, you may have been downsized① or your company may have been acquired by another, or you may be comfortably employed but looking for your next challenge at your present company or another one. People who have always felt secure in their positions and have never considered themselves "job seekers" are now brushing up on these skills "just in case." An executive I know makes it a point to go to at least one interview every six months or so, to keep up to date on the industry, keep his interviewing skills sharp, and to "test the waters" to be sure that his current position is the most ideal.

Although the last thing you want to do when you're job hunting is to incur more expenses, there are a few necessities that will make your job hunt much more effective. Most breaches of etiquette occur not because people intend to be disrespectful or discourteous, but either they didn't know the appropriate etiquette, or they weren't properly equipped. Being late with a thank-you note because you're out of stationery or showing up dressed inappropriately for a lunch or interview because all of your suits

---

① downsize [ˈdaunsaiz] *vt.* 减员

面试涵养考察指标

也许你刚刚开始大学毕业后的第一份工作，也许你已经被裁员，也许你的公司已经被另一家公司吞并，也许你高枕无忧但又觊觎着本公司的其他岗位，甚或其他公司的岗位。人们总以为在自己的岗位上安然无恙，从未想到自己会成为“求职者”，但他们眼下也开始磨砺技能，“以防万一”。我认识的一位执行官特别看重每6个月至少一次的面试，为的就是跟上业界的潮流，保持面试技巧的水准，并通过“试水”来确定目前的职位是否是最理想的。

尽管你找工作时最不想做的事情是承担更多的费用，但有几件必做之事却会大大提高你找工作的效率。大多数违反礼仪的做法并不是因为人们刻意表现出来的无礼或失礼，要么是因为他们对礼仪规范知之甚少，要么是因为他们没有正确掌握这些礼仪。感谢信回复迟了，是因为你的信纸用完了；出席午餐或面试的着装不合适，是因为你所有的套装还在洗衣店。这些行为也许是无意识的，但是未来的雇主仍然通常会认为你对公司不尊重，或者并不在意你申请的这个职位。

are at the cleaners may be unintentional, but is still usually perceived by a perspective employer as a lack of regard for the company or for the position you're applying for.

Here are some things you will probably need:

For men:

Conservative dark navy or gray two-piece business suit. If you only have one or two suits, make sure you make some differences with your tie or shirt in subsequent interviews.

A white long-sleeved button-down dress shirt.

A conservative silk tie.

Clean, well-polished dress shoes.

If the company you're interviewing with is less formal, or for social networking, nicely pressed dress slacks and a conservative sport jacket may be more appropriate than a suit.

For women:

Many employers still think that a skirted suit is still the most conservative choice for a female candidate, although suits with pants are becoming more popular and might be a good choice for the less-conservative and traditional industries. Pick a conservative color such as dark blue, dark gray, or brown; and a rich fabric such as wool. Skirt length should be a little below the knee.

Blouses should be white or light colored.

Shoes should be clean, well-polished and in good repair, with closed toes and low heels.

下面的这些小贴士也许是你可能需要注意的地方：

男士着装：

保守的藏青色或灰色两件套商务西装。如果你只有一套或者两套西装，一定要在后续面试中换条领带或者衬衣以示区别。

白色长袖且领尖钉有纽扣的礼服衬衫。

保守的丝质领带。

干净、锃亮的皮鞋。

如果你面试的公司并不那么正式，或者是做社交网络的公司，平展的休闲裤和保守的运动夹克可能比西服更合适。

女士着装：

尽管西服配裤子越来越流行，并且在应聘不太保守和传统行业时可能是一个不错的选择，但许多雇主仍然认为套裙装对女性候选人来说是最保险的选择。挑一个保险的颜色，如深蓝、深灰或者棕色，以及羊毛这样的厚料子。裙长应该略过膝。

女衬衣应该选白色或浅色。

皮鞋应该干净，擦亮，完好无损，不露脚趾，低跟。

完美无瑕的裤袜。

随身携带公文包，不要拿手提袋。

电话

联系工作时要给很多人打电话。我认识的一位项目经理就是通

Flawless pantyhose①.

Carry a briefcase rather than a purse.

Telephone

Many of the contacts that you make will be on the phone. One project manager I know was hired solely on the basis of phone interviews for a job in a distant city.

When you are looking for a job, the phone number you use on your contact information should always be used in a professional way, since you never know whether the person ringing is a hiring manager or HR representative.

Make sure your answering machine, if you use one, is in good order. Make your greeting conservative and professional. Don't use humor, music, or cute greetings from your kids.

Turn off cell phones while in business lunches, interviews or job fairs-or at least switch it to a silent mode.

Return calls from a land-line in a quiet room, rather than a cell phone, which might not sound as clear if at all possible.

Treat a phone interview with the same formality as you would an in-person interview. Be prepared.

Make sure there are no distractions. Even though the other person can't see what's going on, they will know if they don't have your full attention while you catch a bus or surf the web while talking with them.

Formal Interviews

These can be one-on-one or meeting a panel of the employers'

① pantyhose [ˈpæntihəuz] *n.* 连裤袜

过电话面试在一个遥远的城市找到了一份工作。

找工作时，作为联系信息使用的电话号码应该始终按专业方式来管理，因为你永远不知道给你打电话的人是招聘经理还是人力资源代表。

一定要有录音电话，如果已经有了，就要保持畅通。打招呼时要沉稳和专业。不要用幽默、音乐或童趣式的问候。

出席商务午餐、参加面试或招聘会时，请关掉手机，或者至少把它调至静音模式。

回电话时尽量在一个安静的房间里使用座机，不要用手机，因为手机有可能听起来完全不清楚。

电话面试与现场面试一样正规。要一视同仁，并做好准备。

一定不要分心。即使面试官看不到正在发生的事情，他们也会知道你是否对他们全神贯注，不管你与他们交谈时是在赶公共汽车还是在网上冲浪。

正式面试

正式面试可能是一对一的面谈，也可能是与代表雇主的一个考察小组见面。通过与人力资源部或行政人员的前期接触，也许在正式面试时才能第一次见到公司的人，或者通过电话、电子邮件或非正式会议等大量的联系之后，这种机会才会来临。

前往面试现场前，了解公司和行业当前的动态。

与接待员或其他负责安排的人聊天，以便了解前往办公室的基

representatives. You may meet someone for the first time in a formal interview, previous contact having been made through the Human Resources department or administrative staff, or it may come after a considerable amount of contact by phone, e-mail, or informal meetings.

Be informed about any current events about the company and industry before you arrive.

Talk with a receptionist or other person making arrangements so that you know the basics of directions to the office, where to park, the estimated length of the interview, the basics of who you will be meeting with and what you might be expected to bring, etc.

Find out as much as you can about your interviewers. Look them up on Google, LinkedIn, and other online resources at a minimum.

Arrive not late, but also not more than ten minutes early.

Be pleasant to the parking attendants, receptionists, or other people you meet at that company, regardless of their position.

Stand when someone enters the room (either gender.)

Stand to be introduced.

Shake hands firmly with your right hand.

Smile.

Make eye contact when appropriate and comfortable.

Carry a briefcase with extra copies of résumés, references, portfolios, work samples, and any other information they may be interested in. Offer them if they seem appropriate.

Do more listening than talking, but ask questions.

Be ready with short (1 or 2 minute) polished answers to common

本情况，包括在哪里停车，面试时间大概有多久，你最有可能见到谁，以及他们希望你能给他们带来什么，等等。

尽你所能了解你的面试官。 在最短时间内通过谷歌、商务化人际关系网或其他的在线资源搜索他们的资料。

不要迟到，但早到也不要超过 10 分钟。

与泊车员、接待员或你遇到的那家公司的其他人愉快相处，不论他们在公司的地位如何。

有人进入房间时要起立（不论男女）。

被人介绍时站起来。

用右手有力地握手。

微笑。

在适当和舒适的时候进行目光交流。

随身带一个公文包，多装几份简历副本、参考资料、文件、工作样本以及应聘官可能感兴趣的任何其他资料，以备在看上去适当的情况下提供给应聘官。

多听少说，但要提问。

对简历中各个项目的常见问题准备简短的（1 或 2 分钟）、无瑕疵的解答，但不要显示“排练”的痕迹。 个人独自陈述经历或技能的时间不可超过 10 分钟。 集中精力介绍他们似乎最感兴趣的话题或技能。

询问关于职位、它的机遇和挑战等问题。 工资、福利等问题留

questions about items on your resume, but don't give a "rehearsed[①]" interview. Don't launch into 10-minute monologues about your history or skills. Concentrate on subjects or skills that they seem the most interested in.

Ask questions about the position, its opportunities and challenges. Leave questions about pay, benefits, etc. until a second meeting, or let the employer bring up the topic.

Make sure the next steps are well-defined. "When shall I check back with you?" is a good opener, because it leaves the control with YOU to call THEM back, without being pushy.

(957 words)

---

① rehearse [riˈhəːs] *vt.* 排演

待第二次见面时商谈，或者让雇主提出这个话题。

确保接下来的步骤稳扎稳打。“我什么时候再来和你确认”是一个很好的开场白，既不受制于人，又不抢风头。

知识链接

Job-hopping 跳槽。职场跳槽指商务人士自愿向高级领导请求辞职，另谋高就。一个人跳槽的动机一般有如下两种：一是被动的跳槽，即个人对自己目前的工作不满意，不得不跳槽，这里又具体包括对人际关系、工作内容、工作岗位、工作待遇、工作环境或工作条件、发展机会的不满意等方面。二是主动的跳槽，即面对更好的工作条件，如待遇、工作环境、发展机会，并且发现了自己真正感兴趣的工作时，经不住“诱惑”而促使自己跳槽，寻求更高的挑战与报酬。

题　记

邂逅成功始于成功者营造的气场，即创造并渲染一种与众不同的神韵。身高只有一米五几的拿破仑，却拥有睥睨天下的气场；雅诗兰黛化妆品公司的创始人兰黛女士，用奢华的穿戴和编造的贵族身世，包装出仪态万方、雍容华贵的气场，频频与达官显贵结交。肢体语言在面对面的商务交往中传递了一半以上的信息，它对如何表现商务人士的气场起着至关重要的作用。身体挺直和有资格占据一席之地会令人肃然起敬；紧紧握住他人的手、最多面对面地摇动三次可以传播积极的气场；保持专注的目光交流不仅能够显示自身的信心，还可以了解他人口头表达的真正含义；微笑可以创造乐观、积极的环境，赢得他人的尊重。商务肢体语言产生的强大气场可以帮助人们赢得市场人脉，是铺垫成功的职场阶梯。

Business Body Language

Your body language, i.e your demeanor[1], impacts your success. It's vital that you know how to act when you get to a conference, after-hours, meeting or trade show to make the most effective and efficient use of your time, and to attract those people whom you want to do with business with and add to your network.

The success of any encounter begins the moment someone lays eyes on you. One of the first things they notice about you is your aura, that distinctive atmosphere that surrounds you. You create it, and you are responsible for what it says about you and whom it attracts. Your aura enters with you and starts speaking long before your open your mouth. Since body language conveys more than half of any message in any face-to-face encounter, how you act is vital to your aura.

1) Posture

One of the first key things people notice is how you carry and present yourself. Do you walk and stand with confidence as your mother taught you? The confidence includes stomach in, chest out, shoulders back and head up. Or do you slouch[2], perhaps with your shoulders drooping, your

---

① demeanor [diˈmiːnə] *n.* 举止

② slouch [slautʃ] *vi.* 无精打采地立、坐或行走

商务肢体语言

你的肢体语言，即举止，影响着你的成功。无论是出席会议还是业余时间，无论是会面还是展销会，为了最有效果和最有效率地利用你的时间，为了吸引那些你想与他们做生意的人，并让他们加入到你的社交网络中来，这一点是至关重要的。

邂逅成功始于人们对你的注视。他们对你的关注源自你的气场，这是首要的特质之一，这种与众不同的神韵萦绕在你的周围。你创造了这种光环，你有责任运用它来展现自己，还有它吸引了哪些人。你还没有开口说话，你周围早就形成了一种气场。由于肢体语言在任何面对面的接触中传递了一半以上的信息，你如何表现对你的气场起着至关重要的作用。

1)姿势

人们关注的最重要的东西之一是你如何发挥能力和展示自己。你是否像母亲教你的那样，自信地走路和站立？ 这种自信包括收腹、挺胸、肩向后伸和抬头。你是否有点弯腰驼背、肩膀向下耷拉、头朝前倾、大腹便便？ 你是否告诉别人你对自己没有把握，遇事难以泰然自若，因此，不是他们应该寻找和了解的那个人？ 你在

head forward and your stomach protruding① ? Are you saying to people that you are not sure of yourself, are not poised② and, therefore, not the one they should seek out and get to know? You may be turning people away without even being aware of it.

Command respect by standing tall and claiming the space to which you are entitled. Plant your feet about six to eight inches apart with one slightly in front of the others. My workshop attendees always remark about how this positioning makes them feel "grounded," "rooted" and "balanced", great ways to start any encounter!

You also tell people through your posture if you are want others to approach you. For instance, if you are talking with one other person and the two of you are forming a rectangle, you will give the message that you have "closed off" your space and don't want to be interrupted. If you doubt me, stand by two people who are in the rectangular position and see how long you go unacknowledged. The two will see you out of their peripheral③ vision, but won't include you until they have finished their "private" conversation. If, on the other hand, the two of you stand with your feet pointed outward like two sides of an incomplete triangle, you will be inviting others into the conversation. You can make that all-important eye contact.

2) Handshakes

Another vital component you need to bring to any interpersonal encounter is a firm handshake. Again, those few seconds you "shake" can

① protrude [prəˈtruːd] *vi.* 突出
② poised [pɔizd] *adj.* 沉着的
③ peripheral [pəˈrifərəl] *adj.* 外围的

毫无意识的情况下将人拒之门外。

身体挺直和有资格占据一席之地会令人肃然起敬。站立时双脚分开，距离在6至8英寸左右，一只脚在另一只脚的前面一点。我举办研讨会时，与会者常说，这种站姿使他们感到“踏实”、“稳重”和“平衡”，这是首次见面展示自我的极好方式！

如果希望别人接近你，你还可以通过肢体语言告诉他们。例如，如果你正在和另外一个人交谈，两人之间呈矩形状，那么传递的信息就是：你已经封锁了“空间”，不希望被打扰。如果你对我产生了怀疑，可以站在两个呈矩形人的旁边，观察一下不受关注的时间有多久。双方可以透过周边视角看到你，但要等到他们结束“私人”谈话后才会与你打招呼。另一方面，如果你们双方脚朝外站立，呈不完整的三角形，那就是表示你希望邀请他人加入你们的交谈。你可以尝试目光交流，这一点非常重要。

2) 握手

任何人与人之间的相遇还需要把握另一个重要的原则，那就是稳重地握手。此外，你“摇动”的几秒钟可以增强或削弱一种关系。男士握手的特点是强劲而坚定，因为他们天生就有较强的控制力。

女士则需要抓住窍门以引起他人的关注！我曾经接待过一个客户，因为我与他握手时，他注意到我握手时的力度，便询问我是怎样做的。并且他果断地决定，现在就聘请我教他的员工如何握手！

熟悉下列的握手技巧，它们将会极大地帮助你协调人际关系方

empower or weaken a relationship. Men's handshakes are typically strong and firm because they naturally have a stronger grip.

Women, get a grip and be noticed! I once got a client because the man I shook hands with remarked about my strong handshake and asked what I did. He decided it was time to hire me to teach his people how to shake hands, too!

Being familiar with the following handshakes will help you immensely in your relationship-building activities:

Controller. A person extends his hand to you and as soon as your hands are linked, he purposely maneuvers his hand onto the top. He's telling you he wants to be in charge. Keep that in mind as the interaction continues.

Sandwich. Use this one only with people you know. When you envelop another person's hands, you are invading their private space, where you are to be only when invited. Society promotes the standard handshake but is not as tolerant of using both hands. By the way, this handshake is also known as the politician's handshake, which may be cause enough for most people to avoid it!

Dead Fish. Imagine rubbing a scaly①, dead fish in your hands, and you got the picture. Your hands typically are wet for two reasons: You are nervous or you have been holding a cold beverage in your right hand and move it to your left just before you shake hands. In either case, it is extremely unpleasant for the receiver. If you experience anxiety, wipe your hands on a napkin, the tablecloth or even lightly on your clothes. What you spend at the dry cleaners will be paid for quickly by the better impression

---

① scaly [ˈskeili] *adj*. 有鳞的

面的活动：

控制器。一个人把他的手伸给你，一旦你们的手连在一起，他故意将他的手挪到顶端。他是在告诉你，他要负责掌控。连续互动时记住这件事。

三明治。只有了解当事人时才可使用这种方式。当你包住另外一个人的手时，你正在入侵他们的私人空间，只有受到邀请时才可以这样做。社会鼓励标准式的握手，但不等于容忍使用两只手。顺便说一下，这种握手也被称为政治家的握手，这可能也是大多数人避之不及的原因！

死鱼。想象一下，手中揉搓一条有鳞片的死鱼，画面出来了吧。你的双手通常很潮湿，这里有两个原因：要么紧张，要么右手一直拿着冷饮料，握手之前刚把它移到左手。不论哪种情况，都会令对方极度不愉快。如果你感到焦虑，可以用餐巾、桌布、甚至衣服轻轻擦手。你留下的良好印象将会使你在干洗店的开销迅速得到回报。至于饮料，使用常识即可。

柔软的手指。女士应该伸展手指而不是整个手掌，这种做法远多于男士。当男士强劲有力地握手迎接她时，伸手的女士却感到痛苦。男士告诉我，这常常会使他们与女士握手时用力较轻。职业女士的反应是她们希望得到同等的对待。解决这种问题的途径之一是始终水平地伸出整个手，即使你握手时用力很轻。

良好的握手要素包括紧紧握住他人的手、最多面对面地摇动三次、保持目光接触以及传播积极的气场。

you make. As for the beverage, use common sense.

Limp Fingers. Women, far more than men, extend their fingers rather than their entire hand. It can be painful for the extender, when she is greeted by a man who shakes with his forceful grip. Men tell me this frequently leads to their giving women a lighter handshake. Professional women respond that they want to be treated equally. One of the ways to combat this syndrome is to always extend you full hand horizontally, even if your grip is light.

Ingredients of a good handshake include that hold the person's hand firmly, shake web-to-web, three times maximum, maintain constant eye contact, radiate positive aura.

3) Eye Contact

Make it and keep it! Not only does focused eye contact display confidence on your part, it also helps you understand what the other person is really saying verbally.

Ralph Waldo Emerson once said, "When the eyes say one thing, and the tongue another, a practiced man relies on the language of the first."

Looking someone in the eye as you meet and talk with him/her also shows you are paying attention. Listening is the most important human relations skill, and good eye contact plays a large part in conveying our interest in others.

When to look. Begin as soon as you engage someone in a conversation. However, you may wish to start even earlier if you are trying to get someone's attention. Continue it throughout the conversation. Be sure to maintain direct eye contact as you are saying "good-bye." It will help leave a positive, powerful lasting impression.

Where to look. Imagine an inverted triangle in your face with the

3) 目光交流

保持目光交流！ 专注的目光交流不仅显示了你自身的信心，也可以帮助你了解其他人口头表达的真正含义。

拉尔夫·瓦尔多·爱默生曾经说过："眼睛说的是一回事，舌头说的是另一回事，注重实际的男人信赖捷足先登的语言。"

与人会面和交谈时注视对方的眼睛也表明了你正在对他表示关注。 倾听是最重要的人际关系技能，而良好的目光交流则在传达我们对他人的兴趣方面发挥着重要的作用。

什么时候看。 一参与谈话就要开始注视对方。 尽管如此，如果你试图得到别人的注意，甚至希望更早一点开始，在交谈过程中要一直保持目光交流。 说"再见"时一定要保持直接的目光交流，这将有助于留下一个积极的、强大而持久的印象。

向哪里看。 想象脸上形成的倒三角形，其底边略高于眼睛。另外两边从它往下延伸，直达鼻子和嘴唇之间，这就是在商务交谈时"目视"对方的建议区域。 从社交角度看，三角形的点降至包括下巴和颈部的地方。 人们"上下"打量你时，可能已经超越他们心中所想的商业或非正式的社交情境！

看多久。 我建议目视的时间在80%—90%之间。 少于这个时间，就可能被理解为忐忑不安、闪烁其词、缺乏信心或感到无聊。凝视的时间较长，可能被解读为太直接、突兀或强迫并使其他人感到不舒服。 只要你的目光迅速回应了对方，可以偶尔向下看。 避免目光越过对方的肩膀，好像你正在寻找更感兴趣的人交谈似的。

base of it just above your eyes. The other two sides descend from it and come to a point between your nose and your lips. That's the suggested area to " look at " during business conversations. Socially, the point of the triangle drops to include the chin and neck areas. When people look you "up and down," it's probably more than business or a casual social situation they have in mind!

How long to look. I suggest about 80—90 percent of the time. Less than that can be interpreted as discomfort, evasiveness, lack of confidence or boredom. When you stare longer, it can be construed① as being too direct, dominant or forceful and make the other person uncomfortable. It's okay to glance down occasionally as long as your gaze returns quickly to the other person. Avoid looking over the other person's shoulders as if you were seeking out someone more interesting to talk with.

4) Smiles

Smiles are an important facial expression. They show interest, excitement, empathy, concern; they create an upbeat, positive environment. Smiles can, however, be overused. Often, men smile when they are pleased; women smile to please. You know which is the most powerful!

To gain and increase respect, first establish your presence in a room, then smile. It is far more professional than to enter a room giggling or "all smiles."

(1,229 words)

---

① construe [kən'struː] *vt.* 解释；分析

4) 微笑

微笑是一种重要的面部表情。他们表现出兴趣、激动、同情和关心；它们创造了乐观、积极的环境。尽管如此，微笑也可能被过度使用。通常，男士感到高兴时微笑；女士通过微笑取悦于人。你知道哪一个最强大！

为了赢得尊重和增加尊重，首先在房间里树立你的形象，然后微笑。这比咯咯地笑或“满脸堆笑”地进入房间更为专业。

知识链接

EQ 情商(Emotional Quotient)。情商包括五个要素：第一，自我意识(Self Awareness)；第二，自我管理/约束(Self Management/Control)；第三，自我激励(Self Motivation)；第四，移情能力(Empathy)；第五，社会交往能力(Social Skills)。

题 记

面试套装虽然不是面试者成败的必然决定因素，但也是能否成功拿到职位的重要一环。对即将参加求职面试的年轻人来说，参考电影明星的着装、准确地断定时髦的“面试套装”是一件有价值的事情。影片《冷暖群芳》中女主角那袖口打折的海军蓝夹克装，袒露出闪光的带圆点花纹的衬里，时髦的女式衬衫与乳黄色帽子相得益彰；电影《打工女郎》将色彩鲜艳、干练、带垫肩的套装恰如其分地发展到顶峰，他们让美国大牌“艾利·塔哈瑞”和“琼斯纽约”也相形见绌，甘拜下风。但面试时穿裤套装、裙套装还是便装，与众不同还是协调一致，模仿他人还是塑造自身的完整形象等问题却要根据招聘方与应聘职位的不同而调整。为了心仪的职位准备良久的求职者千万不要在面试着装上“小河沟里翻了船”。

The Return of the Interview Suit

This is possibly a bad moment to bring up a 1959 film called "The Best of Everything." But, oh, was that a glorious period for the interview suit. It's hard to imagine rejecting Hope Lange for a job when she walked into 375 Park Avenue, and the breeze caught her cuffed[1] navy jacket, revealing a flash of its polka-dot lining and a smart blouse that matched her cream hat.

"Working Girl," in 1988, reflected another moment for the interview suit, appropriately enough during the pinnacle of the broad-shouldered, brightly colored power suit, when Elie Tahari and Jones New York were staples of a career woman's wardrobe.

It was so much simpler then.

For a generation of young people who were recruited to technology, financial and news media fields right out of college, and who may now be competing to hold onto the jobs they have or to find any that might be available, figuring out what exactly is the modern day "interview suit" is not so easy to do without looking like Melanie Griffith. Walking downtown

---

① cuff [kʌf] *vt.* 给……上袖口

面试套装的回归

把1959年的一部影片《冷暖群芳》拿出来说事可能不太合时宜。但那的确是面试套装的辉煌时刻。霍普·兰格走进派克大街375号，微风吹起她那袖口打折的海军蓝夹克装，袒露出闪光的带圆点花纹的衬里，时髦的女式衬衫与乳黄色帽子相得益彰。很难想象她的这身装束在求职时会遭到拒绝。

1988年的电影《打工女郎》折射出面试套装的另一个重要时刻，当美国品牌“艾利·塔哈瑞”和“琼斯纽约”占据职业女性衣橱之时，色彩鲜艳、干练、带垫肩的套装恰如其分地发展到顶峰。

从那以后，事情就变得简单多了。

年轻人大学毕业后直接进入科技、财经和新闻媒体等领域就职，他们目前也许正在努力地保住已有的工作，也许还在寻找可得到的工作机会。对这一代人来说，完全不参考梅兰妮·格里菲斯等电影明星的着装，就准确地断定时髦的“面试套装”并不是一件容易的事情。不久前的一天，设计师尼古拉·米勒在市中心逛街时，突然注意到一位魅力十足的年轻女性，当时她正在走向华尔街。这位女士穿着灰色的裤套装，这套服装吸引了设计师的目光，因为在

the other day, the designer Nicole Miller noticed an attractive young woman who was headed toward Wall Street. The woman was wearing a gray pantsuit, which caught the designer's eye because, for much of the last decade, corporate fashion has pulled so far away from the polished, two-piece look that the outfit, while professional, seemed dated.

"I hadn't seen anybody in a pantsuit for so long that I thought it looked wrong," Ms. Miller said.

But with the unemployment rate in America at a 14-year high and more than half a million jobs lost in the last three months alone, there has been a detectable shift in the way people are dressing for work. In the financial sector, certainly, the tone has become more serious, and as a predictable result, somber suits are making a comeback. Companies like Men's Wearhouse and Tahari are reporting an upswing in suit sales, particularly for those classic navy or gray pinstripe styles they classify as "interview suits." Arthur S. Levine, known as the suit king of Seventh Avenue who now designs a collection of women's career clothes in a joint venture with Mr. Tahari, said he sold 1.8 million outfits this year, almost 10 percent more than he had expected.

"We are back to a time when every company expected both women and men to wear suits and we didn't have a Casual Friday," said Gloria Mirrione, a managing director of A-L Associates, a financial services placement firm. "They are looking for a sharper style. I recommend a strong suit that says you are collected and ready to work."

Still, there are a lot of possibilities for error, and even fashion professionals differ in their opinions about what style will make the best

过去10年中的大部分时间里，光鲜精练的两件套早已远离公司的时装样式，尽管这种套装非常职业，但看上去仍然显得过时。

米勒尔先生承认："我太久没有看到人们穿套装，以至于我都以为自己看错了。"

但是，美国的失业率14年来居高不下，仅在过去的3个月中，就有50多万人丢掉了工作，人们的工作着装发生了明显的变化。当然，金融业的氛围变得更加严肃，正如预期的一样，压抑的工作套装正在回归。据报道，"男人屋"和"淑女屋"等公司的职业套装的销售额正在增加，尤其是那些经典的海军蓝或灰色细条纹系列，它们被归类为"面试套装"。著名的"第七大道"套装之王阿瑟·S.莱文声称，他今年卖出了180万美元的套装，比预期几乎高出了10个百分点。他现在与塔哈瑞先生开办了一家合资企业，设计女式套装系列。

金融服务就业公司A-L合资公司的经营主管格洛尼亚·米若尼认为，"我们重新回到了男士和女士身着职业套装的时代，我们不再有'星期五便装日'，这正是各家公司所期待的。他们正在寻找一种更激进的设计式样。我推荐一款强势的套装，穿上它你会显得镇定自若，并为工作做好准备。"

尽管如此，仍然可能出现很多失误，即便是时装专家们也会对哪种风格的服装更能产生最好的印象莫衷一是。举例来说，在裤子与裙子的大争论中，休闲品牌"香蕉共和国"的创意主管西蒙·克宁建议："我肯定赞同裤套装，因为这种套装更显身材。"

impression. For example, on the great debate of pants versus skirt, Simon Kneen, the creative director of Banana Republic, had this advice: "I would definitely go with a pantsuit because that gives a better silhouette① ."

Ms. Miller said the opposite: "I'm really against pants. They look too casual in most situations."

Who to believe? There isn't always a right answer, but each decision an applicant makes—pants or skirt, bright color or neutral, heels or flats—sends a subtle message that may play a role in how she will be perceived in an interview. To relieve some of that pressure, designers and career counselors offered some points to consider when deciding what to wear.

PANTSUIT, SKIRT SUIT, OR NO SUIT?

"There is no one right way to dress," said Karen Harvey, a recruiter for top fashion and retail jobs. "But there are a lot of don'ts." The key is to research the corporate culture to learn what a potential boss might expect. But on a basic level, "it doesn't have to be a suit at all. I recommend clean and simple lines — anything that doesn't distract the interviewer from understanding the qualities you bring to the table."

Jenna Lyons Mazeau, the creative director of J. Crew, said a pencil skirt or tailored trousers, worn with a simple cardigan (preferably cashmere) and a beautiful necklace, looks as sophisticated as a pantsuit. A more individualized look is also a modern way to approach an interview, she said, suggesting that the applicant is creative, free-thinking and

---

① silhouette [ˌsiluˈet] *n.* 轮廓

米勒女士则持相反的意见："我真的反对裤套装。它们在大多数场合看上去不太正式。"

应该相信谁呢？并不总是有正确的答案，但是求职者做出的每一个决定都传递着微妙的信息——无论是裤套装还是裙套装、亮色还是中性色、高跟还是平底，而这些信息可能在面试中别人如何感知她起着作用。为了减轻这些压力，设计师和职业顾问们提供了一些需要思考的要点，作为面试着装选择的参考。

裤套装，裙套装还是便装？

高级时装和零售业的招聘人员卡伦·哈维认为，"并不是说哪种着装方式就一定正确，但是有很多禁忌"。关键是研究那个企业的文化，从中了解潜在的老板可能期待什么。但是在最基本的层面上，"并不一定非穿套装不可。我推荐整洁、简单的条纹装，任何不会分散面试官的注意力、并能了解应试者品质的着装均可"。

时尚服装品牌 J. 克鲁公司的创意总监吉娜·里昂·马祖认为，铅笔裙或者是裁剪讲究的裤子，配上简单的开襟羊毛衫（开司米更适宜），再加上一条漂亮的项链，看上去像裤套装一样成熟优雅。她相信，更为个性化的外表也是参加面试的流行做法，这种方式表明，求职者富有创意、思想自由和自信。但是，这也要看不同的领域，运动服装整体看起来可能最适合创意领域。对于公司面试来说，选择的范围仍然很小，通常要求某种类型的套装。

克宁先生辩解说，裤套装的优势在于使腿显得修长，他认为"身着裤装是全职业化的方式"。他推荐一种双面纤维织物，比细

confident. But it also depends on the field, and the sportswear ensemble① look may be best suited to creative fields. For corporate interviews, the options are still slim, and usually require a suit of some sort.

Mr. Kneen argued that the advantage of a pantsuit is that it elongates② the legs, and "it's all business when you're wearing pants," he said. He recommended double-face fabrics, which look more expensive and feminine than pinstripes. Another traditional choice would be a solid wool crepe dress worn with a matching blazer, as long as the dress is well fitted and flattering.

"And if you decide to wear a white shirt, make sure it is pristinely③ clean," he said. "A new shirt is always the whitest."

TO STAND OUT OR TO BLEND IN?

"I'm a big fan of sticking with navy or gray pinstripes," said James Purcell, a onetime Seventh Avenue designer who now works as an image strategist for executives and politicians. "But avoid a solid black suit. It's the worst thing a woman could wear because it shows any sign of dandruff and every gray hair that you have."

But color can be a tough call. The majority of human resources professionals recommend wearing the classics—navy, black or gray—but, then again, playing it safe can also run the risk of looking too uniform.

"To me, the most important thing is give people something to

---

① ensemble [ɑnˈsɑmbl] *n*. 全套服装
② elongate [ˈiːlɔŋgeit] *vt*. 加长
③ pristinely [ˈpristainli] *adv*. 原始状态地

条纹西裤显得更加昂贵和妩媚。另外一种传统的选择是纯羊毛丝绸裙搭配颜色鲜艳的运动上衣，只要裙子协调和讨人喜欢即可。

他说："如果你决定穿白色衬衣，要确保它洁白干净。新衬衣往往是最白的。"

与众不同还是协调一致？

詹姆士·波赛尔曾经是"第七大道"的设计师，现在是执行官和政治家形象策划顾问。他说，"我是海军蓝或灰色条纹西裤的狂热追捧者。一定要避免纯黑色的套装。对女性而言，穿黑色套装是最糟糕的，因为它会显露你已有的头皮屑或者白发"。

但是，挑选颜色也可能是一种艰难的抉择。大多数人力资源专家推荐穿经典色系，如海军蓝、黑色或灰色，但他们一再强调，谨慎小心的做法也可能使大家看起来千篇一律。

里昂·马祖女士声称："对我来说，给人留下印象是最重要的事。很多人在那儿竞争一份工作，所以与穿灰色的套装相比，还不如选一个其他颜色。"但是颜色不宜太亮。她说："对白肤金发碧眼的女人来说，粉红看上去不那么高贵。这并不意味着你要穿霓虹灯般的亮色。"

棕色或者深蓝色之类的朴实颜色，会使气质与众不同又不至于锋芒毕露。但是一定要对淡色系多加小心。她说："我认为，除非绝对完美，否则淡色系套装往往给人有点热情奔放的感觉。"

美国女性服饰制造商安·泰勒公司的高级设计副总裁妮莎·埃里克森认为，多彩多姿的饰件是给基本套装增添色彩的另一种方

remember," Ms. Lyons Mazeau said. "There's going to be a lot of people out there competing for a job, so pick a color, as opposed to wearing all gray." But no brights, she said, and "if you are a blonde, pinks can look less expensive. This is not about wearing a neon sign."

Earthier colors, like brown or a rich blue, impart a distinctive personality without coming off as overpowering. But beware of pastels: "I think that lightly colored suits, unless they are absolutely perfect, can feel a little Eastery," she said.

Lisa Axelson, a senior vice president of design at Ann Taylor, said colorful accessories are another way to add color to a basic suit without risking an outfit so loud that the candidate appears out of place in a conservative environment. Prints, meanwhile, are discouraged. As Ms. Miller said, "They'll remember you better, but what you want is for them to remember your personality, not to be totally distracted by that person who came in wearing the loud print."

ISN'T THERE SOMEONE TO COPY?

Take cues from what powerful women are wearing, as in Michelle Obama or Sarah Palin. Mrs. Obama wore a J. Crew cardigan with a textured skirt on "The Tonight Show with Jay Leno" that demonstrated a classy combination of polish and ease. And Governor Palin, despite the controversy surrounding her campaign clothes, was most often wearing sensible suits from Tahari, Arthur, and S. Levine that she had mixed and matched. Mr. Levine was upset that news programs were so impressed with a red suit with a ribbon belt that they assumed it was by the likes of Oscar de la Renta, not the Tahari suit sold at Neiman Marcus for about $ 498.

式，他们不会使套装过于张扬，又不至于使求职者在保守的环境中显得格格不入。同时，不鼓励穿印花布料的着装。正如米勒尔女士所言：“他们会对你印象更为深刻，但是你想要的是让他们记住你的个性，而不是被一个身着花哨印花图案的人分散了注意力。”

有可以模仿的人么？

米歇尔·奥巴马或者萨拉·佩林等强势女性的穿着告诉我们该怎么做。奥巴马夫人在“杰·雷诺今夜脱口秀”节目上身着J.克鲁的开襟羊毛衫和织纹裙，展示了高雅与随和的经典组合。佩林主管参加各种商业活动时的着装备受争议，除此之外，她在很多时候都是明智地选择套装，包括艾丽·塔哈瑞品牌、亚瑟王品牌和S.莱文品牌，她喜欢混搭。佩林女士穿着配有缎带的红色套装在新闻节目中出镜，给人印象深刻，公众认为这件套装是奥斯卡·德拉伦塔之类的品牌，而不是以经营奢侈品为主的高端百货商店曼·马库斯售价约498美元的艾丽·塔哈瑞品牌，这件事令莱文先生感到沮丧。佩林女士穿过的其他20款左右的系列套装价位都不到198美元。

莱文先生认为，“关键是你可以看上去穿着由设计师专门设计的服装，而不需要花很多钱。”

怎样塑造完整的形象？

埃里克松夫人认为，“你携带的手提袋是关键。你不会希望拎着一个破旧的购物袋招摇过市。你渴望拥有一个漂亮、时髦的手提袋，里面装着你的黑莓手机和简历。建议身着黑色套装的人在手提袋里装一小卷粘尘器”。

About 20 other suits from his collection worn by Ms. Palin cost less than $ 198.

"The point is, you can look like you are wearing designer for not a lot of money," he said.

HOW TO FINISH A LOOK?

"The bag you carry is key," Ms. Axelson said. "You don't want to be walking in with an old shopping bag. You want a beautiful, chic① tote that carries your BlackBerry and your résumé. A tip for people who wear black suits is to pack a small lint roller in your tote bag."

And if there's room, some designers advise packing a nice pair of heels to change into just before arriving at the interview, so that they remain unsoiled.

"There's nothing wrong with wearing flat shoes and bringing heels," Mr. Purcell said. "Maria Shriver has somebody who carries her shoes for her. High heels help your stance. The American Orthopaedic② Association may say I'm crazy, but the right heels will help you get a job."

(1,405 words)

---

① chic [ʃiːk] *adj*. 时髦的

② orthopaedic [ˌɔːθəˈpiːdik] *adj*. 整形外科的

如果包里还有空间，有些设计师建议再装一双精致的高跟鞋，可以在面试前换上，这样它们看上去一尘不染。

波赛尔先生认为，“穿平底鞋再换上高跟鞋并没有什么错。玛丽亚·施赖弗甚至安排了专门替她带鞋的人。高跟鞋有助于你的站姿。全美整形协会的人说我疯了，但是高跟鞋会帮助你获得工作”。

知识链接

Oscar de la Renta “奥斯卡·德拉伦塔”是一个备受社交界尊崇的时装品牌，以设计名贵华丽的礼服、讲究工艺质感又强调高贵品位著称。奥斯卡·德拉伦塔品牌经营的时装品类繁多，其中高级时装和晚礼服最为有名，女鞋也堪称精品。奥斯卡·德拉伦塔公司的总部在美国纽约，创立于1973年，创立人奥斯卡·德拉伦塔是美国十大设计师之一。

Jones New York “琼斯纽约”是美国纽约时尚巨头Jones集团的核心女装和配饰品牌，与Nine West属姐妹品牌，其优雅的设计，经典的风格，深得美国白领女性的欢迎。

Melanie Griffith 梅兰尼·格里菲斯曾获奥斯卡奖和金球奖。在1988年的一部电影中，梅兰尼·格里菲斯在其中扮演女主角Tess，一个在华尔街工作的女秘书，穿着带垫肩的西服。

Seventh Avenue 美国纽约市曼哈顿的第七街，也是美国时装业的中心。

Neiman Marcus 曼·马库斯是美国一家以经营奢侈品为主的高端百货商店。

Maria Shriver 美国加州前州长阿诺德·施瓦辛格的妻子，也是著名的媒体人和新闻记者，美国前任总统约翰·肯尼迪的侄女。她已宣布与阿诺德·施瓦辛格分居。

题　记

不论客户是男士还是女士、妈妈还是爸爸抑或私营企业、即将上市的新公司，或是英特尔、国际纸业或威讯公司之类的商业巨头，主办商务晚餐的基本要素大同小异。首先，要确保合适的聚餐时间：提前打电话给餐厅经理，说明商务宴会的重要性；宴会前一天给客户打电话确认时间；聚餐当日提前到达餐厅。其次，在客户到达前安排好座次，保证客户有最好的位置，比如可以观赏水和天际线的座位。再次，用餐时限制酒量，明智的做法是适量饮酒，小酌一口，品尝一下即可，最多不要超过两杯。用餐时的举止可以决定商务交往中的成败，只要真心实意，坚守诚信，竭尽所能满足客户的需求，令其欢欣而来，满意而归，达成交易就是顺理成章的事情。

Hosting a Business Dinner

When you host a business dinner, remember one crucial point: You're in charge.

Doing business over dinner is a good way to introduce yourself to clients, build relationships and seal the deal. Get it right, and it's duck soup. Get it wrong, and you're dead in the water.

"Always be familiar with the restaurant so there won't be any surprises," says Lydia Ramsey, author of Manners That Sell. "Show up on time, dress appropriately, don't drink too much, keep the conversation going, and you'll be fine."

As the host, everything falls to you. Extend the invitations to a business dinner at least one week in advance, and, for a breakfast or lunch, at least three days ahead of the scheduled date.

Helpful Hint No. 1: Be sure the date works for you.

This seems obvious, but if you have to postpone or cancel, you'll look disorganized and will have wasted your clients' time.

Always call ahead and make it clear to the maitre'd that you will be hosting any important business dinner. Stress that everything must be perfect and that you'll pay the bill.

If possible, make arrangements with the restaurant to pay the bill

主持商务宴会

主持商务宴会时，请记住至关重要的一点：你是主人。

聚餐时进行商务交流是一种有效的方式，你可以把自己介绍给客户，建立人际关系，签订合同。如果事情进展顺利，主持商务宴会易如反掌。如果出现差错，就会把事情搞砸。

《礼仪之道》一书的作者莉迪亚·拉姆齐认为，“对餐厅了如指掌才能遇事不惊。一定要准时到场，穿着得体，不要喝太多，并保持谈话顺畅，而你也会处之若泰”。

作为主人，事无巨细，你都需要安排。至少要提前一周发出商务宴会邀请，对于早宴和午宴来说，至少要比预定日期提前三天发出邀请。

提示1:确保合适的聚餐时间。

显而易见，如果你不得不推迟或取消聚餐，别人会认为你安排不当，同时也浪费了客户的时间。

任何时候都要提前打电话，对餐厅经理说明你即将主持的重要商务宴会，强调不能出任何差错，并且你会买单。

如果有可能，与餐厅商定在餐前付账。拉姆齐认为，最好在宴

prior to the dinner. Ramsey says it's best if the bill doesn't come to the table. But if the restaurant won't accept advance payment, make sure you grab the bill first. Check it briefly, but don't quibble① .

When selecting a restaurant, stick with top-of-the-line joints and avoid the latest hot spot. What you're looking for is a restaurant that's relaxed and conducive② to good conversation. For starters, think oak paneling and high-back chairs; that will eliminate loud music or heated arguments booming from the kitchen.

Also, be sure to call your clients the day before to confirm the dinner. If there's a mixup on their end, be gracious and reschedule.

When preparing for the event, dress in appropriate business attire, and kick it up a notch③ . This underscores your seriousness about the clients and their business. It's better to be a little over-dressed than woefully under-dressed.

On the day of the meal, get to the restaurant ahead of time so you'll have a chance to attend to any last-minute details. This is the time to give the restaurant your credit card, and to gently remind the maitre'd what's at stake. A tip in advance never hurts.

Helpful Hint No. 2: Don't forget seating strategy.

Work out the seating before your guests arrive. Make sure the guests have the best seats—those with a view of the water or skyline, for example.

---

① quibble [ˈkwibl] *n.* 斤斤计较

② conducive [kənˈdjuːsiv] *adj.* 有益于

③ notch [nɔtʃ] *n.* 凹口;刻痕

会结束前买单。但是，如果酒店拒绝提前结账，一定要抢先拿到账单，简要地看一下，但不要斤斤计较。

选择餐厅时，定位在高级的娱乐场所，不要去最近的热门餐厅。你要找的是可以休闲放松、并有益于愉快商谈的餐厅。首先，考虑安排橡木镶板的高靠背椅，这样可以消除喧闹的音乐声和厨房传来的激烈争吵声。

同时，一定要提前一天给客户打电话，确认宴会时间。如果客户最终难以抽身前往，要表现出彬彬有礼的姿态，重新安排时间。

赴宴时，要穿合适的商业正装，以提升自己的形象。它表示你对客户及这笔业务的重视程度。着装略微正式比太过于随便要好得多。

聚餐当日，要提前到达餐厅，这样你就有机会关注最后的细节。此时，你可以把信用卡交给餐厅，并且礼貌地提醒大堂经理绝不能掉以轻心。事先提示绝对没有坏处。

提示 2：牢记座次策略。

在客户到达前安排好座次。保证客户有最好的位置，比如可以观赏水和天际线的座位。别让客人面对墙壁、厨房或洗手间。如果餐桌不合适，可以要求换个更好的位置，不要不好意思。

商务会餐时，不要在餐桌上大声喧哗。如果只有一个客户，你可以挨着他坐。如果有两个客户，让其中一个坐在你的对面，另一个坐在你的旁边。

拉姆齐认为，“如果你坐在他们之间，试着跟上双方的谈话节奏

You don't want your guests facing the wall, kitchen or restrooms. If the table isn't suitable, don't be bashful about asking for a better one.

This is a business dinner, and you don't want to shout across the table. If you have one client, sit next to each other. If you have two clients, seat one across from you and the other to your side.

"If you sit between them, you'll feel like you're watching a match at Wimbledon as you try to follow the conversation," Ramsey says.

When ordering, Ramsey suggests that the host make a few suggestions. This indicates the price range and opens the evening to appetizers and an appropriate wine. The recommendation can be as simple as, "I've always enjoyed the veal" or "This restaurant has an excellent selection of California wines."

Let your guests order first. There's no need to comment on their selections because they have excellent taste, you've taken them to a first-class restaurant and everything on the menu is good.

Ramsey says it's important to be aware of time, but don't keep checking your watch. As a general rule, a business dinner should be wrapped up in two or three hours; lunch should be about an hour-and-a-half and breakfast about an hour.

Helpful Hint No. 3: Limit the amount of alcohol you and your guests consume at dinner.

The meal is about business, not high times at your old school. It might be wise to stick with wine. Sip and savor① it, and plan to have no more

① savor [ˈseivə] *vt.* 品尝

时，感觉就像是在观看温网比赛”。

拉姆齐表示，主人在点餐时可以提出少许建议，即指出价格范围，开胃菜和合适的葡萄酒，以此拉开晚宴的帷幕。可以如此这般地简单推荐：“我一直都喜欢这里的小牛肉”，或者“这家餐厅有极好的精酿加州红酒。”

让客户先点餐。没有必要评论客户挑选的食物，因为它们都是美味佳肴。在一流的酒店请客，菜单上的菜品样样赏心悦目。

拉姆齐认为，留意时间非常重要，但是切忌不断地查看手表。一般来说，商务晚餐大约持续两至三小时，午餐大约一个半小时，早餐一个小时即可。

提示3:用餐时限制你和客户的酒量。

宴请是为了业务，不是重温母校的美好时光。明智的做法是适量饮酒。小酌一口，品尝一下即可，最多不要超过两杯。如果其中一个客户有难处，那么你可以出面解围，小心谨慎地要求侍者别再倒酒或再来一瓶。如果你必须解围的话，只可在两道菜之间提出要求。

作为主人，你要把握商谈业务的时机。晚餐是社交场合，所以等到主菜上齐后再谈论具体细节。午餐时等到点完菜之后再说，这样你就不会被打断。若是早餐，就可以直奔主题。

如果就餐过程中有什么问题，可以请求离席，找餐厅工作人员私下协商。如果你当着客户的面抱怨，他们会觉得不舒服。永远不要在公共场合训斥员工。

than two glasses at most. If one of your guests is getting into trouble, excuse yourself and discreetly ask your server to refrain from refilling the glasses or bringing another bottle. If you must excuse yourself, do so only between courses.

As the host, you determine when to discuss business. Dinner is a social occasion, so wait until the main course has been completed before getting down to details. At lunch, wait until you've ordered so you won't be interrupted. At breakfast, get to the point quickly.

If something goes wrong, excuse yourself and discuss the problem privately with the restaurant staff. Your guests will feel uncomfortable if you complain in front of them. Never berate① staff members in public.

The basics for hosting a business dinner are the same whether your clients are Mr. and Mrs. Mom and Pop, a privately held enterprise, a new company about to go public or a giant like Intel, International Paper or Verizon Communications.

"Your conduct during the meal can determine your professional success," Ramsey says. "If you've handled all the small details correctly and made every effort to see that your clients had a pleasant evening, they will assume that you will handle their business the same way. You could have them eating out of your hand before long."

(902 words)

---

① berate [biˈreit] *vt.* 斥责

不论客户是男士还是女士、妈妈还是爸爸抑或私营企业、即将上市的新公司，或是英特尔、国际纸业或威讯公司之类的商业巨头，主办商务晚餐的基本要素都是相同的。

拉姆齐认为，“用餐时的举止可以决定你事业的成败。如果你在所有的细节上都处理得当，并且尽一切努力让客户度过一个愉快的夜晚，他们会认为你将以同样的方式对待他们的业务。不久他们就会成为你的囊中之物。”

知识链接

International Paper 美国国际纸业公司是一家业务遍布全球的造纸和包装行业公司。公司业务包括非涂布纸、工业和消费品包装和林产品。公司全球总部位于美国田纳西州孟菲斯市。

Verizon Communications 威讯公司是一家美国的主要电信公司，总部位于纽约市。公司的主要业务为语音通话、固定宽带和无线通信。

题 记

轻松获得新客户的诀窍之一就是具备良好的举止和恰当的商业礼仪。无论你从事什么行业，合适的商业礼仪并非可随意选择，因为它是人们必须每天遵守的准则。但是，使用恰当的商业礼仪可以凸显人的优雅和职业，给客户留下精通业务、充满自信的印象。保持待人接物和自我介绍的最佳状态是吸引潜在客户的必要手段，根据场合着装会给潜在客户留下积极的信息和良好的印象，适当使用商业名片帮助潜在客户顺利地记住公司的标识和名称，礼貌的交流和沟通可以帮助潜在客户应对面临的一切挑战。在日常工作中践行商务礼仪，可以快速促成一种领导气质，它是金钱与威望望尘莫及的光环。正如约翰逊所言：“礼貌像只气垫：里面可能什么都没有，却能奇妙地减轻我们的颠簸。”

Easy Ways to Gain New Clients

When meeting with prospective clients and discussing your products or services, three elements are keys: knowing about your company, knowing about your competitors and knowing how to treat others professionally. Of those three important elements, the latter is lacking in many circumstances.

These days, good manners and proper business etiquette make good sense. Aside from being educated about your products and industry, you must also know how best to meet people and make introductions, how to dress for the occasion, how to use your business cards properly and how to converse with your clients. Improve these skills today in order to ensure long-term business growth.

Meet People and Make Introductions

In order to build your client base, you need a steady flow of prospects. That means meeting new people on a constant basis and introducing them to your business. Many people shy away from this practice because they're afraid of appearing pushy or too "marketable." The truth is, they have simply never learned how to meet people or how to network.

You can meet people virtually anywhere—at a networking event, a cocktail party, in line at the bank or in a waiting area. Use your self-

轻松获得新客户

与潜在客户会面和讨论产品或服务时，需要把握三个关键元素：了解公司，了解竞争对手，了解如何专业地对待他人。当然，在这三个重要元素中，后者在很多情况下存在欠缺。

在当下，良好的举止和恰当的商业礼仪具有重要意义。除了接受与产品和行业相关的培训，你还必须了解如何达到待人接物和自我介绍的最佳状态，如何根据场合穿着打扮，如何得体地使用名片，以及如何与客户交谈。为了确保长期的业务增长，提高这些技能是当务之急。

待人接物和自我介绍

为了建立客户群，需要源源不断的潜在客户流。这意味着在稳定的基础上会见新客户，以便将你的业务推荐给他们。许多人羞于这么做，因为他们担心自己的表现被认为是爱出风头或者太过于“市场化”。而事实真相是，他们只是从来没有学会如何与人打交道或如何与人交流。

实际上，你在任何地方都要与人打交道，包括处理网络事件，参加鸡尾酒会，在银行或等候区排队。自我介绍是一种分享信息而不是推销的方式。典型的自我介绍可以这样说：“你好。我是约翰·史密斯，我公司的代尼尔纤维产品提供方便、轻型的商品展示

introduction as a way to share information, not make a sale. A good example of a self-introduction is: "Hello. My name is John Smith, My company, CMD Products, offers convenient, lightweight trade show displays to make your booth① setup easier."

Your self-introduction need only be a 10-second description of who you are and what you do. Be selective about the words you use to describe your company or business. Work to refine your self-introduction so it will provide information and also interest others.

Dress for the Occasion

Before you speak a word, your clothes have already spoken volumes. As the old saying goes, "You never get a second chance to make a first impression."

Many people mistakenly believe that whatever they wear to the office is acceptable to wear after hours or when meeting clients. That's fine if your office dress code matches your after-hours or meeting event; however, many times work clothes are either too casual or too formal for an out-of-office meeting. Dress too casually and your prospects may not perceive you as professional or knowledgeable. Dress too formally and they may see you as "stuffy②" or "out of their league."

As a business executive, you have a responsibility to send the best professional message you can to be successful. If necessary, bring a change of clothes to the office so you have something appropriate to wear to your event. Remember, the way you dress shows respect for yourself, your

① booth [buːð] *n.* 展位
② stuffy [ˈstʌfi] *adj.* 沉闷的

架，可以使你的展台设置更容易。”

自我介绍只需要十秒钟的描述，说明你是谁以及你是做什么的。描述公司或业务时注意斟词酌句。自我介绍要讲究精练，既能提供信息，又能引起别人的兴趣。

根据场合着装

开口说话之前，你的着装已经胜过千言万语。正如俗话所说，“你永远不会有第二次机会再造第一印象”。

许多人错误地认为，无论他们在办公室穿什么，下班后或会见客户时也是可以接受的。如果办公室着装与下班后或会见活动相符的话，那是可以的。然而，很多时候，对于办公室外的会面来说，工作装要么过于随便，要么过于正式。着装过于随便，潜在客户可能会认为你不够专业或精通业务。着装过于正式，他们可能会认为你“沉闷”或者“不是他们的同盟者”。

作为企业主管，你有责任尽可能成功地发出最好的专业信息。如果有必要，带一套替换服装到办公室，这样你就可以在参加活动时恰当着装。请记住，着装方式显示出你对自己、你的业务、你的公司以及你的产品或服务的尊重。仔细整理你的衣柜，你会给潜在客户留下积极的信息。

适当使用商业名片

每个人都需要拥有充足的商业名片。它们的印刷成本相当便宜，但它们代表着你和公司的长久印象。想一想你握手之后留下的商务名片。

基本信息应该放在商业名片正面显眼的位置，包括姓名和头衔、公司名称和标志、地址、电话号码。

business, your company and your products or services. Plan your wardrobe carefully and you'll leave your prospects with a positive message.

Use Your Business Cards Properly

Everyone needs to have an adequate supply of business cards. They're fairly inexpensive to print, and they present a long-lasting impression of you and your company. Think of your business card as the handshake you leave behind.

Business cards should have essential information easily visible on the face of the card. This could include your name and title, company name and logo, address, telephone.

It is not necessary to leave the back of the card blank. Many people utilize this space to list the products or services offered, give a description of the business or share an interesting quote or statistic.

After you introduce yourself to a prospective client and determine that you'll be able to help that person, offer one of your business cards as a reminder of who you are, what you do and where you can be reached. Business cards can also be used as a forwarding agent when attached to an information kit① newspaper clipping, or something you promised to send. Everyone likes to be remembered, so make sure your business card helps you to be remembered favorably.

Converse with Your Prospects

When you meet with new people, always spend time conversing and getting to know them. Too many executives, especially salespeople, rush into the sales part of the meeting without first learning the clients' needs.

① kit [kit] *vt.* 装备

没有必要让名片的背面留出空白。很多人利用这个空间列出提供的产品或服务，描述业务，或者分享有趣的报价或统计。

对潜在客户做完自我介绍并确定可以给他提供帮助时，递给他一张名片，以此提醒他你是谁、你是做什么的以及怎样与你联系。也可以将商业名片当做一种传递媒介，附上资料袋剪报或你承诺发送的信息。每个人都希望能被记住，所以，确认你的商业名片帮助你顺利地留在他人的记忆中。

与潜在客户交流

与新客户见面时，常常要花时间谈话，并了解他们。太多的主管特别是销售人员，事先不了解客户的需要就仓促进入销售谈判环节，这种做法只会带来灾难性的结果。

人们总是与他们了解、喜欢和信任的那些人打交道。为了让潜在客户与你做生意时感到舒服，他们需要知道，你在意他们，并且愿意帮助他们应对面临的一切挑战。你要通过会话艺术来完成这项任务。

因为人们通常喜欢谈论自己，所以可以向你的潜在客户提一些非打扰性的问题来了解他们。了解他们的公司，他们的需要，他们过去做过什么项目，以及将来他们需要完成什么项目。如果你认为你的产品或服务可以帮助他们达到目标，然后，也只有在那时，你才应该进入完整的展示环节。

请记住，你是在创造并维持一种关系。在表达礼貌和尊重的同时，还要友好和使用常识。避免使用行业术语。如果能避开行业特殊术语，谈话和交流的气氛会更融洽，思想会表达得更清楚。毕竟，所有交流的目的都是为了增进了解，而不是制造混乱。你的潜

This is a road to disaster.

People do business with those they know, like and trust. In order to get prospective clients to feel comfortable doing business with you, they need to know that you care about them and want to help them solve whatever challenge they may have. You accomplish this through the art of conversation.

Because people generally like to talk about themselves, ask your prospects non-intrusive questions to get to know them. Find out about their company, their needs, what projects they've done in the past and what they need to accomplish future projects. If you think your products or services can help them achieve their goal, then and only then should you move into your full presentation.

Keep in mind that you are creating and maintaining a relationship. Be friendly and use common sense while being courteous and respectful. Avoid using industry jargon. You'll have a better conversation and communicate your ideas more clearly if you avoid industry specific terms. After all, the goal of all communication is to enhance understanding, not to confuse. Your prospects will appreciate your efforts.

No matter what business you're in, proper business etiquette is not optional; it is something you must use every day. In fact, using proper business etiquette will help you appear polished and professional, causing clients to view you as knowledgeable and confident. By practicing your business etiquette on a daily basis, you'll soon develop a leadership style that money and prestige can never buy. As a result, your business and career will grow beyond your wildest dreams.

(945 words)

在客户会对你的努力表示感谢。

无论你从事什么行业，合适的商业礼仪并非可随意选择。它是人们必须每天遵守的准则。但是，使用恰当的商业礼仪可以凸显人的优雅和职业，给客户留下精通业务、充满自信的印象。在日常工作中践行商务礼仪，可以快速促成一种领导气质，它是金钱与威望望尘莫及的光环。结果是生意和事业比肩发展，共同超越辉煌的梦想。

知识链接

Cocktail Party 鸡尾酒会。场面隆重的商务发布会常伴有鸡尾酒会，大多安排在发布会开始之前，在演出大厅外的空间。参加商务发布会的人一般遵守主流社会规定的礼仪：鸡尾酒会场面豪华，食品精致小量；客人们衣冠楚楚、彬彬有礼，男士要穿西服，女士要化妆着正装，等等。鸡尾酒会上要小声说话、小口啜饮、少量进食。

题记

尽管旅途劳顿、美元疲软，但美国的高管们仍然频繁地穿梭于海外，乐此不疲地享受着异国文化带来的愉悦。日本人身穿三件套的西服前往商务谈判会场，美国人却身着不合时宜的卡其装和马球装。中国人对颜色有特别的讲究，而美国人却喜欢色彩绚丽的服装和珠光宝气的配饰。阿根廷商人之间的肢体接触比大多数美国人习惯的肢体接触要频繁得多，而亚洲人在与人打交道时却很少使用肢体语言和手势。澳大利亚人的商务着装相对保守，但他们在商务洽谈时会直奔主题；超长时间的握手在巴西习以为常，但美国人有些豪放不羁的行为在巴西人看来却不那么文雅；德国人倾向非常正式的称呼，对商务专业头衔一丝不苟，面面俱到；而阿拉伯人却将猪皮产品、酒类或任何含酒精的商品视为禁忌。国际商务礼仪传递着丰富、复杂、微妙的信息，商务人士只有做到“入国问禁，入乡随俗，入门问讳”才能游刃有余。

When in Rome, Do as the Romans Do

International business meetings become more frequent as global trade grows. Despite travel travails① and the weak dollar, U.S. executives are traveling overseas more frequently all the time. However, there are rules to follow, and not everyone knows them. Business protocol varies from country to country, and knowing what it is could mean the difference between making and breaking the deal.

"This is extremely important for the American businessman to know," said Margaret Burke, principal with Key Point Protocol, an online firm that promotes training in business communications and protocol. "Be sensitive to and be very cautious about everything from training on the cultures of the country to the food that they would be experiencing."

In order not to offend meeting hosts in foreign countries, it is necessary to know the do's and don'ts, according to Lisa Grotts, founder of the AML Group and an etiquette consultant. "We're completely different and have a different perspective than our counterparts are used to," she added. "Failing to recognize it, I think, could spell disaster."

One of the main differences involves the clothing worn during meetings. Americans, Grotts said, have a tendency to dress more casually

---

① travail [ˈtræveil] *n.* 辛苦

入 乡 随 俗

随着全球贸易的增长，国际商务会议变得越来越频繁。尽管旅途劳顿、美元疲软，但美国的高管们却仍然频繁地穿梭于海外。然而，并不是所有人都了解应该遵循的规则。商务礼仪因国而异，了解它的细则可能意味着交易成败之间的区别。

礼仪要点公司的负责人玛格瑞特·伯克声称："对美国商人来说，了解礼仪细则极为重要。无论是熟悉他国的文化，还是可能要品尝的食物，他们都要格外敏感，谨慎小心。"礼仪要点公司是一家促进商务沟通和礼仪培训的在线企业。

AML 集团创始人和礼仪顾问丽莎·葛奥茨认为，在国外，为了不得罪会议的东道主，有必要知道哪些可以做、哪些不可以做。她补充说："与同行们养成的习惯相比，我们完全与众不同，持有不同的观点。我认为，如果意识不到这一点，可能会引起麻烦。"

主要的分歧之一涉及会议期间的着装。葛奥茨指出，与日本或中国等国的商人相比，美国人更青睐随意的装束。她补充说："与日本人举行会议时，美国本土有很多人身着卡其装和马球装，这是不合适的。与会的日本人身穿三件套的西服，所以你也应该穿套装。"

中国是一个习俗与美国大相径庭的国度。专攻中国、日本和英

than businesspeople in countries such as Japan or China. "There are a lot of people here in the United States who would have meetings with the Japanese wearing khakis and a polo," she added. "That's inappropriate. The Japanese are going to come in a three-piece suit. You should be in a suit as well."

China is one country where the customs differ greatly from those in the U.S. Grotts, who specializes in Chinese, Japanese and British business etiquette, said one should dress more conservatively in China, avoiding loud colors and flashy jewelry. "Also, the color of white is really a no-no," she added. "White is the color of funerals in China, and you never want to wrap a package in white if you're giving a gift, because it means death." Avoid red too, Grotts said, as it is reserved for brides.

One of the most important meeting etiquette rules to remember is associated with business cards, an important part of business meetings and something you should never leave home without. "When you're overseas, you're going to have two passports," Grotts said. "One the U.S., and the other, your business card."

In China, she added, business cards are handed out using two hands, with one's thumbs on either corner and the name facing toward the person receiving the card. Grotts, who is the former director of protocol for the city and county of San Francisco, also said that when conducting meetings in foreign countries, it is best to have your information translated into the language of the country and printed on the back. "When you present it," she added, "you should present it on the foreign side. That way they can understand it."

Gestures and body language can be troublesome in some countries. Elena Brouwer, director of the International Etiquette Centre, agreed, that in Argentina, businesspeople are much more "touchy-feely" than most

国商务礼仪的葛奥茨认为，在中国，着装要更加谨慎，避免色彩绚丽的服装和珠光宝气的配饰。她补充说："此外，白颜色确实是一个禁忌。在中国，白色是葬礼的颜色。如果你要送礼，千万别用白颜色的包装，因为白色意味着死亡。"葛奥茨认为，还要避免红色，因为它是新娘的专用颜色。

需要牢记，最重要的会议礼仪规则之一与名片相关，它是商务会议的重要组成部分，也是出门时一定要随身携带的物品。葛奥茨认为，"出国时需要备两本身份通行证，一本是美国护照，另一个是商务名片。"

她再次强调，在中国，双手递出名片，拇指放在名片两边的角落，名字朝向接收名片的人。葛奥茨是旧金山市的前任礼宾司司长。她还提醒大家，在外国参加会议时，最好将你的信息翻译成该国的语言，并印刷在名片的背面。她补充说："递名片时，应该出示外国语言的那一面。这样，他们就可以读懂名片了。"

手势和肢体语言在有些国家可能造成麻烦。国际礼仪中心的主管艾琳娜·布劳威尔赞同这种观点。在阿根廷，商人之间的肢体接触比大多数美国人习惯的肢体接触要频繁得多。她说，通常在握手之后，阿根廷男士还会拍打同事的肩膀，表达相互之间的问候，即便他们只是通过电话或电子邮件通信建立的关系。

另一方面，她注意到，亚洲人在和别人交谈时，很少使用肢体语言和手势。布劳威尔说："他们说话时很冷静。无论在什么地方，你都必须学习与人相处之道，因为礼仪让他人感觉舒服。"

葛奥茨认为，使外国东道主感到安逸的一种方法，就是融入他们的文化，这一点在中国尤为重要，尤其是在吃饭的时候。葛奥茨

Americans are used to. She said often after shaking hands, Argentinian men will greet colleagues by touching their shoulders even if they have established relationships only through phone or e-mail correspondence.

Asians on the other hand, she noted, use very little body language and few gestures when speaking to others. "They aren't animated when they speak," Brouwer said. "No matter where you are, you have to learn the protocol of the people that you're with, because manners is making other people feel comfortable."

One way to make foreign hosts feel at ease, according to Grotts, is by partaking in their culture, something important in China, especially when it comes to dining. Grotts said, unlike in America, it is a sign of rudeness to eat everything on your plate as it signals your host that you want more. She added that cleaning one's plate is a nonverbal way of showing dissatisfaction.

"You should always leave a little on your plate in China when you're eating," Grotts said. "If you don't, they're going to keep giving you seconds, thirds and fourths. Oftentimes food is a way of showing themselves off and showing off their country, so for you not to partake in it is saying you don't want to partake in their culture."

When in Rome, Do as the Romans Do. Proper business meeting etiquette varies from country to country and even city to city. Tradeshow Week spoke with a number of experts on international business etiquette to get their tips on how to act in some of the world's busiest tradeshow cities.

Sydney, Australia

Business dress in Sydney is conservative. Men are expected to wear a dark business suit and tie, while women should stick with a dress or skirt and blouse.

Punctuality is the name of the game down under. Don't be surprised

说，与美国不同的是，在中国吃光盘中餐是一种粗鲁的表现，因为这会提示主人，你还想要更多。她补充说，吃光盘中餐是表达不满的非语言方式。

葛奥茨说："在中国吃饭时，你通常应该在盘子里留一点。如果你不这样做，他们会一次、两次、三次、四次地为你添加食物。美食通常是他们炫耀自己和炫耀他们国家的一种方式，所以，如果你不分享美食也就意味着你不愿分享他们的文化。"

入乡随俗。恰当的商务会议礼仪因国而异，甚至因城市而异。"贸易展会周刊"采访了一些国际商务礼仪专家，得到了一些世界上最繁忙的贸易展览城市的活动建议。

悉尼，澳大利亚

在悉尼，商务着装相对保守。男士最好穿深色商务西装和打领带，而女士一定要穿裙装或裙子和女式衬衫。

守时在这个国家非常重要。当你的联系人跳过聊天、直奔主题时，请不要感到惊讶。

头衔很重要，尤其是在与政治领导人打交道的过程中。一定要用合适的头衔称呼你的联系人。

尽管晚餐会议正在成为一种广受欢迎的建立业务关系的方式，工作早餐和上午8时的会议在这个国家仍然很普遍。

圣保罗，巴西

穿三件套西服的男士是主管，穿两件套西服的男士通常是办公室的工作人员。不要把公文包和钱包放在地上，因为当地迷信的观念习俗认为，这样做你的钱会流失。

超长时间的握手在巴西习以为常，如果你的同行比你有更多的

when your contacts skip the chit-chat and get straight to the point.

Titles are important, especially when dealing with political leaders. Make sure you call your contacts by their proper moniker.

Working breakfasts and 8 a.m. meetings are common in this country, although dinner meetings are becoming a popular way of building business relationships.

Sao Paulo, Brazil

Men should wear a three-piece suit to suggest they are an executive; two-piece suits are associated with office workers. Refrain from placing briefcases and purses on the ground as local superstition holds that your money will run away.

Extra-long handshakes are the norm in Brazil, and don't be surprised if your counterparts are more touchy-feely than you. Brazilians tend to frequently touch arms, elbows and backs. Watch your hand gestures, as some everyday American movements may have rude connotations.

Titles are important in this country, but often first names will be used in a business setting.

Brazilians are extremely punctual, but you should allow the host to start the meeting as casual conversations are expected beforehand.

Berlin, Germany

Business dress in Germany is quite restrained. Men and women both should wear dark, solid colors with white shirts. Men always should wear ties, and keep them conservative.

Be on time for a meeting with German clients, as punctuality is respected. Tardiness① may be seen as an insult to your hosts.

Germans tend to shake hands at both the beginning and end of a

---

① tardiness [ˈtɑːdinis] n. 迟到

肢体接触，不要感到惊讶。巴西人往往频繁地触摸他人的胳膊、肘部和背部。留神你的手势，因为有些美国人的日常动作在巴西人看来不那么文雅。

头衔在这个国家很重要，但是处理商务时可以直呼其名。

巴西人特别守时，但你应该允许主人按照事先的安排，以一种随意谈话的方式开始会议。

柏林，德国

商务服装在德国相当拘谨。男士和女士都应该穿深色、单色的服装，并搭配白衬衫。男士任何时候都要系领带，以使自己显得传统。

德国人崇尚守时，所以与德国客户见面要准时。迟到被视为对主人的侮辱。

德国人在商务会议开始和结束时往往会握手，并可能伴随着轻微的点头或鞠躬。请务必回应，并直视对方的眼睛，如果不这样做，无意中就会犯错。

德国人倾向非常正式的称呼。即使同事们在一起工作了很长一段时期，他们彼此之间仍然中规中矩地称呼“先生”。如果客户有一个以上的专业头衔，务必介绍所有的称呼。

迪拜，阿拉伯联合酋长国

商务着装非常保守，穆斯林传统规定，男士和女士的大多数身体部位都不可外露。男士最好穿夹克和打领带，女士应该穿低调的女装，高领口，长度直达脚踝底缘。

等待主人与你打招呼。虽然有些男士会和女士握手，但大多数男士不会。做手势和握手时，请不要使用左手，因为这样做不卫

business meeting, and the handshake may be accompanied by a slight nod or bow. Make sure to reciprocate① and look directly into your counterpart's eyes, as failure to do so could get you off on the wrong foot.

Germans tend to be very formal with titles. Even when colleagues have worked together for a lengthy period, they still greet one another with the formal "Herr." If a client should have more than one professional title, make sure to include all of them in introductions.

Dubai, United Arab Emirates

Business dress is very conservative, and Muslim tradition dictates that most body parts on men and women should be covered. A jacket and tie is best for men; women should dress modestly, with high necklines and ankle-length hemlines.

Wait for your host to initiate contact in a greeting. Although some men will shake hands with women, most will not. When gesturing and shaking hands, do not use your left hand as it is considered unclean and used only for hygienic② matters.

Gift-giving, although unnecessary, is often appreciated. Some gifts, however, should be avoided: pigskin products, alcohol or anything containing alcohol and gifts depicting or holding images of dogs.

In meetings, the one who asks the most questions tends to be the least important member of the group. The person in charge often is silently observing.

(1,266 words)

---

① reciprocate [riˈsiprəkeit] *vi.* 回应;互换

② hygienic [haiˈdʒiːnik] *adj.* 卫生的

生，只有上厕所时才用左手。

虽然不需要送礼，但礼品往往受到赞赏。然而，一定要规避猪皮产品、酒类或任何含酒精的商品，以及描绘和带有狗头像的礼物。

在会上，提问最多的人往往是这群人中最不重要的成员。负责人通常在默默地观察。

知识链接

Muslim 穆斯林。信奉伊斯兰教的人统称为“穆斯林”，意为“顺从者”。伊斯兰教是与佛教、基督教并列的世界三大宗教之一，7 世纪初产生于阿拉伯半岛。

题 记

潜在的商务失礼不仅会使商务人员的良好个人形象毁于一旦，也折射出所在企业的企业文化水平和企业的管理境界。本文列举的五种失礼行为就超出了从事商业活动的商务人员在商业交际中必须遵循的礼仪规范：电子邮件没有标点符号且充满拼写错误；邀请客户共进晚餐时信用卡被拒；销售代表在鼻子上镶嵌金箍；在没有受到邀请的情况下带着家人出差；商务会议结束时恰逢大雨倾盆，是否与客户共伞难免会让人进退两难。即使你拥有工商管理硕士文凭和翩翩风度，不注重细节也难以成为最新的客户代表并赢得他们的尊重。由此可见，良好的商务礼节能营造良好的商务交往氛围，为企业的合作奠定良好的基础。相反，潜在的商务失礼可能给企业造成不良的影响和带来巨大的损失。

Potential Faux Pas of Business Etiquette

Read on to see five more potential faux pas of business etiquette and what you can do to avoid them.

An MBA and charming manners aren't enough to win your newest rep the respect of clients. His e-mails are barren of punctuation and rife① with misspellings.

Every day sales executive Linda receives at least one e-mail that is entirely lower case, a product of IM② and chat room culture. "There's a sense you can leave things lower case and skip punctuation," he says. "I see no reason for that. It's just as important as a letter in terms of presenting a professional face to a client. People who are sloppy in their e-mail may be sloppy in other places too." Not only can poor punctuation and grammar mar③ a rep's professionalism, it can also offend the recipient. "It's a sign of disrespect to the person with whom you're

① rife [raif] *adj.* 充满的；充斥的

② IM：即时通信(instant message)

③ mar [mɑː] *vt.* 损毁；玷污

潜在的商务失礼

仔细阅读商务礼仪中五种潜在的失礼行为，然后思考如何避免失礼。

工商管理硕士文凭和翩翩风度并不足以使你成为最新的客户代表并赢得他们的尊重，因为你的电子邮件没有标点符号且充满拼写错误。

销售主管琳达每天至少收到一封全部是小写字母的电子邮件，这无疑是即时通信和聊天室文化带来的产品。他说：“有人认为可以使用小写字母并跳过标点符号，我认为这是没有道理的。电子邮件呈现给客户的是一副专业面孔，它和普通信件一样重要。电子邮件写得杂乱无章的人，处理其他事务同样也会很草率。”拙劣的标点符号和语法不仅玷污了销售人员的专业精神，而且也得罪了收件人。巴尔的摩一家广告公司的广告媒体执行副总裁奇克·戴维斯声称：“这是对与你通信的人不尊重的标志。”

销售代表应该使用合适的标点和语法，因为他们的信息可能被转发给其他人。礼仪专家彼得森认为，“人们没有意识到的是，电子邮件常常会被复制或打印，然后给其他人看。如果你没有加标点，或者有错误拼写，别人会觉得你没有文化”。商务电子邮件常常必需附上称谓和完整的签名，而且标题行的长度不应该超过 7 个

communicating," says Chic Davis, executive vice president of Advertising Media Plus, an advertising agency in Baltimore.

Reps also should use proper punctuation and grammar in case their messages are forwarded to other people. "What people don't realize is that e-mail often gets copied or printed—other people see it," etiquette expert Petersen says. "When you don't punctuate and when you misspell, you look illiterate." Business e-mails must always have a salutation and full signature, and subject lines should be no longer than seven words.

Your credit card gets rejected while picking up a client's dinner.

Craig Poms, vice president for a financial products provider based in Brentwood, Tennesee, ran into this very situation with one of his reps. "He (the rep) had reserved a premium car for a week, and through a glitch on the car rental company's end, they had somehow charged it two or three times," recalls Poms. "Of course he couldn't take care of it all at the restaurant. He was taking to dinner one of our best clients, who he had been with for years and had a great relationship with. The client just laughed and picked up half of the bill. But imagine if it had been a prospect!"

If this happens with a client or prospect who would not be so forgiving, excuse yourself from the table and speak with the maitred or the manager in private. You can give them your driver's license and your address so they know you're not going to run out on them. Or you can call home and get your partner's credit card number. Or a lot of restaurants now have house accounts, where you can be billed after the fact. The best

单词。

邀请客户共进晚餐时,信用卡被拒。

总部位于田纳西州布伦特伍德的一家金融产品提供商的副总裁克雷格·波姆斯说，他的一名销售人员恰好遇到了这种情况。波姆斯回忆说："那个销售人员将一辆高档汽车预留了一个星期，由于汽车租赁公司终端的一个小故障，不知为什么收了两到三次车费。当然，就餐时他完全不可能处理此事。他当时正在与我们最好的客户之一共进晚餐，这位客户与他交往多年，有着良好的业务关系。这位客户听说此事之后只是付之一笑，付了一半的费用。但是请想象一下，那可是我们潜在的大客户啊。"

如果恰巧你碰到的客户或潜在的客户并不是那么宽容，就找个借口离席，私下与服务台主管或经理交换意见。你可以把驾照押给他们，并留下你的地址，让他们明白，你不会就这么不负责任地离开。或者你可以给家里打电话，拿到配偶的信用卡号。现在很多餐厅都有账号，你可以记账，并在这件事之后付款。当然，避免这种尴尬局面的最好方法就是事先安排好要支付的账单。礼仪专家托尼认为："事先付账会让你看起来很高效、很能干和很强势。"

你的销售代表在鼻子上嵌了一个金箍,你认为这可能会得罪部分客户。你告诉他取下来吗?

礼仪专家彼特森认为，文身和穿孔等问题已经成为热门话题，特别是在强调传统和优雅外表的公司中，因为这对处理客户的关系至关重要。一家猎头公司近期向彼特森寻求帮助，他们的一位接待员在被雇佣三个月后开始穿戴眉环。这位接待员是个优秀的员工，但是穿环这一举动让客户不知所措，他们想知道，这家传统的公司

way to prevent embarrassment, however, is to arrange for payment ahead of time. "Having the bill taken care of ahead of time makes you appear very efficient, very capable, and powerful," etiquette expert Toney says.

Your rep has a gold hoop dangling from his nose that you think might offend some of his clients. Do you tell him to take it out?

Especially in a company where a conservative and refined appearance is vital to client relationships, the issue of tattoos and piercings can be a hot-button① topic, says etiquette expert Petersen. An executive-search company recently contacted Petersen for help with its receptionist, who had started wearing an eyebrow ring about three months after the company hired her. The receptionist was a star employee, but her piercing was causing clients to wonder if the conservative company was shifting its focus and priorities. Although the company was able to solve the problem by gently suggesting that the woman remove the ring, the real solution to the problem of distracting accessories is to put your policy in writing.

To salespeople with tattoos or piercings, Petersen advises consideration for employers. "Find out if it is appropriate with the company, and consider the clients of that company."

Your husband, a die-hard ski bum②, wants to accompany you on your business trip to Colorado.

Bringing family members on business trips is acceptable at most

---

① hot-button 热门话题

② bum [bʌm] *n.* 迷;无赖

是否正在调整业务重点和优先顺序。虽然公司能够通过提出温和的建议解决问题，让接待员摘下眉环，但根本的解决方案还是要以书面形式列出公司的政策方针，去掉分散注意力的配饰。

彼特森建议，要考虑那些文身或穿孔的销售人员的感受。"首先要看这种行为是否符合公司的文化，然后再考虑那家公司的客户。"

你的丈夫是一个铁杆滑雪迷，他想陪你到科罗拉多州出差。

虽然很多公司允许带家人一起出差，但是一定要提前获准。弄清楚晚上和休闲时间需要做哪些工作。并且事先与上司谈谈你如何支付机票的费用。如果晚上的活动安排是出差公务的一部分，那么除非家人受到邀请，否则最好不要带他们一道前往。如果有些活动不包括儿童在内，一定要确保你能够安排和照顾孩子们的行程。

你的销售代表正准备离开商务会议。时逢大雨倾盆。他只有一把雨伞，但他的两个客户都没有带雨伞。共伞还是不共伞就成了一个问题。

位于北卡罗来纳州格林斯博罗一家商务礼仪公司的主管觊茜·约翰逊认为，要依赖常识来解决这个难题。她说："如果你们有一辆汽车，那么把伞给那个开车的人。然后他可以拿到车，并开车回来接你们。"如果当时没有车，把伞给最年长的客户。约翰逊警告说，最好不要简单地因为她是女性就把伞给她，因为这样会被理解为想让她欠你的人情。

知识链接

An executive-search company 猎头公司。"猎头"是一种十分流行的人才招

companies, but make sure you approve it beforehand. "Find out what is required for evenings and leisure time. Be real up front with your manager about how you're covering the cost of airfare. If there are evening events scheduled as part of your trip, don't bring any family members along unless they're invited. And make sure you'll be able to make child care arrangements if children aren't included in some of the events.

Your rep is leaving a business meeting. It's pouring. He has an umbrella, but his two clients do not. To share or not to share, that is the question.

To solve this conundrum, Cathy Johnson, director of CorProtocol, a business etiquette firm in Greensboro, North Carolina, recommends relying on common sense. "If you're getting in a car, give the umbrella to the person who's going to drive," she says. "Then they can get the car and drive back to pick you up." If the situation does not involve a car, give the brolly to the client with the most seniority. Avoid giving it to someone simply because she is female, Johnson warns, because that could be construed as condescending.

(866 words)

聘方式，意指“网罗高级人才”。猎头公司的猎物对象是高级管理人才。一般来说，主要是举荐总裁、副总裁、总经理、副总经理、人事总监、人事经理、财务经理、市场总监、市场经理、营销经理、产品经理、技术总监、技术经理、厂长、生产部经理、高级项目经理、高级工程师、博士后、博士、工商管理高级人才、其他高级顾问及其他经理级以上的人才。

题　记

职场升迁难免让商务人士牵肠挂肚，怀才不遇者比比皆是。实际上，谋求升职的礼仪与处理任何其他的事情完全一样，犹如摆弄餐桌上的盐。你可以运用“摆餐桌”的原理谋求升迁——把握时机，谋篇布局：老板正谈得兴起时，不要谋求餐桌上的盐，因为他的双手忙得不可开交，嘴巴正在狼吞虎咽；按晚宴单的要求去做，趁还有盐的时候取盐，不要等盐瓶空了或者食物凉了再讨盐，届时已经为时太晚。你可以运用“游戏”的技巧谋求升迁——当机立断，破釜沉舟：如果就餐时发现盐似乎被藏起来了，想方设法追讨，沉着冷静应对，直到你在任何情况下都可以保持心跳正常并想象成功。在典型的工作场所，“盐”会深藏不露，你可能不知道其他人摄取了多少，也无法知道还有多少剩余。因此，在达到梦寐以求的升职目标之后，为了生意的缘故，不要对外声张，因为你不会希望在任何伤口上撒盐。

Don't Rub Salt in Any Wounds

In some offices, your relationship with the boss is so good all you have to do is say, "Hey, I need a raise," and you'll get one. But in most cases, where the workplace isn't that informal, etiquette can guide you through a successful negotiation

The etiquette of asking for a raise is exactly like the etiquette of asking for anything else—say, salt at the dinner table. The only difference is that in typical offices, the "salt" is hidden, not to mention hoarded, so you may have no idea how much everyone else is getting or how much is available.

Indeed, since "salary" is a word that derives from the salt allowance given as payment to Roman soldiers, the analogy is even more apropos[1].

Set the Table

First of all, money is a measure of value, and since value is fluid, timing is everything.

You wouldn't ask for the salt at the dinner table when your boss is in the middle of a conversation, his hands are occupied and his mouth is full—so keep the same in mind for a work context. Approach your boss to open negotiations at a time and in a setting that places your boss at ease,

---

① apropos [ˌæprəˈpəu] *adj.* 恰当的

不要在伤口上撒盐

在有些部门，你和老板的关系很铁，只需要说一句："嗨，我该升职了"，然后就会得到提拔。但在大多数情况下，工作场所并非那么随意，只有凭借礼仪的指导才能谋求成功升迁。

实际上，谋求升职的礼仪与处理任何其他的事情完全一样，犹如摆弄餐桌上的盐。唯一不同的是，在典型的工作场所，"盐"深藏不露，更不必说储藏，因此你可能不知道其他人摄取了多少，也无法知道还有多少剩余。

事实上，由于"工资"一词源自给罗马士兵支付的盐津贴，所以这个类比更显得贴切。

摆餐桌

首先，金钱是衡量价值的一种尺度，由于价值千变万化，所以时机就是一切。

老板正谈得兴起时，不要谋求餐桌上的盐，因为他的双手忙得不可开交，嘴巴正在狼吞虎咽。所以在工作环境中，大脑里也应该保持相同的画面。找一个让老板感到惬意的时间和环境，最好是在他为新签订的合同感到兴奋，并且对你为得到这份合同所做的出色工作表示感谢之时，和他开诚布公地协商。

在更广泛的公司背景下，把握时机也很重要。此外，像晚宴单的要求一样，你必须趁还有盐的时候去取盐，不要等盐瓶空了或者

preferably when he is flush with a new contract and already thanking you for a job well done in getting it.

Timing is also important in a broader company context. Again, like a dinner-table request, you must ask for salt while it's still available—not after it's too late, when the shaker is empty or your food is cold. Ask while the moment is right—not right after the company releases bad earnings numbers.

Whenever the opportune moment is set up and you're actually asking for a raise, break it down. If you were at dinner, you'd never demand "Salt! Now!" of your dining companion. You'd ask nicely. So proceed with negotiations as you would all business dealings: use a softened start-up, evidence and an open question—or perhaps even better, an open statement.

The soft start-up approach follows the same formula as a constructive complaint. When you begin the process with a compliment, your audience will be much more receptive. As you pass into framing evidence of the problem, the onus transfers to your boss to imagine himself in the same situation. Then, when you conclude with an open question, your boss can be free to brainstorm solutions.

It works because the conversation is structured so that you're working together on a solution, instead of turning yourself into one more burdens your boss has to shoulder alone.

For example, if you were at a dinner where the salt appeared to be hoarded, you might say, "This soup is intriguing, but something's missing. As one who brought in 15% more salt this year than last, I think my broth① needs a sprinkle."

---

① broth [brɔθ] *n*. 肉汤

食物凉了再讨盐，届时已经为时太晚。在正确的时候谋求升职，当公司发布糟糕的业绩数字之后谋求升迁是不恰当的。

只要时机成熟，而且你确实渴望升职，那就破釜沉舟。假设你是在吃饭，你绝不会对就餐同伴要求“盐！现在就要！”你一定会举止得体。所以，像做所有的商业交易一样，继续你的谈判：用一种温和的语气来开始彼此的谈话，然后拿出证据，再直接说明问题，也许直奔主题会更好。

作为建设性的倾诉，软启动的方法遵循同样的规则。当你用恭维话开始诉求时，听众会更容易接受。当你开始组织问题证据时，责任就转到老板身上，他会设身处地考虑这个问题。然后，当你在结束谈话时提出悬而未决的问题之后，老板会轻松地提出解决方案。

谈话安排得当就会产生效果，你可以和老板共同制定解决方案，而不是让自己成为老板不得不独自承受的额外负担。

例如，如果你在就餐时发现盐似乎被藏起来了，你可能会说：“这汤挺诱人的，但还缺了点什么。我今年摄入的盐量比去年多了15%，我觉得我的肉汤还需要撒点盐。”

开始游戏

一旦谈判开始，要有耐心。

大多数工资谈判达不到雇员期望的目标，主要是他们出于恐惧而过早地结束了谈判。

因此，要源源不断地出示证据，包括你创造效益的具体例子、开发的新项目的图表或清单等都是优质素材，但最重要的是，与老板和睦相处。这个目标不只是保持礼貌，而是要热情，不仅是因为它会使你的老板放松警惕。

Let the Games Begin

Once negotiations begin, be patient.

Most salary negotiations fall short of the employee's goals because they end too soon—mostly out of fear.

So keep your evidence coming, any specific examples of your productivity, including charts or lists of new projects you've initiated, are excellent fodder, but above all, remain friendly. The goal is not to remain merely polite, but warm—and not just because it keeps your boss off guard.

If you allow your boss's posturing to upset your warm regard for him or the company, it can hinder the relationship. On the other hand, if you maintain your best, most charming characteristics, the Old Salt will go the extra mile to keep you happy. It's a game, so play along. The boss is just doing his job, keeping costs down. If he didn't do that, his own salary would be on the line.

The ultimate preparation is to calm yourself. Practice and role-play with nonwork friends, not colleagues, until you can get through any number of scenarios without raising your heart rate. Visualize success. Assume the attitude that your boss wants to help, but realize that he's got to have exactly the right ammunition to make achieving your goal OK with his bosses.

As you negotiate, keep coming back to the mantra of etiquette: Your boss is perfect in every way, so practice being flattering and funny. The last thing you want is to win the negotiation but sour the relationship. Alternately, if it's just not working out this time around, save your ammunition for the next.

And when you do get the raise you were aiming for, for business' sake, keep it to yourself. You don't want to rub salt in any wounds.

(771 words)

如果你让老板言不由衷的姿态扰乱了你对他或公司的热情，就会妨碍你们之间的关系。另一方面，如果你保持最佳状态，最有魅力的特点，经验丰富的老板就会付出额外的努力，让你觉得开心。这是一场游戏，所以需要与人合作。老板只做他分内的事，即保持成本降低。如果他不这样做，他自己的工资就会朝不保夕。

终极准备工作是使自己沉着冷静。与非工作关系的朋友们做游戏和角色扮演，不要与同事在一起练习，直到你在任何情况下都可以保持心跳正常。想象一下成功。假设老板持愿意帮助的态度，但要意识到，他必须恰好拥有正确的论据，才能与他的老板们共同促成你的目标。

谈判时，坚持回到礼仪准则：老板在各方面十全十美，所以要练习奉承和逗笑的能力。最糟糕的事莫过于赢得了谈判，却输掉了交情。如果这次没有达到目标，继续努力，为下次升职储备力量。

当你达到梦寐以求的升职目标时，为了生意的缘故，不要对外声张。你不会希望在任何伤口上撒盐。

知识链接

Value Investing 价值投资。价值投资是投资者通过比较股票内在价值与现实价格的差异，选择被市场低估价值的股票进行投资而达到稳定收益的一种股票投资方法。价值投资理论由哥伦比亚大学的本杰明·格雷厄姆创立，经过伯克希尔·哈撒威公司的执行总裁沃伦·巴菲特的使用发扬光大，备受人们的推崇。价值投资有三大基本概念，也是价值投资的基石，即正确的态度、安全边际和内在价值。

题记

商务人士出差在外期盼的“家外之家”是五星级酒店，这些繁华奢侈的住所让他们在疲惫不堪的旅途中舒适地栖身。他们在工作场所享受的“家外之家”是办公室里温馨的卫生间和浴室，这些体贴的设置让他们在任何特定的时间内在此刷牙、用牙线洁牙、给头发吹风、做直发造型、有时候甚至修面。工作场所的“家外之家”为公司员工准备了单间浴室，给那些想避开交通拥挤时间、在破晓时分出门的白领们提供了到办公室完成早上洗漱的便利条件，使他们在接待客户时身上不至于散发出难闻的气味。工作场所的“家外之家”为公司员工准备了在办公室刷牙清洁口腔的空间，他们养成的这种习惯既可以避免餐后的余味在办公室弥漫，又可以去除牙缝中嵌有的食物残渣，从而保持体味和口味的清新。“家外之家”为商务人士打造出细意浓情的人性化管理和服务礼仪。

Home Away from Home

The workplace bathroom is no longer just for, well, going to the bathroom.

Like the gym bathroom, the office restroom has become a home-away-from- home bathroom. At any given time, someone is in there brushing their teeth, flossing, blow-drying, hair straightening and sometimes even shaving. Simply put, if you're looking for a quiet place to think, you might as well think again.

Longer workdays are partly to blame. For employees who work late and then have an evening function, they want to smell fresh and look clean. Others don't want to fight rush-hour traffic, so they leave home at the crack of dawn and complete their morning hygiene regimen at the office.

In Pictures: Home Away From Home?

Some companies now require their executives and other staffers who have significant client interaction to brush their teeth before a meeting. Jacqueline Whitmore, author of Business Class: Etiquette Essentials for Success at Work says one of her wealth management clients asked that she lead a seminar on proper personal hygiene for the workplace.

"My clients would rather see their employees brush teeth at work

家外之家

工作场所的浴室不再仅仅是为了去浴室而去浴室。

像健身房的浴室一样，办公室的更衣室已经成为家以外的另一个家用浴室。在任何特定的时间内，都会有人在里面刷牙、用牙线洁牙、给头发吹风、做直发造型，有时候甚至修面。简言之，如果你想找个安静的地方，不妨考虑利用一下办公室的更衣室。

越来越长的工作日是部分原因。 对那些工作到很晚然后还有夜间任务的员工们来说，他们希望自己散发出清新的气息，看上去干净整洁。 还有些人想避开交通拥挤时间，所以他们在破晓时分出门，到办公室完成早上的洗漱。

这是家外之家的画面吗?

有些公司现在要求经理主管们和其他职员在会见重要客户前要刷牙。《老板不说，但你要做到的事》一书的作者杰奎琳·惠特摩尔认为，她的一位财富管理客户要求她举办一次研讨会，讨论工作场所的合适的个人卫生。

指导棕榈滩礼仪学校礼仪研讨会的惠特摩尔说:“我的客户们宁愿看到他们的员工上班时刷牙，而不愿他们在接待客户时发出难闻的气味。”

这种心态并不只局限于企业界的高层。 康涅狄格州一所私立大

than breathe dragon breath on their clients," says Whitmore, who leads etiquette seminars through The Protocol School of Palm Beach.

This mentality is hardly restricted to the upper ranks of the corporate world. Melissa O'Brien, a career counselor at a private college in Connecticut, views it as a public service of sorts. She doesn't want to offend anyone with after-lunch breath. "It's out of mutual respect," says O'Brien, who has brushed on-the-go since she was in college.

This is what Cleveland-area dentist Matthew Messina calls "social brushing." "It's a 30- to 45-second wave of the toothbrush across visible parts of the teeth," he says. And while that's fine for eliminating food particles and odors, he's quick to remind that the American Dental Association recommends twice daily brushings and once a day flossing to remove plaque① and bacteria.

People who brush their teeth at work don't necessarily do so for the reason you might expect. Take Jacqueline F. Gray, assistant public information officer for the City Council of Birmingham, Ala. She brushes daily at work to prevent herself from eating the sweets and baked items that frequently make their way into the office.

Like with orange juice, "Once you brush your teeth, sweets don't taste as good for some reason," says Gray, a workplace tooth-brusher for about five years.

As anyone who works in a large office knows, the workplace restroom is sometimes less than desirable. Gray has learned to contend with that

① plaque [plæk] *n.* 牙菌斑

学的职业顾问梅丽莎·奥布莱恩认为，它属于某种类型的公共服务。她不想因为午餐后的呼吸冒犯任何人。奥布莱恩说："这是出于相互尊重。"上大学的时候她就在学校梳洗。

这就是克里夫兰地区的牙医马修·梅西纳所说的"社交洗漱"。他认为，"这是一个对牙齿可见部分30-45秒的洗漱"。尽管这种做法对清除食物颗粒和气味有效，但他还是随即提醒大家，美国牙医协会建议每天刷两次牙，每天做一次牙线，以去除牙菌斑和细菌。

你并不一定能够推测人们在工作场所刷牙的原因。以阿拉巴马州伯明翰市议会的助理新闻官杰奎琳·F.格雷为例。她经常吃糖和烧烤，为了避免这种气味在办公室弥漫，她每天在工作时刷牙。

格雷指出，比如喝橘子汁，"刷牙过后，甜味就会因为某种原因不那么明显"。她在工作场所刷牙已有5年左右。

任何一个在大办公室工作的人都知道，工作场所的卫生间有时候并不那么称心如意。格雷已经学会了对付这种情况。她声称："如果卫生间臭气熏天，就会使我厌恶至极，我将会去另外的楼层找卫生间。我在午餐后花点时间刷牙。有时候我会从一层楼找到另一层楼。"

与其说感到恶心不已促使她刷牙，还不如说另有原因。格雷参加过很多会议，不止一次看到过男男女女的会议出席者的牙缝中嵌有食物残渣。她绝不想成为那种人，而薄荷糖并不总能去除牙缝中的生菜。

她认为，"薄荷糖似乎增加了更多的脏物，还不如清洁口腔。漱口水又过于苦涩。你站在老板的旁边，身上散发着欲盖弥彰的气味，只有用薄荷香型的牙膏才能完美地掩饰这一切"。

issue. "It grosses me out if the smell is bad in the bathroom, and I'll search out a restroom on a different floor," she says. "I put the time in after lunch to brush my teeth. Sometimes I have to go from floor to floor."

Speaking of being grossed out, there's another reason she brushes. Gray has attended more than one meeting in which the presenter has food particles stuck in his or her teeth. She never wants to be that person, and a mint doesn't always kill the piece of lettuce wedged between your teeth.

"It seems like mints are adding more stuff than cleaning," she says. "And mouthwash is too harsh. You stand next to your boss and you smell like you're trying to hide something. Toothpaste is minty perfect."

Penelope Trunk, author of Brazen Careerist, takes the opposite perspective.

"It's preposterous," says Trunk. "You don't have bad breath just from existing during the day. Have a mint after lunch, and brush your teeth at night." She goes on to say that being that attentive to hygiene may be a sign of a larger problem than bad breath. "It's a sign of perfectionism and that's one of the biggest causes of depression at work," Trunk says. "It's like you're chasing a carrot you can never reach. You can't always be perfect at work, but you do the best you can. It seems innocuous, but it's obsessive."

That may be true, but what if someone points it out? Chuck Schotta is a licensed specialist in school psychology in Bridgeport, Texas, and has had more than one child tell him he has coffee breath. "I handle those remarks with humor," says Schotta, who now brushes at work daily. "I say, 'I know, and can you smell the onions?' Since I started brushing my teeth

《厚脸皮的野心家》的作者佩尼洛普·图朗克持相反的观点。

图朗克声称，“这真是荒谬。你白天待在那儿不会有口臭。午餐后吃颗薄荷糖，晚上再刷牙”。她接着说，注意卫生可能释放一种信号，是个比口臭更严重的问题。图朗克认为：“这是一种完美主义的征兆，而完美主义是工作中导致抑郁情绪的最大原因之一。这就像你在追求一个你可能永远得不到的胡萝卜。你在工作中不可能尽善尽美，但是你可以尽力做到最好。这看起来并无伤害，但还是会让人感到压力。”

这也许是真实的，但有人把口臭指出来后又会怎么样呢？查克·斯科塔是德克萨斯州布里奇波特的一位在校心理专家，不止一个孩子告诉过他，他有咖啡味口臭。斯科塔说：“我幽默地对待这些言论。我说，‘我知道，你能闻到洋葱味么？’因为我已经开始刷牙，这个问题已经不重要了。”他现在每天工作的时候都要刷牙。

除了保持口气清新，斯科塔也喜欢在其他方面把自己拾掇得体面可人。因为得克萨斯州的气候酷热，他中午一般会在男士更衣室梳洗一番，包括冲凉后再用修脸润肤露、洗头和洗脸。

幸运的是，大多数学校都为教职员工准备了单间浴室。尽管如此，“大多数男卫生间还是脏得令人恶心”。为了抵制这种恶劣的环境，他把纸巾放到柜子里，把牙刷放到柜子的顶部，没有放到无遮蔽的柜子中。

马修·吉尔斯认为，他工作场所洗手间的日常状况也是如此。他在澳大利亚布里斯班的一家合作银行工作，在夏天，当温度高达华氏 86 度时，他出门前往工作地点，途中他会大汗淋漓。吉尔斯走到火车站，下车后再走到工作地点。

it's a non-issue."

Aside from having fresh breath, Schotta likes to be presentable in other ways too. Since it's so hot in Texas, he generally stops in the men's room for a midday freshening up that includes applying a dash more aftershave, brushing his hair and washing his face.

Luckily, most schools have single bathrooms for the faculty. Still, "most men's rooms are notoriously① nasty." To combat that, he puts a paper towel onto the counter and then places his toothbrush on top of it instead of putting it on the bare counter.

Matthew Giles thinks of his workplace bathroom routine similarly. He works in a credit union in Brisbane, Australia, and in the summer when it's 86 degrees, by the time he leaves for work, he gets quite sweaty en route. Giles walks to the train station and then from the station to work.

He found a space in the office to store lockers and he keeps all his "freshening-up" equipment there. That includes a week's worth of freshly pressed work attire② . Giles goes to work in casual clothes and shaves, bathes and changes when he gets there.

Trunk may not approve, but Giles says his co-workers prefer him smelling clean.

(932 words)

---

① notoriously [nəu'tɔːriəsli] *adv*. 众所周知地；声名狼藉地

② attire [ə'tair] *n*. 服装

他在办公室找了一个空间，存放他的储物柜，然后把所有“使人焕然一新”的洗漱用具放在那里。柜子里装着足够一周穿的气味清新的工作装。吉尔斯身穿休闲服去上班，到达工作地点后再刮胡子、洗澡和换装。

图朗克可能不赞成这种做法，但吉尔斯说，他的同事们更喜欢他身上那种干净的气味。

知识链接

Brushing method of business people 商务人士刷牙方法。最新研究表明，商务人士的科学刷牙时间应为 2 分钟、用力1. 5牛。刷牙时最好采用温水(水温35℃左右的水)。正确的刷牙方法是顺着牙齿生长的方向刷，先将牙刷平放在口腔里，刷毛轻压牙龈的边缘，然后轻轻转动手腕将刷毛逐渐转向牙面，上牙从上往下刷，下牙从下往上刷，反复刷动。每刷一个地方，需要往返 5~10 次，这样既能清洁牙齿表面和牙缝，又能使牙龈得到适当的按摩。

题 记

不同的国家有不同的习惯和风俗，同一种行为在不同的国家表示不同的意思。商务出差经常要与陌生人打交道，不愉快的偶然事件往往直接导致从商的成败得失。完美的商务旅行需要熟悉世界各国的社会规范和礼仪准则：美国风格的OK手势在巴西象征淫亵和粗俗；墨西哥人出席商务会议习惯迟到，而日本人却会提前到达；澳大利亚人在商务会议上直截了当地陈述观点，泰国合伙人则采取迂回的方式阐述意见；在新加坡用双手奉上名片，在非洲用右手递交名片，而在日本双手或单手递交名片均无伤大雅。即使是握手、眼神交流和送礼这种简单的事，也充当着改善商务关系的手段。所以，旅行礼仪既可以增强人际关系，也可以破坏人际关系。正如任何一位商人所知道的那样，人际关系为社交网络提供燃料，而社交网络引领着纷至沓来的业务。

Traveling around the World on Business Errand

Before you step into another country, it is imperative that you become familiar with their social norms.

Mr. X, in Japan on his first trip abroad, has just disembarked at Tokyo. Receiving him at the airport is Mr. Y. Mr. X and Mr. Y meet. Mr. X extends his hand for the customary handshake. Simultaneously Mr. Y bows, as is the wont in that country. Taking the cue, Mr. X bows. Unfortunately, Mr. Y extends his hand at the same time. Mr. X, bent, looks up and sees Mr. Y's hand. He stands erect and extends his hand. Unfortunately, Mr. Y bows at that precise moment…

In fact, you might have already seen this scene in a number of movies. Cultural differences and mannerisms like these have been grist to the mill[1] for comedians since time immemorial. Unfortunately, once in a while, reality comes home to bite.

Kunal Guha, an engineering student in the US, still remembers the pin drop silence which followed, when, once on a trip to Brazil, in the midst of a get-together with some local acquaintances he signaled OK in

---

① be grist to one's mill 对某人有好处

商务周游世界

在去另一个国家之前，当务之急是要熟悉该国的社交规范。

X 先生第一次出国去日本，刚在东京下飞机。 Y 先生在机场迎接他。 X 先生和 Y 先生见面。 X 先生习惯性地伸出手去跟 Y 先生握手。 此时，Y 先生按照本国习惯正在给 X 先生鞠躬。 看到这种情况，X 先生也开始鞠躬。 不幸的是，Y 先生此时伸出了手。 X 先生弯下腰，往上一看，看到了 Y 先生的手。 他立即站直，伸出手。 不幸的是，就在这个时候，Y 先生却又在鞠躬……

事实上，你或许已经在很多电影中看到过这种情景。 自古以来，像这样的文化差异和特殊习惯一直是喜剧演员青睐的表演素材。 不幸的是，现实生活中偶尔也会出现这样的剧情。

库纳尔 · 古哈仍然记得那针掉下来都能听到的沉寂。 事情发生时，他是一名在美国攻读工程学的学生。 在一次前往巴西的旅行中，他与当地的一些熟人开联欢会，中途兴起时，他用标准的美国风格做了一个 OK 的手势，即用大拇指和食指围成一个圆圈。 他说：“在巴西，你不可能犯比这更大的错误了。 当地人认为我用的这种手势极其淫亵和粗俗。”

the standard US style-a circle of first finger and thumb. He says, "You can't make a bigger blunder① in Brazil. The gesture which I used is considered completely obscene and vulgar."

A misdemeanor like this might be overlooked between friends but, on a business trip, when you are dealing with strangers, such happenstances might have unpleasant repercussions; it could spoil a relationship.

Therefore, if going abroad, it would be wise to brush up on the rules guiding the social behavior of the country you are visiting. In other words get your travel etiquette right.

"If you are planning a trip, getting your travel etiquette right not only helps save you the embarrassment but also helps you maintain your poise in a situation where you would have otherwise reacted angrily," says Sanjay Anand, a software programmer, who is at present in Singapore on a project. He goes on to add, "For example, in some countries like Mexico, if a meeting is scheduled for a particular time, it is only a rough estimate of the period when you will meet. If the time fixed is 2 pm, don't be surprised if nobody turns up till 4 pm. But it is pointless to take umbrage at② anyone because that is the way things work out there. Contrary to this, in a country like Japan, if the meeting is fixed for 2 pm, then be sure to be there 15 minutes early otherwise you will offend your hosts."

Ann Marie Sabath, in her book, International Business Etiquette: Asia and the Pacific Rim, writes that the most important reason for becoming knowledgeable in every country's "silent language" of etiquette is to

---

① blunder [ˈblʌndə] *n.* 愚蠢的错误

② take umbrage at 埋怨

朋友之间可能不会计较此类不雅行为，但是，商务出差时你是在与陌生人打交道，这种偶然事件可能会引起不愉快的反响。它可能会破坏你们之间的关系。

因此，如果你要出国，明智的做法是温习你即将出访国家的规则，并运用它们来引导你的社交行为。换句话说，掌握正确的旅行礼仪。

桑吉·阿南德认为，“如果你正在计划旅行，掌握正确的旅行礼仪不仅可以帮助你避免尴尬，还可以帮助你万一要生气时保持淡定”。桑吉·阿南德是一名软件程序员，他目前在新加坡做项目。他继续补充道：“例如，像墨西哥等一些国家，如果会议定于某一特定时间，这只是你们开会的粗略估算时间。如果时间定在下午2点，直到4点才有人出现你也不必感到奇怪。埋怨任何人都毫无意义，因为这是当地习惯的方式。与此相反，在一个像日本这样的国家，如果会议时间定在下午2点，就要确保提前15分钟到达，否则就会得罪东道主。”

安·玛丽·萨芭丝在她的书《国际商务礼仪：亚洲和环太平洋地区》中写到：熟悉每个国家礼仪中“无声语言”的最重要的原因就是为了在海外建立良好的业务关系，其中的一个主要因素就是注意你在会议上的行为举止。

举例来说，在澳大利亚，明智的做法是直截了当地在商务会议上陈述观点。人们只接受你的话的字面意思，他们希望澳大利亚人所说的话也按字面意思来理解，不要附加任何内容。即使是闲聊，

develop good business relationships overseas and a major factor in this is to mind your meeting manners.

In Australia, for instance, it is advisable to be direct during a business meeting. Your words are taken at face value and it is expected that what the Australians say is also taken literally without any added dimensions attached to it. Though there is small talk, it is minimal.

Conversely, the Thais are considered to be informal but asking if there are any questions or opinions from your Thai associates should be done in an indirect manner. Blunt questioning is considered inappropriate, which is somewhat like in Japan where phrases like " We will think about it", " We will see", " Perhaps"-which you might take for a " Yes"-might indeed mean " No".

Travel etiquette starts from the first handshake and exchange of cards to holding the chopsticks at the farewell dinner. Says Anand, " In Singapore, visiting cards are usually presented with both hands. The name should face the recipient." In Japan you must face your counterpart, bow slightly and hand over the card with either hand or both hands together. Just don't shove it into the back pocket of your trousers after receiving it-that's offending. In Africa, on the other hand, you hand over the card with the right hand.

Even handshakes change from place to place. Frederica Care Kussin in her book AllEtiquette.com-A Power Guide writes " in Africa a light warm handshake is the acceptable form of greeting when you meet and when you leave", but in Europe " shake hands with a firm grip when you meet and when you depart". And whilst in North America, a proper handshake is " a full hand grip that is firm and warm with an understated downward

也要尽可能直接。

相反，人们认为泰国人非常随意，询问泰国合伙人是否有任何问题或意见时，则应该采取迂回的方式。直率的提问被认为是不恰当的。这有点像日本的短语“我们会考虑这个问题”，“到时候再说”，“也许”等，这些话有可能让你以为是肯定的回答“是”，也有可能让你认为是否定的回答“不是”。

旅行礼仪始于初次握手，接下来是交换名片，再到欢送晚宴上持筷子的方式。阿南德说：“在新加坡，通常要用双手奉上名片。名字应该面对接收者。”在日本，你必须面向对方，微微鞠躬，单手（哪只手都可以）或双手一起递交名片。收到名片后，不要把它放到裤子后面的口袋里，这样做会令对方不愉快。另一方面，在非洲，你要用右手递交名片。

即使是握手也会随地点的不同而改变。弗雷德里卡·卡尔·库辛在她的书《礼仪全攻略——权威指南》中写道，“在非洲，初次见面或离别时，稍微热情的握手是可接受的问候方式”，但是在欧洲，“见面或离别时要紧握对方的手”。然而在北美，适当的握手方式是“紧紧地、热情地完全握住对方的手，然后轻轻地放下分开。”

因此，在谈判过程中，除了对地区特征做好必要的准备工作之外没有别的选择。你必须小心谨慎，不要冒犯对方，但也不能显得过于顺从。眼神交流是一个很好的例子。在美国和加拿大，与人交谈时，眼神交流是一件好事。它建立了信任，增强了亲和力，避免眼神交流表示你隐藏了什么东西。但是在非洲，你必须避免强烈的眼神交

snap."

So, during negotiations, there is no alternative to some good homework on regional traits-one must be careful about not offending but you cannot also appear too submissive. Eye contact is a good example. In the United States and Canada, eye contact is a good thing when speaking to someone. It builds trust and affinity and avoiding eye contact implies that you have something to hide. However in Africa, it is strong eye contact which must be avoided. Another factor which must be kept in mind during negotiations, is the pace of the meeting. Hurrying things up will go against you if you are meeting the Indonesians. Go armed with patience and diligence because Indonesian businesspeople are slow and deliberate when it comes to making decisions. If you attempt to rush them through the negotiation process, you risk being regarded unfavorably. Haste makes waste in such cases.

If you do not get your etiquette right, then even your good intentions might backfire. Take something as simple as a gift, which is a means to improve relations. The global rule is of course that it is completely unethical, if not illegal, to pass off a bribe as a gift. But what if your intentions are strictly honorable, and it still gives the wrong impression.

Mayuresh Kelkar, joint managing director, remembers an incident. " I once gave a gift wrapped in white paper to a Chinese acquaintance. Though he accepted it, I instantly sensed that something was wrong. Later, I made enquiries and found that a faux pas had been made. The color white stands for death in China and gifts are never wrapped in white paper there," he says.

It is fairly common knowledge that pork and alcohol are anathema

流。谈判中必须谨记的另一个要素是会议的节奏。如果你与印尼人会晤，急匆匆地将事情做完会得不偿失。一定要耐心和勤奋，因为印尼商人做决定时喜欢缓慢而慎重。如果你试图在谈判进程中催促他们，就有可能被认为不合时宜。在这种情况下，欲速则不达。

如果你没有正确地使用礼仪，那么即使你满怀好意也可能会适得其反。比如送礼这种简单的事，它是一种改善关系的手段。当然，国际惯例认为，把贿赂当做礼物是完全缺乏职业道德的行为。但是，假使你的意图确实非常正当，那又怎么样呢，它仍然会给出错误的印象。

联合总经理马苏瑞卡·科尔卡记起了一件事。他说："我曾经给一个中国熟人一份用白纸包装的礼物。尽管他收下了礼物，我立刻意识到有点不对劲。后来，我咨询了一下，才知道我犯错了。白色在中国代表死亡，在那里从不用白色包裹礼物。"

猪肉和酒精在信仰穆斯林的国家是禁忌，这是公认的常识，但是我们有多少人知道，在拉丁美洲，任何带有刀或剪刀的礼物，不仅不会加强你们之间的联系，反而会产生完全相反的后果。这两件物品都意味着友谊的破裂。

所以，旅行礼仪既可以增强人际关系，也可以破坏人际关系。正如任何一位商人所知道的那样，人际关系为社交网络提供燃料，而社交网络又可以带来业务。

但是，最后要说的是：不要冲昏头脑，把事情混为一谈。也许你已经改正了规则，并给你的中国东道主留下了不错的印象，即当

among Muslim and in Muslim countries but how many of us know that in Latin countries, any gift items having knives or scissors, will instead of firming up your association, have exactly the opposite effect. Both articles signify the breaking of a friendship.

Travel etiquette is therefore something which can make or mar your relationships. Relationships fuel the network and the network is what brings in the business, as any businessman knows.

But, as a final word, don't be carried away and mix things up. You might have got your rule book correct and suitably impressed your Chinese hosts, when once the waiter or business associate has refilled your tea cup, you sign your appreciation by taking two fingers of your left hand and tapping it lightly thrice on the table close to the tea cup. But try to do the same thing in front of a Vietnamese audience, and you will be signaling a "Master-Servant" relationship. Definitely not something recommended, if you want them to sign that deal.

(1,222 words)

服务员或生意合伙人重新斟满你的茶杯时，你用左手的两根手指在桌子上离茶杯不远的地方轻轻敲三下，以此表示你的感谢。但是，如果在越南人面前做同样的事情，大家会认为你们之间是“主仆”关系。如果你想让他们签署协议，这种方法绝对不值得推荐。

知识链接

Social norms 社交规范。社交规范指人们社会行为的规矩，社会活动的准则。它是人类为了社会共同生活的需要，在社会互动过程中衍生出来，相习成风，约定俗成，或者由人们共同制定并明确施行的。它的本质是对社会关系的反映，也是社会关系的具体化。

题记

越来越多的公司日益关注商务人士平时积累的涵养和礼仪修养，重视企业对客户的人性化服务和关爱。纽约长岛周围的公司对公司礼仪和国际礼仪的热情正在持续发酵，大多数企业从事礼仪咨询顾问的专业人士迅速增加，他们提供培训计划，帮助学生和管理人员专心致志地研究商业礼仪的策略。美国大通曼哈顿银行举办了商业礼仪和跨文化意识研讨会，集中讨论了介绍和维护职业形象的恰当礼仪；美国旗舰银行将商业礼仪并入了销售培训计划，指导新员工磨炼沟通技能，以便他们与顾客和谐相处；哈帕克工业协会对长岛大约800家公司的会员提供教育项目和服务，加强海外营业公司跨文化复杂知识的培训；派克电子系统公司一直密切地关注礼仪的国际化趋势，为员工开设了文化礼仪研讨班。商务礼仪日趋上升的地位驱使礼仪培训服务成为全球炙手可热的行业。

Honing Employees' Etiquette

Louis Paolillo had done it. Hoping to land the business of a large insurance company, Mr. Paolillo, then 24, had wrangled a meeting with a managing partner of the insurer. They were to have lunch in the company's executive dining room

The meeting went fine at first, but then Mr. Paolillo, an underwriter, ordered a stuffed artichoke①.

As Mr. Paolillo pulled the artichoke leaves through his teeth and repeatedly wiped oil and bread crumbs from his fingers with his napkin, he saw the managing partner glowering at him.

"I was so focused on the appetizer and how messy it was that I couldn't concentrate on the discussion," recalled Mr. Paolillo of Rockville Centre, now 34, and a senior underwriter with the same firm. The lunch ended and so did any chance of Mr. Paolillo landing the company's business.

The etiquette lesson: Don't order finger-food at a business lunch.

Companies around the Island, realizing that their executives may need similar lessons, are turning to experts to teach employees corporate

① artichoke[ˈɑːtitʃəuk] *n.* 朝鲜蓟(形似百合果的绿果)

提高员工的礼仪修养

路易斯·保利洛做过这样一件事。为了获得一家大保险公司的订单，时年 24 岁的保利洛先生与保险公司的任事股东会面时发生了纠葛。他们当时在公司的高管餐厅共进午餐。

会面起初进展顺利，然而，当保险商保利洛先生点了一份满满的洋蓟之后，情况发生了变化。

当保利洛先生把洋蓟叶子塞进嘴里，并再三地用餐巾擦拭手上的油和面包屑时，他发现任事股东对他怒目而视。

任职于洛克维尔中心、现今 34 岁的保利洛回忆说："当时我的注意力都放在开胃菜上了，没能专注于商谈，真是太糟糕了。"保利洛现在是这家公司的资深保险人。那次午餐结束的时候，保利洛也错失了获得那家公司订单的机会。

这就是一门礼仪课程：不要在商务会谈的餐桌上点需要用手指抓食的菜肴。

纽约长岛周围的公司意识到，他们的高管可能需要类似的课程。这些公司正在求助于专家，希望他们来公司给员工们教授礼仪技能。许多有海外业务的公司也在雇用顾问，给员工辅导国际礼仪。纽约长岛的有些大学甚至提供培训计划，帮助学生和管理人员专心致志地研究商业礼仪的策略。

etiquette skills. Many companies that do business overseas are also hiring consultants to coach employees on international protocol. And even a few Long Island colleges are offering training programs to help students and executives bone up on the strategies of corporate etiquette.

"It is all about outclassing the competition," said Dorothea Johnson, director and founder of the Protocol School of Washington in McLean, Va.

Experts say the surge in interest in corporate and international etiquette among Long Island businesses is growing and mirrors a national trend. The number of businesses around the Island consulting etiquette professionals has risen about 25 percent during the last two years, said Dominique Isbecque, president of the Association of Image Consultants International in Manhattan, a trade group.

Chase Manhattan Bank, for example, runs business etiquette and multicultural awareness seminars for its employees, including those on Long Island. Topics for new hires focus on proper decorum in introductions and maintaining a professional appearance. Senior executives are taught to fine-tune restaurant manners and mixing and mingling.

"At a cocktail reception food is not the objective, rather networking and the opportunity to develop business," said Lauren Solomon, vice president for professional and expert programs at the bank. "Honing communication skills means listening more effectively to the customer, not just to make a sale but to develop the relationship."

The bank also instructs its employees on high-tech etiquette-the rules that govern E-mail, voice mail, pager, phone and fax manners. Guidelines include setting pagers on vibrate① and leaving only concise messages on

---

① vibrate [ˈvaibreit] *n.* 振动

弗吉尼亚州麦克利恩市华盛顿礼仪学校的创始人兼董事长多萝西娅·约翰逊认为，“这都是为了在竞争中胜出”。

专家们认为，长岛的公司对公司礼仪和国际礼仪的热情正在持续发酵，这种浪潮反映了一种全国性的趋势。曼哈顿贸易集团的国际形象顾问协会主席多美尼克·伊莎贝克指出，在过去的两年里，长岛周围大多数企业从事礼仪咨询顾问的专业人士增加了25%。

比如，美国大通曼哈顿银行举办了商业礼仪和跨文化意识研讨会，参与者包括长岛地区在内的雇员。面向新雇员的讲座集中讨论了介绍和维护职业形象的恰当礼仪。他们还指导高管们调整餐厅礼仪，并让他们参加各种活动。

大通曼哈顿银行的职业与专家项目副总裁劳伦·所罗门声称：“我们在鸡尾酒会上的目标不是餐饮，而是建立社交关系和寻找拓展业务的机会。培养沟通技能意味着更有效地听取客户的建议，不仅要促进销售，还要建立关系。”

这家银行还指导员工掌握高科技礼仪，即管理电子邮件、语音信箱、寻呼机、电话和传真礼仪的规则，包括将呼机调成振动和只在语音信箱中留下简短信息的指南。

美国旗舰银行将商业礼仪并入了销售培训计划。销售管理部副总裁凯瑟琳·多尔蒂表示，之前的企业文化只包括“微笑送给顾客，保持眼神交流”等组成部分。她认为，现在的计划更具有实质性的内涵，可以指导新员工磨炼沟通技能，以便他们与顾客和谐相处。

专家们表示，尽管这些技能在海外做生意时也非常重要，但了

voice mail.

Fleet Bank incorporated business etiquette into their sales training program. Previously, the corporate culture component consisted of "smiling to customers and maintaining eye contact," said Kathleen Doherty, vice president of the sales management group. Now the program is more substantive, she said, and instructs new hires to sharpen communication skills so they can build rapport with customers.

While those skills are also important when doing business overseas, understanding the nuances of foreign culture is much more crucial, especially with Long Island companies doing so much business abroad, experts say The International Trade Association of the United States Department of Commerce reported that exports totaled about $ 3.7 billion from Nassau and Suffolk Counties, up 31 percent from last year.

The Hauppauge Industrial Association, which provides educational programs and services to its nearly 800 company members on Long Island, held an international protocol seminar. William A. Laraque, vice president and regional trade officer for Marine Midland Bank and a member of the association, said a number of the association's companies that conduct business abroad sensed they needed "increased multicultural sophistication" for their businesses to grow.

Failing to learn the rules of etiquette before conducting business abroad "almost guarantees failure," said Ms. Johnson. She said the success rate among American business ventures overseas was less than 30 percent.

A Long Island company paying close attention to international etiquette is Parker Electronic Systems of Smithtown, a division of the Cleveland, Ohio-based Parker Hannifin Corporation. This summer the company, which manufactures and distributes aerospace electronics

解外国文化的细微差别更加至关重要，特别是对长岛涉及大量海外业务的公司来说。美国商务部国际贸易协会的报告显示，自去年起，纽约拿骚和沙福克郡的出口总额上涨了31%。

哈帕克工业协会对长岛大约800家公司的会员提供教育项目和服务，并举办了一次国际礼仪研讨会。海丰银行副总裁和地区贸易官威廉·A. 拉腊克是该协会的一名会员，他指出，该协会很多在海外经营业务的公司感到，为了业务的增长，他们需要“加强跨文化的复杂知识”。

约翰逊女士认为，如果在海外做生意之前没有学习礼仪规则，就“几乎意味着生意失败”。她指出，美国的海外公司的业务成功率还不到30%。

长岛史密斯镇的派克电子系统公司一直在密切关注国际礼仪，这家公司是总部设在俄亥俄州的美国派克汉尼汾公司在克利夫兰的分部。今年夏天，作为世界航空电子产品的生产商和销售商，公司为长岛350名雇员中的部分人开设了第一届文化礼仪研讨会。人力资源部主管阿斯特丽德·西博思表示，为期4天的研讨会涉及几个国家的公司文化，讨论了面对面交流、远程交流以及管理风格的做法和禁忌。

培训部经理基利·柯林斯声称，长岛万豪酒店和会议中心开办了一个项目，从服务员到高级管理人员等各种层次的员工都参加了培训，教授文化多样性问题和重新了解外国的风俗习惯。

长岛的一些大学和商业学校正在大量开设商务礼仪和国际礼仪的课程。道林学院是位于奥克达尔镇道林大学的分部，提供继续教

worldwide, offered its first cultural protocol seminar to some of its 350 Long Island employees. The four-day seminar covered the corporate culture of several countries and discussed the do's and taboos of face-to-face communication, long-distance communication and management styles, said Astrid Sipos, director of human resources.

The Long Island Marriott Hotel and Conference Center runs a program that instructs employees, from bellhops to senior executives, in cultural diversity issues and reviews foreign customs and practices, said Keely Collins, training manager.

Courses on business etiquette and international protocol are also proliferating at some of Long Island's colleges and business schools. The Dowling Institute, a continuing education and corporate training division of Dowling College in Oakdale, began a course in business, dining and social etiquette, said Elana Stern, assistant provost and executive director.

"At business lunches and dinners I have seen American businessmen unfamiliar with the rules of etiquette," Ms. Stern said. "They would ask me which fork should they use or which way should they pass the bread."

The Katharine Gibbs School recently opened a corporate training center geared to tweak employees' business skills and includes courses in computer training, office and high-tech etiquette. School officials said employees from companies including Pepsi-Cola of Long Island, Fala Direct Marketing in Melville and Recognition Systems, a Port Washington manufacturer of photographic supplies, have registered for the program.

Molloy College in Rockville Centre is helping students navigate the right's and wrong's of international etiquette through a federally①

---

① federally [ˈfedərəli] *adv*. 联邦地；同盟地

育和企业培训，其助理教务长兼执行理事艾蕾娜·斯特恩说，学院开设了一门关于商务、用餐和社会礼仪的课程。

斯特恩女士说："在商务午餐和晚餐上，我碰到一些不熟悉礼仪规则的美国商人。他们会问我应该用哪个叉子，或是应该用什么方式分发面包。"

凯瑟琳-吉布斯学院近期开设了一个企业培训中心，主要用来调整员工的业务技能，包括计算机培训、办公室和高科技礼仪方面的课程。学院的官员表示，包括长岛百事可乐公司、梅尔维尔法拉直销公司以及华盛顿摄影器材港口供应商"识别系统"在内的员工，已经注册参与该项目的培训。

洛克维尔中心的莫洛伊学院借助联邦资助项目，鼓励学生参与模拟公司的运营，培训他们驾驭国际礼仪正误行为的能力。为了帮助学生洞悉海外经商的规则，他们还启动了国际交换生项目。

奔赴海外经商之前，学生们需要参加外国风俗和习惯讲习班。研修主题包括馈赠礼物的误区和解释国际手势语。企业管理部门的助理教授朱迪·奥尔森举例说，**OK** 的手势在日本代表钱，在德国则有淫秽之意。

长岛大学波斯特分校的职业体验和规划项目主管珍妮特·葛尼尔说，在学院举办的年度餐饮礼仪研讨会上，学生们边吃烤鸡胸和山羊奶酪沙拉，边学习餐桌礼仪。

她认为，"大学生和刚走出校门的毕业生都是双收入家庭的产物，他们是吃着快餐和微波食品长大的一代。他们还不习惯定期出席正式的宴会"。

financed program that has the students running simulated companies. An international exchange program also helps students gain insight into doing business overseas.

Before traveling abroad, students enroll in workshops on foreign customs and practices. Topics include gift-giving gaffes and interpreting international gestures. For example, the O.K. gesture in Japan means money, and in Germany it is an obscenity, said Judy Olsen, assistant professor in the business management department.

At C.W.Post/Long Island University's annual dining etiquette seminar, students learn table manners while eating stuffed breast of capon and goat cheese salad, said Jeanette Grill, director of professional experience and placement at the college.

"College students and new graduates are products of two-income families who have been reared on fast food and microwave meals," she said. "They are not accustomed to formal dinners on a regular basis."

Experts said that business people not steeped① in manners could be held back in the workplace.

"New graduates are finally realizing they will not make it in business unless they have etiquette skills," Ms. Johnson of the Protocol School said.

(1,093 words)

---

① steeped [ˈstiːpt] *adj*. 充满的，浸泡的

专家们表示，没有受过礼仪熏陶的商人会在工作中遇到麻烦。

礼仪学校的约翰逊女士指出："刚毕业的大学生们最终会意识到，只有熟谙礼仪技巧才可能取得成功。"

知识链接

Chase Manhattan Bank 美国大通曼哈顿银行，是美国大型的商业银行，1955 年由大通银行和曼哈顿银行公司合并而成，总部位于纽约。2000 年美国大通曼哈顿银行和摩根银行合并。两家银行合并后，大通曼哈顿银行主要经营信用卡、发放购买房屋和汽车贷款等业务，摩根银行主要从事股票承销业务。

Marriott Hotel 万豪国际酒店是全球首屈一指的国际酒店管理公司，在美国和其他 69 个国家及地区拥有2 800多个业务单位。万豪国际集团的总部设于美国首都华盛顿，员工人数约128 000名。

题　记

求职礼仪是征服面试主考官的利器，它帮助求职者将自身良好的气质和渊博的学识等静态因素转变成动态的竞争力。求职在很多情况下将与面试官进行最直接的“短兵相接”，所以，一举一动、一言一行，都让面试官尽收眼底：关闭手机，对面试者表示尊重；不要随便动老板的东西；展现良好的风度；检查交往信件中的错误；懂得如何倾听；穿着得体；不要在面试中言行轻浮；就餐时注意礼貌；了解你应聘的是什么工作；做好面试前的准备工作；不要对面试官撒谎；注意细节等。所以，怀揣求职礼仪的锦囊妙计才能让应聘者步步为营，成功获得梦寐以求的职位。

Not-Too-Subtle Advice on Etiquette for Job Hunting

Did you hear the one about the accountant who squashed① a bug in a job interview? Or the woman who wrote a letter to a prospective boss that began, "Dear Blah Blah?" Or the aspiring lawyer who went to interviews in tennis whites?

No, they are not jokes. They happened. And they hold a lesson for job seekers in these difficult economic times: it really does matter how you behave in those friendly chats with would-be employers. They will notice your indiscretions② and probably hold them against you.

Of course, some stories told by hiring managers about the gaffes③ they have witnessed are so outlandish④ that the garden-variety goofs committed by most people seem harmless by comparison. Even so, they are only extreme infractions of the basic rules of job hunting. Here is an unscientific list of dos and don'ts.

Turn Off the Cellphone

"We've had a lot of candidates blow interviews because of cellphone

---

① squash [skwɔʃ] *vt.* 压扁

② indiscretion [indis'kreʃən] *n.* 不谨慎的行为

③ gaffe [gæf] *n.* 失态;过失

④ outlandish [aut'lændiʃ] *adj.* 奇异的

求职礼仪的锦囊妙计

你听说过某个会计在求职面试时踩死虫子的故事吗？或者听说过某位女士给未来的老板写信以“亲爱的某某某”开头吗？又或者是某个踌躇满志的律师身着白色的网球服去参加面试吗？

实际上，它们不是笑话，它们真实地发生在我们身边。在经济陷入低迷时期，它们给找工作的人好好上了一课：如何与你未来的雇主在友好的氛围中谈话是相当重要的。他们会细心观察你的不雅行为，而这可能会让你最终丢掉工作的机会。

当然，招聘经理讲的这些故事都是他们在面试过程中的亲身经历，面试者的一些过失很令人奇怪，相比之下，大多数人犯下的普通错误看起来则显得微不足道。即使如此，它们也是找工作时对基本准则的极端违规行为。下面列出一些非学术性的准则，说明哪些是该做的，哪些是不应该做的。

关闭手机

安妮·马克斯菲尔德是曼哈顿一家人力资源公司项目清偿部的总裁，她指出：“因为手机的原因，应聘者搅乱面试现场的例子不胜枚举。”她想起了一件事情，有一个高级职位应聘者先在工作人员那里报到，坐下后就开始给他母亲打电话，“他大声聊天，谈论如何去牙医那里修补了牙龈”。当经理最后会见他时，这位应聘者说道：“等几分钟再说。”

usage," said Anne Maxfield, president of Project Solvers, a Manhattan staffing firm. She recalled a senior-level candidate who checked in with the receptionist, sat down, called his mother and began "a loud conversation about how he had just gone to the dentist to have his gums trimmed." When a manager finally greeted him, the applicant said, "I'll be with you in a few minutes."

Don't Play with the Boss's Stuff

Alan Towers, president of Towers Group, a Manhattan public relations firm, interviewed a woman who struck him as intelligent and poised. When he escorted her back to the reception area, he noticed the furniture had been rearranged.

"I thought maybe the cleaning lady or a secretary had done it. When she asked me how I liked it, I realized with a shock that it was her doing," he said. She was a take-charge individual, but there are limits. My last words to her were: "We'll call you."

Show Good Manners

Anthony P. Carnesi, owner of Profitability Consulting in Manhattan, was surprised by the disheveled appearance of a woman he was interviewing. Even so, her résumé was impressive, and he kept an open mind.

Until she plopped her canvas bag on its side on a table, that is, and a large water bug scurried out. "I was shocked, but she reached out and slammed her hand down right on top of the little critter①," Mr. Carnesi said. "I was impressed by her swiftness. She then wiped her hand on the napkin that her coffee cup was on, turned to me and continued answering my question as if nothing had happened." But something had: She had just blown her chance to get the job.

---

① critter [ˈkritə] *n.* 生物;家畜

不要随便动老板的东西

曼哈顿一家公共关系公司塔牌集团的总裁艾伦·陶尔斯曾经面试过一位女士，这个人给他留下了既聪明又稳重的印象。当他把那位女士送回接待区的时候，他注意到家具被重新摆放过了。

他说："我想这也许是清洁女工或秘书做的吧。但当她问我是否喜欢这样的摆设时，我忽然明白了这都是她做的。"她是个有领导才能的人，但是做任何事情都应该有尺度，所以最后我对她说："我们会给你电话的。"

展现良好的风度

曼哈顿一家咨询公司的老板安东尼·P. 卡纳西居然碰到一位衣着凌乱的女士前来参加面试，这真是出乎他的意料。即便如此，由于她的简历让人眼前一亮，所以卡纳西还是给了她面试的机会。

她刚把帆布包扑通一声放到桌子边上，一只蟑螂突然跳了出来。卡纳西说："我吓了一跳，但她却伸出手，直接拍到小虫子顶部。她的动作之敏捷真让我惊叹。随后她用咖啡杯旁的纸巾擦了擦手，然后转向我继续回答问题，仿佛什么都没有发生过一样。"但有些事情却不言自明：她已经丢掉了这份工作的机会。

检查信件中的错误

一位应聘《美食与美酒》杂志助理编辑的人给两位面试过她的编辑写了一封感谢信。但是她的粗心大意却置她于死地：在套用信函格式中，她忘记插入其中一位编辑的名字。

《美食与美酒》杂志的主编达纳·科文说："一封信里她写对了名字。另一封信却题为'亲爱的某某某'。收到'某某某'信函的女士真有一种被轻视的感觉。"

懂得如何倾听

纽约米尔伍德市一家索诺星投资公司主席大卫·莫尔回忆了一

Check Correspondence for Errors

A candidate for an editorial assistant's job at Food & Wine magazine wrote thank-you notes to both editors who had interviewed her. But her carelessness did her in; she forgot to insert the name of one of the editors in her form letter.

"On one letter she got the name right," said Dana Cowin, Food & Wine's editor in chief. "The other letter was written to Dear Blah Blah. The woman who got the Blah Blah was really insulted."

Know How to Listen

David Moore, chairman of Sonostar Ventures, a venture capital firm in Millwood, N. Y., recalls a prospective employee's 40-minute monologue about himself. "He hardly came up for air," Mr. Moore said. "At the end of the meeting I said, 'Do you have any questions for us?' He said, 'No, I think you've answered all of my questions.' But he hadn't asked any. This is not the kind of person you want around."

Dress Appropriately

When he was at the Harvard Business School, before the era of casual dress in the workplace, Mr. Moore and the five law students he lived with often compared notes about their job searches.

One morning, a housemate came downstairs in a tennis outfit and announced he was going to an interview. "He said, 'I go to all my interviews dressed like this. Hey, this is who I am; if they don't like me, they won't hire me,' " Mr. Moore said. "To the best of my knowledge, no one ever did."

Don't Flirt in Interviews

About a year ago, Mr. Moore was interviewing a woman dressed in a sexy black dress for an executive assistant's position and wondered why she started talking about all the times she had gone out to dinner with her former boss.

次面试经历，当时一位潜在的应聘者独自滔滔不绝地讲了40分钟。莫尔先生说："他几乎就没停过。在面试快结束时我说，'你有什么问题要问我们吗？'他说，'没有，我觉得你已经回答了我所有的提问'。但他根本就没有问任何问题。这种人当然不是你想要的。"

穿着得体

摩尔先生在哈佛商学院读书时，工作场所休闲服装的时代尚未到来，他和五个法学院的学生住在一起，他们经常就找工作时遇到的问题交换意见。

一天上午，一位室友穿着网球套装走下楼来，宣布他要去参加面试。摩尔先生表示："他说，'我参加所有面试都穿这身套装。嗨，这就是我。如果他们不喜欢，他们不雇用我就是了。'据我所知，还没有人那样做过。"

不要在面试中言行轻浮

大约一年前，摩尔先生在面试时遇到一位穿着黑色性感长裙的女士，她应聘的职位是行政助理，面试开始后，她就一直大谈和前老板外出去吃饭的事情，这让摩尔先生颇为意外。

他说："很明显，她不反对在另一份工作中复制和以前一样的氛围。但这显然不是我应该仿效的方式。"

就餐时注意礼貌

纽约欢乐谷《读者文摘》的副总顾问马克·史洛塔回忆道，他曾经和一个顶级律师事务所的几个合伙人一起外出吃饭，想应聘一个夏季实习生的职位。他先吃了点简单的食物，然后点了一盘裹着巧克力汁生奶油的巧克力松露甜点。他刚拿起勺子用力舀时，松露突然从盘中飞脱而出。

服务员清理餐桌、收拾残局时，史洛塔先生坐在原地一动不

"But then it became clear that she was not opposed to reproducing that situation in another job," he said. "It was clear this wasn't a path I should go down."

Watch What You Eat

Mark Sirota, an associate general counsel with Reader's Digest in Pleasantville, N.Y., was taken to lunch once by several partners of a white-shoe law firm seeking to fill a summer associate's position. He kept to simple fare-until he ordered chocolate truffles① in a bed of whipped cream covered with chocolate sauce for dessert. As he pressed down on the first truffle with a spoon, it flew off his plate.

Mr. Sirota sat motionless while the waiter pulled out the table to clean up the mess, then joked about the need to observe job candidates at lunch "to make sure we won't embarrass the firm in front of clients." The lawyers laughed politely. Mr. Sirota didn't land the job.

Know What the Job Is

Janet Lee, fitness director at Fitness Magazine in Manhattan, remembers trying to get a job as a summer intern② at the Federal Reserve Bank in Washington when she was studying accounting in college.

She was asked in an interview what she hoped to do. "Well, I really don't like working with numbers," she replied. She realized her goof immediately and tried to talk her way out of it, to no avail. "Since then, I've definitely polished my interviewing skills," she said.

Do Your Homework

Fred Neurohr, a researcher for the Nassau County Youth Board in Hempstead, N.Y., tells this story about a job interview he had at Publishers

---

① truffle [ˈtrʌfl] *n.* 松露

② intern [ˈintəːn] *n.* 实习医师

动，随后开玩笑地说，我们需要观察求职者在午餐时的表现，“以确保公司不至于在客户面前难堪”。律师们礼貌地大笑。史洛塔先生没能获得那份工作。

了解你应聘的是什么工作

曼哈顿一家《健身杂志》的健身主管珍妮特·李回想起她的一次经历，当时她在大学学习会计，准备在联邦储备银行找一份暑期实习生的工作。

在面试时，她被问到希望做什么事情。她回答说：“说实话，我很不愿意与数字打交道。”她随即意识到自己说错了，试图纠正过来，但为时已晚。她说：“从那以后，我绝对在不断地打磨我的面试技巧。”

做好准备工作

纽约州亨普斯特德市的“拿骚县青年委员会”研究员弗雷德·纽诺讲了一个求职面试的故事。他当时谋求一份出版商清算所的工作，是抽奖活动信封提供的机会。

为了打破面试官的沉默，他问道：“艾德·麦克马洪常来这儿吗？”没有回答。他仍然坚持问道：“你们见过他吗？”又是沉默，他继续说道：“我敢打赌，他肯定外出休假旅行去了。”直到这时，面试官才回答说：“他外出参加比赛服务工作去了。”

说来也奇怪，他得到了那份工作，继而成为出版商清算所的首席研究员。他后来发现，大多数美国人错误地将麦克马洪先生与出版商清算所联系在一起。

不要撒谎

要敢做敢当。《美食与美酒》杂志的科文女士仍然记得，有个人声称他有大学文凭，但实际上并不完全正确。

Clearinghouse① , the mailer of sweepstakes② offers. To break the ice with the interviewer, he asked, "Is Ed McMahon around a lot?" Getting no answer, he persisted. "Have you met him?" Meeting more silence, he tried again. "I bet he's a trip at the holiday party." Only then did his interviewer reply, "He works for the competition."

Oddly enough, he got the job, going on to become Publishers Clearinghouse's head researcher. He later discovered that most Americans mistakenly associate Mr. McMahon with Publishers Clearinghouse.

Don't Lie

And if you do, admit it. Ms. Cowin of Food & Wine magazine remembers a man who acknowledged his claim to have a college degree was not exactly right.

"And I said, 'You either have a degree or not.' Finally, he said he almost got the degree, falling one credit short." She hired him anyway because of his terrific work. "What made the difference is that he admitted it," she said.

Check Your Zipper

It may be the stuff of jokes, but it happens. Ask Linda Gilleran, a principal consultant for Hewlett-Packard in New York. She left an interview for an associate's position at Lazard Frères, the investment bank, some years ago thinking she had made a great impression.

Once outside, she said, "I looked down to find my fly wide open with just the fluttering silk of my underwear between me and the world." She didn't get the job.

(1,250 words)

---

① clearinghouse [ˈkliəriŋhaus] *n.* 票据交换所

② sweepstake [ˈswiːpsteik] *n.* 彩票

“我问道：‘你到底拿到学位没有？’最后，他说他差点就获得了学位，但因为差一个学分而前功尽弃。”但不管怎样，由于他工作表现极其出色，科文女士还是雇用了他。她说：“正是因为他承认了这件事，才使我做出了有别于他人的决定。”

检查你的拉链

这可能是讲笑话的猛料，但确实发生过这样的事。不信你去问纽约惠普公司的高级顾问琳达·吉勒冉恩。若干年前，她参加了拉扎德投资银行一场面试，应聘一个助理的职位，离开时她认为自己给面试官留下了深刻的印象。

面试出来的时候，她说道：“我向下看了看，发现衣服扣子敞开了，内衣的蕾丝边居然飘在光天化日之下。”当然，她没有得到那份工作。

知识链接

Lazard Frères 拉扎德投资银行。拉扎德是近几十年来最好的国际投资银行之一。它由亚历山大·拉扎德(Alexandre Lazard)、艾里·拉扎尔(Elie Lazare)和西蒙·拉扎德(Simon Lazard)兄弟三人于1848年共同创立，从开始在新奥尔良经营纺织品业务，逐渐转向银行及外汇业务，并在巴黎、伦敦和纽约设立分行。在整合之风日盛的美国金融界，拉扎德几乎是绝无仅有地保持独立、并未将业务线过分延展的金融机构。

题 记

英国女王曾经告诫查尔斯王子："着装帮人塑造外在形象，人们会根据这个形象判断内在的心理状态。人们可以欣赏你的外表，却难以窥视你的内心。"商业技能和经验很重要，但是个人外表和第一印象同样也很重要，人们的穿着方式向他人积极传递着事业心、人品、能力等信息。商务男士的职业着装是充分展示自我的一种方式，目的是让客户感觉舒适并对你有信心，它对时尚的追求从一季到下一季的变化并不明显。商务女士的职业着装需要符合女性的行业以及行业内的职位和头衔，展现女性优雅得体的商务公关能力。商务服装有别于周末装束和晚礼服。对商务衣橱的慷慨投资是对职业前途的一种投资。对那些认为不是着装、而是能力创造了成功的人来说，是重新思考这个问题的时候了。

Shape You Outward Sign

Do you ever wonder where all the dress rules have gone? Depending on when and where you are on any given business day, the words "distant past" might come to mind. It's difficult to decide if people don't know what to wear to work or if they have lost sight of the relevance of appearance to professional success.

The Queen of England is reported to have told Prince Charles, "Dress gives one the outward sign from which people can judge the inward state of mind. One they can see, the other they cannot." Clearly, she was saying what many people are reluctant to accept; that people judge us by the way we dress. In all situations, business and social, our outward appearance sends a message.

Try going to a busy restaurant at lunchtime. Look around you at what people are wearing and see if you don't make judgments about who they are, their line of business, their personalities and their competencies. Think about how you feel when you are dressed in your usual business attire as opposed to casual dress. Your choice of business apparel speaks to your professional behavior and credibility. It is important to understand how to dress for business if you wish to promote yourself and your organization in a positive manner.

How you dress depends on four factors: the industry in which you work, the job you have within that industry, the geographic area in which

塑造外在形象

你有没有想过，所有的服装规则已消失在何方？ 随便哪个工作日，根据时间和地点的不同，服装规则也许会以“遥远的过去”这样的字眼出现在你的脑海。 如果人们不知道穿什么去上班，或者对外表与职业成功的关系视而不见，那么确实很难判断什么是得体的着装。

据说，英国女王曾经告诫查尔斯王子：“着装帮人塑造外在形象，人们会根据这个形象判断内在的心理状态。 人们可以欣赏你的外表，却难以窥视你的内心。”显然，她说的话是很多人不愿意接受的：即人们根据我们穿着的方式判断我们的言行。 无论是商界还是社交领域，不管什么情况，我们的外表在向他人传递信息。

不妨在午餐时间走进一家繁忙的餐馆。 观察一下周围人的穿着，看你是否能从外表上判断他们是谁、他们从事什么行业以及他们的个性和能力。 想一想你穿着平常的职业装和休闲装时那种截然相反的感觉。 职业服装的选择表达了你的职业行为和信誉。 如果你希望以积极的姿态提升自我和自己的事业，了解如何着装至关重要。

you live; and most importantly, what your client expects to see.

Professional Dress for Men

In men's clothing, fashion does not change significantly from season to season but business attire is about being professional and not about being fashionable. It's about presenting yourself in a way that makes your clients feel comfortable and confident with you. Dressing for success is still the rule. The professional businessman should keep in mind these few points when deciding what to wear to work.

Choose a conservative suit in navy, black or gray either pinstripe① or solid. The quality of the material speaks as loudly as the color and can make the difference between sleaze② and suave③ .

A solid white or blue dress shirt with long sleeves offers the most polished look. The more pattern and color you add, the more the focus is on your clothing, rather than your professionalism.

Ties should be made of silk or a silk-like fabric. Avoid the cartoon characters and go for simple and subtle if you want to enhance your credibility.

Socks should be calf-length or above. Make sure they match not only what you are wearing, but also each other. A quick glance in good light before heading out the door can save embarrassment later in the day. Check for holes as well if you'll be going through airport security and removing your shoes.

Shoes should without question be conservative, clean and well

① pinstripe [ˈpinˌstraip] *n*. 细条纹
② sleaze [sliːz] *adj*. 廉价的
③ suave [swɑːv] *adj*. 文雅的

怎样着装取决于四个因素：你所从事的行业，你在行业中的职位，你生活的地理位置，最重要的是，你的客户期待看到什么。

男性的职业着装

在男性服装领域，时尚从一季到下一季的变化并不明显，但是商务着装是为了职业化而非时尚。它是展示自我的一种方式，让客户感觉舒适并对你有信心。为成功而着装才是硬道理。职业商务人士在决定穿什么上班时应该记住这几点。

选择保守的细条纹或紧致的海军蓝、黑色或者灰色套装。面料的质量与颜色一样重要，质薄廉价的面料与温和婉约的面料效果会大不相同。

紧致的白色或蓝色长袖衬衫给人最优雅的形象。你增加的款式和颜色越多，人们就会越关注你的着装，而不是你的职业能力。

选择丝质或丝质类面料的领带。如果你希望提升你的信誉度，切忌将自己打扮成卡通人物，追求简单和精细即可。

短袜需要齐及小腿或略长。袜子不仅要与身上穿的衣服搭配，而且还要搭配得当。出门前在明亮的光线下打量一下自己，可以避免当天晚些时候的尴尬。最好检查一下袜子上是否有破洞，以免通过机场安检脱鞋时出现尴尬的状况。

毫无疑问，鞋子要保守、干净和锃亮发光。选择系带的鞋，不要穿休闲鞋或拖鞋。不要有丝毫的闪失，以为别人不会注意你的鞋子。很多人还来不及关注你的脸就已经看到你的脚了。

polished. Lace-up shoes are the choice over slip-ons or flip flops. Don't think for a minute that people don't notice shoes. Many people will look at your feet before your face.

Belts need to match or closely coordinate with your shoes. Once again, quality counts.

Keep jewelry to a minimum. In a time when men sport gold necklaces, bracelets and earrings, the business professional should limit himself to a conservative watch, a wedding band and maybe his college ring.

The finishing touch for the business man is his choice of accessories: briefcase, portfolio and pen. When it comes to sealing the deal, a top of the line suit, a silk tie and a good pair of leather shoes can lose their affect when you pull out the ball point pen you picked up in the hotel meeting room the day before.

Professional Dress for Women

When women entered the workplace in the 1970's and 1980's in greater numbers than ever before and began to move into positions which had traditionally been held by men, many of them believed that they needed to imitate male business attire. The result was women showing up at the office in skirted suits or coordinated skirts and jackets with tailored blouses finished off with an accessory item that looked very much like a man's tie. Happily those days are gone. While the business woman may now wear trousers to work, she does it out of a desire to appear professional and at the same time enjoy the flexibility and comfort that pants offer over skirts. Her goal is no longer to mirror her male colleagues.

The same overall rules apply to women's work attire as apply to men's. Business clothing is not a reflection of the latest fashion trend. A

皮带需要和鞋子配套，或搭配得几乎天衣无缝。再次提醒，皮带的质量要上乘。

尽量少戴首饰。在这个男人也喜欢佩戴金项链、手镯和耳钉的时代，商务职业人士应该限制自己，只戴传统的手表，结婚戒指以及大学纪念指环等饰品。

最后，商务男士还需要注意公文包、文件夹和钢笔等配饰的选择。签署协议时，掏出前一天在酒店会议室随手拿的圆珠笔，高档西服、丝绸领带和搭配合适的皮鞋创造的美好形象瞬间烟消云散。

女性的职业着装

自20世纪70年代到80年代以来，女性进入职场的数量比以前大大增加，并且开始进入传统上属于男性的岗位，她们中的很多人认为，她们需要仿效男式商务装。结果，女士在办公室身着西装裙套装，或配套的裙子和夹克，里面是剪裁讲究的女士衬衫，领口配有装饰物，看上去非常像男人的领带。所幸这样的时光已经一去不复返了。虽然职业女性也许现在穿着长裤去上班，但她们希望在着装显得职业的同时，也能享受柔韧性和舒适，这就像相对于裙子，裤子更适用一样。她们不再一味模仿男人。

整体上来说，男性工作装的规则同样适用于女性。商务着装不是为了追赶最新的时代潮流。人们需要关注女性，包括她是谁，她有什么样的职业能力，而不是她身着什么样的服饰。她的商务着装需要符合她的行业以及行业内的职位和头衔。

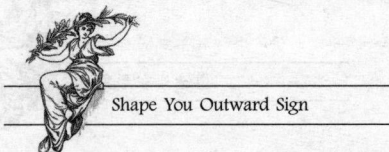

woman should be noticed for who she is and her professional skills rather than for what she wears. Her business wear should be appropriate for her industry and her position or title within the industry.

Start with a skirted suit or pants suit for the most conservative look. A skirted suit is the most professional. With a few exceptions, dresses do not offer the same credibility unless they are accompanied by matching jackets.

Skirts should be knee-length or slightly above or below. Avoid extremes. A skirt more than two inches above the knee raises eyebrows and questions.

Pants should break at the top of the foot or shoe. While Capri pants that come in assorted lengths from mid calf to ankle are the latest trend, they are out of place in the conservative business environment.

Blouses and sweaters provide color and variety to woman's clothing, but they should be appealing rather than revealing. Inappropriate necklines and waistlines can give the wrong impression.

Women need to wear hose in the business world. Neutral or flesh-tone stockings are the best choices. Never wear dark hose with light-colored clothing or shoes. Keep an extra pair of stockings in your desk drawer unless the hosiery store is next door or just down the street from the office.

Faces, not feet, should be the focal point in business so chose conservative shoes. A low heel is more professional than flats or high heels. In spite of current fashion and the sandal rage, open-toed or backless shoes are not office attire. Not only are sandals a safety hazard, they suggest a certain official agenda.

When it comes to accessories and jewelry, less is once again more. Keep it simple: one ring per hand, one earring per ear. Accessories should

首先，西服裙套装或西裤符合最传统的形象。西服裙套装是最典型的职业装。当然也有些例外，女装要想给人信赖感一般要配上合适的夹克衫。

裙子应该长及膝盖，或略在膝盖之上或之下。不要过长或过短。裙子如果比膝盖短两英寸以上，容易引人侧目和非议。

裤子的长度应该刚好盖住脚背或鞋子。虽然紧身裤的长度从小腿到脚踝不等，迎合了最新的潮流，但在传统的商业环境中却显得不合时宜。

色彩绚丽和款式多样的衬衣和毛衣使女性服装魅力纷呈，但她们的造型应该优雅迷人而不是袒胸露肩。如果领口和腰围不合适会让人产生错觉。

在商界，女性需要穿长筒袜。中性或肉色的长袜是最好的选择。决不可穿黑色的长筒袜搭配浅色的衣服或鞋子。如果办公室隔壁或附近的大街上没有出售袜类的商店，最好在办公桌的抽屉里准备一双备用的长袜。

在商务活动中，人们一般关注面部而不是脚部，最好选择保守一点的鞋子。低跟鞋比平底鞋或高跟鞋更职业。尽管当前的时尚趋势风行凉鞋，但露趾鞋和无后跟的鞋并不适合办公室着装。凉鞋不仅会带来安全隐患，也不符合正式场合的着装规范。

再一次强调，佩戴饰品和珠宝应该越少越好。保持简约的风范：每只手戴一枚戒指，每只耳朵戴一只耳环。饰物要能彰显你的

reflect your personality, not diminish your credibility.

Business attire is different from weekend and evening wear. Investing in a good business wardrobe is an investment in your professional future. For those who think it's not what you wear but who you are that creates success, give that some more thought. Business skills and experience count, but so does personal appearance and that all-important first impression.

(1,129 words)

个性，而不是毁坏你的形象。

商务服装有别于周末装束和晚礼服。对商务衣橱的慷慨投资是对职业前途的一种投资。对那些认为不是着装、而是能力创造了成功的人来说，是重新思考这个问题的时候了。商业技能和经验很重要，但是个人外表和第一印象同样也很重要。

知识链接

Competency Model 素质模型。素质模型是为完成某项工作，达成某一绩效目标所具备的一系列不同素质要素的组合，包括不同的动机表现、个性与品质要求、自我形象与社会角色特征以及知识与技能水平。这些行为和技能必须是可衡量、可观察、可指导的，并对员工的个人绩效以及企业的成功产生关键影响。

题 记

商务礼仪的钟摆不停地摆来摆去。在过去的20年间，职场的环境已经变得越来越随意，让人们释放出真实的性格。路易斯·梅南也不免一声叹息："一个英国女人教训美国人怎么用分号，倒有点像美国人教训法国人怎么做沙司酱汁一样。"人们再也无须恪守职场的陈规陋习，但仍然遵照老祖宗的叮嘱从事：穿什么服装就扮演什么角色。尽管近几十年成长起来的年轻人生活中往往缺乏礼仪教养，如餐桌礼仪、相互介绍的基本惯例，他们甚至对何时以及如何写感谢信都知之甚少，但那些简单的、自上而下的改变可以改善职场礼仪，并在商务交往的人群中营造一个相互尊重的氛围。良好的行为与不良的行为如出一辙，它们具有同样的感染力，让商务礼仪的钟摆在正确的轨道上运行。

The Pendulum Is Swinging Back

Think business etiquette and you're liable to focus on how your employees interact outside of your organization, from interactions with clients to networking with other professionals.

But sometimes your employees can check those good manners at the door when they return. Most of us have encountered bad or boorish behavior at one time or another in the workplace.

"People can get lazy at work," notes Amy Palec, owner of Mind Your Manners, a business protocol and etiquette consulting firm in Cedarburg.

Palec often consults for corporate clients on how to improve external polish, but interestingly enough, she is usually asked to also touch on office decorum.

"The pendulum① is swinging back," she says in terms of more formal expectations of employees. "It's like the old adage about corporate dress: You dress the part, you'll also act the part. During the past 20 years, many workplace environments have become more casual, and that casualness lets people's true colors come through."

A co-worker of mine used to use his lunch hour to regularly clip his

① pendulum [ˈpendʒələm] *n.* 钟摆

钟摆不停地摆来摆去

思考商务礼仪时，人们易于关注员工在公司之外如何互动，包括与客户的交往到与其他专业人士建立关系网等环节。

但有时你可以趁员工返回之际，检查这些良好的礼仪习惯。我们中的大多数人都曾经在职场碰到过恶劣或粗鲁的行为。

位于赛达堡的一个商务协议和礼仪咨询公司——“注意礼貌”公司的老板艾米·帕莱克表示，“人们可以在工作时偷懒”。

帕莱克经常为企业客户咨询，传授如何改善外部形象的秘笈，但有趣的是，人们还常常邀请她讲授办公礼仪。

她在谈及员工对正装的期待时说：“钟摆不停地摆来摆去。关于公司的着装，有一句老话是这样说的：穿什么服装就扮演什么角色。在过去的20年间，许多职场的环境已经变得越来越随意，让人们释放出真实的性格。”

我的一个同事习惯利用午餐的时间定期修剪指甲，修剪的声音传入各个隔间的角落，让棕色便当袋里的食物瞬间变得索然无味。

我还做过另一份工作，为夫妻档的小业主提供服务。妻子为了拉拢员工，会与他们分享婚姻和与丈夫亲密的细节。这不仅加大了为她工作的难度，而且集中精力处理好她丈夫对我说的任何事情也变得加倍困难。

nails, a sound that cuts through the din of any cube farm and makes any brown-bagged lunch instantly unappetizing.

At another job, I worked for husband-and-wife small business owners. In an attempt to connect with her employees, the wife would share intimate details about her marriage and her husband. Not only did it make it difficult to work for her, it made it twice as hard to concentrate on anything her husband said to me.

Unfortunately, some employees come to the workplace with an inherent disadvantage.

"It's more and more apparent with younger, greener employees," she says.

The lessons learned by those growing up in previous decades-think table manners, basic rules of introductions, even knowing when and how to write a thank-you note-are often absent from their lives. "These are behaviors that really do start at home."

Topics formerly thought to be verboten in polite conversation-from politics to sex-also now seem to be part of the conversational landscape, even at work.

They shouldn't be. Your workplace neighbor, boss or employee may not be quite as comfortable talking about these issues as you perceive them to be.

"Personal is personal," stresses Palec.

She notes that the natural, human inclination is to give an immediate response to a question or statement, regardless of whether it is suitable for discussion.

"There are many ways to very politely step out of conversations like these instead of responding," she says.

In my case, I tried to busy myself with a task whenever my female

不幸的是，有些员工就职时即存在固有的劣势。

她表示，“很显然，越来越多的年轻人缺乏礼仪教养，特别是新手”。

近几十年成长起来的年轻人在生活中往往缺乏礼仪教养，如餐桌礼仪、相互介绍的基本惯例，他们甚至对何时以及如何写感谢信都知之甚少。“这是一些本应该从小就在家中养成的习惯。”

以前被认为在礼貌会谈中不允许出现的话题，例如政治和性，现在也似乎成为了会话景观，甚至在职场也不例外。

这种现象本不应该出现。职场的同事、老板或员工并不像你感觉的那样，他们在谈论这些问题时会感到不太自在。

帕莱克强调说：“个人有个人的观点。”

她指出，人有种天生的本能，会对某个问题或声明直接做出反应，甚至不顾这个观点是否适合讨论。

她表示：“可以运用多种方法礼貌地避免这种交谈，根本无需做出任何回应。”

在我看来，只要我的女老板直言相谏，我就会竭尽全力拼命工作。如果这还不奏效，我会在脑子里反复唱“星条旗”这首国歌。虽然我的沉默回应常常会让她拖延一到两分钟再来一次歇斯底里的发泄，但也并不总能平息事态。

无论是对员工还是客户而言，恪守不良的公司内部礼仪只会产生意想不到的严重影响。

帕莱克认为，“如果不礼貌的行为将客户拒之门外，你也许永远不会知道。在公司内部，同样的事情发生在老板或经理身上也不足为奇。如果人员流动量太大，老板却不知道为什么会如此，就有可

boss had her candid moments. When that didn't work, I'd sing through the "Star Spangled Banner" in my head. It didn't always work, though my mute responses usually made her move on after a minute or two of full disclosure①.

Bad internal workplace decorum can have just as critical of an impact on employees as it has on clients.

"If bad manners put off a client, you'll never know," she says. "Internally, that same thing can happen with a boss or manager, too. If there's a tremendous amount of turnover and the boss has no idea why, it can be issues like lack of respect for employees, inappropriate workplace actions or low standards for behavior."

"It's a delicate issue to talk about," she says. "People are fearful that they will burn a bridge by bringing it up."

The good news is that simple, top-down change can improve workplace decorum and increase a shared sense of respect among members of your environment.

"A lot of CEOs and managers don't take charge of or enforce workplace etiquette," she says. "They have no idea how much power they have, and how their interactions with employees really do set the pace."

Lasting change often takes time to happen. But a good place to start is with yourself. Treat others as you'd like to be treated, or better.

Like bad behavior, good behavior can be infectious②.

(662 words)

---

① disclosure [disˈkləuʒə] *n.* 泄露

② infectious [inˈfekʃəs] *adj.* 传染的

能是缺乏对员工的尊重、不恰当的职场表现抑或低水准的行为等问题”。

她声称：“这个问题谈起来很微妙。人们担心，提出这个问题会影响双方的关系。”

好消息是，那些简单的、自上而下的改变可以改善职场礼仪，并在你周围的人群中营造一个相互尊重的氛围。

帕莱克指出：“许多首席执行官和经理们并没有负责或执行职场礼仪。他们根本不知道他们拥有多少权力，以及他们与员工的互动如何真正起到带头作用。”

持久的变化常常需要时间做支撑，但是，良好的开端应该从自己做起。善待别人正如你期待被别人善待一样，或者做得更好。

良好的行为与不良的行为如出一辙，他们具有同样的感染力。

知识链接

Professional Trainer in business etiquette 礼仪培训师。按通用的社会礼节、礼规标准，完善和矫正学员的社会形象和行为规范，经考试获得国家形象设计协会《注册礼仪培训师证书》的专业人士，统称为礼仪培训师。礼仪培训师要具备以下素质：一是形象要好，气质要佳；二是要讲职业道德；三是内容要专业；四是知识面要宽；五是要有亲和力，要有风度；六是自我简介应该实事求是。

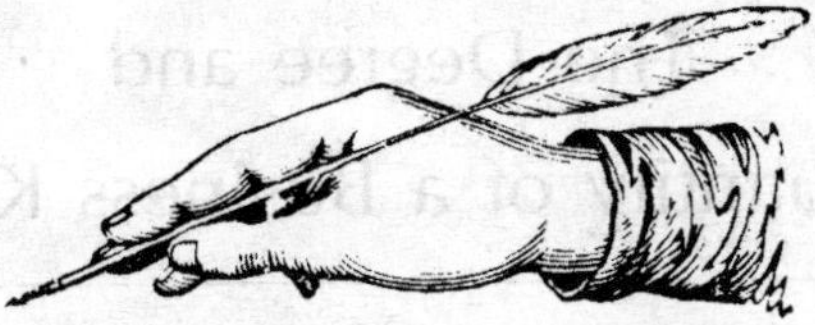

题　记

经典电影《相见恨晚》里有一个场景，男女主人公在威灵顿车站分别时，曾深情拥吻。无数人为此流下眼泪，更有不少疯狂的影迷专门跑去坐火车，在站台上接吻，体验这份浪漫。在方兴未艾的全球化浪潮的冲击下，商务接吻大有异曲同工之妙。接吻的冲动代表了一种文化现象，司空见惯的飞吻或感情色彩浓厚的商业接吻使传媒业的影响力在当代社会持续上升。工作场所的接吻使人们更容易感受到同事之间真诚的热情，晚宴之后的接吻能表达彼此间的相互尊重，晚会上跳舞时女士率先主动接吻可以减少男士的尴尬，与不同国家和不同地区的人做生意时礼貌接吻让全球文化产生了新的交集。当加尔各答的呼叫中心忙于处理英国信用卡的咨询电话之时，当巴黎的大街小巷飘逸着清淡美味的美国咖啡之际，商务接吻礼仪也大张旗鼓地传遍了全球的每一个角落。

The Degree and Quantity of a Business Kiss

Call centre operatives in Calcutta is dealing with British credit card queries. Weak American coffee is being served in Paris. All in all, globalization has a great deal to answer for. But perhaps the most troublesome side effect of the fading significance of international borders has been mass confusion over the role of the kiss in business.

There used to be a time, within Anglo-Saxon companies at least, when a handshake was the only physical contact between colleagues of the opposite sex. Come to think of it, there was a time, in parts of the United Kingdom, when a handshake was the only physical contact between spouses. But nowadays a work social is just as likely to begin or conclude with a kiss on the cheek, a kiss on both cheeks, a handshake and a kiss on the cheek, two kisses on each cheek, or an air kiss accompanied with a "mwah". Recently, to the visible horror of the recipient, who looked like she was passing a painful kidney stone, I even witnessed someone end a business lunch by kissing the hand of a female client.

Indeed, the only certainty is that there is no certainty. If what I have observed recently is anything to go by, at the crucial moment people

商务接吻的度与量

加尔各答的呼叫中心，操作员正忙于处理有关英国信用卡的咨询电话。巴黎的大街小巷，清淡的美国咖啡美味飘香。总而言之，全球化引起的巨大变化对此责无旁贷。但是，随着国际边界意义的逐渐淡化，这种现象最棘手的副作用或许是接吻在商界的作用，它让人们感到困惑不解。

曾经有一段时间，至少在盎格鲁-撒克逊人的公司中，握手是异性同事之间唯一的身体接触。回想一下，曾经有一段时间，在英国的部分地区，握手是夫妻之间唯一的身体接触。然而，现在的社交活动就只可能以接吻开始或结束，要么亲一边脸颊，要么两边脸颊都亲，要么握手和亲一边脸颊，或者每边脸颊都亲两下，或者“吮哇”一声，给人一个飞吻。最近，我甚至亲眼目睹某人在结束商业午餐时，亲吻一位女客户的手，很明显，被吻的客户对此极度厌恶，看上去就像肾结石发作那样痛苦不堪。

的确，唯一的确定性就是不存在确定性。如果我最近观察到的是需要遵守的事，无论人们身处何地，在关键时刻都会踌躇不前，优柔寡断地摇头，本打算亲脸颊的却亲在鼻子、嘴巴或者耳朵上了，人们无法判断，此时给出的亲吻是看起来开心还是出于自我防卫的发泄。

everywhere are floundering[1] in around, jerking their heads indecisively, delivering a kiss meant for a cheek to the nose and/or mouth and/or ear and, when the kiss is planted, are unable to decide whether to look pleased or lash out[2] in self-defense.

The confusion extends to the highest levels-President George W. Bush attracting derision when he planted smackers on his two female cabinet nominees. Condoleezza Rice was given two kisses on the cheek when Mr. Bush introduced her at the White House as the secretary of state, while Margaret Spellings, the new education secretary, was congratulated rather bizarrely with a peck on a corner of the lips when she was presented the next day.

Some may attribute the increase in, and confusion over, social kissing to factors other than globalization: the rising influence of the media industry, for instance, where air-kissing is the norm, or the emotionalizing of business. Nowadays it's not good enough just to be in business-we have to show passion, too. Meanwhile, I have just read a piece that put the blame for the arrival of "the corporate kiss" firmly at the stiletto-clad feet of the increasing number of women in the workplace.

However, I think globalization is a more significant factor. I have two reasons: my most awkward social kisses have been with people from different countries and research conducted by Vaughn Bryant, an

---

① flounder [ˈflaundə] *vi.* 挣扎

② lash out 猛击

乔治·W. 布什总统亲吻他的两位女性内阁成员时就闹过笑话，让这种困惑达到顶峰。布什先生在白宫任命康多莉扎·赖斯为美国国务卿时，在她脸上亲了两口；令人相当诧异的是，新任教育部长玛格丽特·史裴琳在第二天上任时，布什只是在她的嘴角匆匆一吻，以示祝贺。

有些人可能会将不断增多和日趋混乱的社交接吻归结于全球化之外的因素。例如，司空见惯的飞吻或商业的感情色彩使传媒业的影响力持续上升。现如今，单单是做买卖已经远远不够，我们还得表现出激情。同时，我刚读过一篇文章，它毫不犹豫地把“企业接吻”的出现归咎于越来越多的职场女性穿细高跟鞋这一因素。

然而，我认为全球化是一个更加重要的因素。最令我尴尬的社交接吻是和来自不同国家的人打交道，得克萨斯州农工大学的人类学教授沃恩·科比的研究表明，从本质上说，接吻的冲动是一种文化现象，而不是明显的女性行为或任何其他显而易见的事情。在一些国家，即使是夫妻之间的亲吻也不被认可。

考虑到我们中的许多人目前在工作中面临着多国文化的交集，令人吃惊的是，这种混乱显得并不那么严重。几乎不可能了解谁期望得到什么。在诺曼底，标准是亲吻四下（每边脸颊亲两下）；其他的欧洲国家亲三下（右边、左边、右边）。有人告诉我，在俄罗斯的部分地区，接吻的次数超过六次，而在其他地区，据说男人毫无顾忌地相互亲吻嘴唇。另一方面，日本人和中国人对噘起嘴唇接吻表现十分冷淡。

那么，该做些什么呢？商务礼仪专家的共识似乎是不主张接吻。不过我发现这很难做到绝对化。我在英国西米德兰地区长

anthropology professor at Texas A&M University, suggests that the urge to snog is essentially a cultural one rather than something distinctly feminine or distinctly anything else. In some countries it is considered a no-no even between couples.

Given how many national cultures many of us now cross at work, it's surprising the confusion isn't even more crippling. It's almost impossible to keep track of what is expected by whom. In Normandy the norm is four kisses (two on each side). Other continentals kiss three times (right, left, right). In parts of Russia, I am told, the number of kisses can exceed six, while in other parts men apparently have no problem kissing each other on the lips. On the other hand, the Japanese and Chinese aren't keen on puckering up at all.

So what is to be done? Well, the consensus among experts in business etiquette seems to be: don't kiss. However, I find it hard to be so definite. Having been raised by Punjabis-not the world's most enthusiastic snoggers-in the West Midlands, where any physical contact that doesn't cause bleeding or bruising is considered unnecessary, a large part of me thinks a hello and a handshake between colleagues is more than enough. At the same time, the Punjabi in me, while not keen kissers, they are extremely fond of the suffocating① bear hug, combined with my profession, I have been to dinner parties in London Media land where even the male host has kissed me goodbye, and a certain amount of neediness makes me think

---

① suffocating [ˈsʌfəkeitiŋ] *adj*. 令人窒息的

大，父母是印度旁遮普人，他们不是世界上最热衷接吻的人。在西米德兰，任何不导致流血和鼻青脸肿的身体接触都被认为是没有必要的，我在很大程度上认为，同事之间一般的问候和握手已经足够了。同时，我作为旁遮普人，虽然不热衷亲吻，却极其喜欢令人窒息的熊抱；我作为职业人，常常出席伦敦传媒界的晚宴，连男主人也会与我吻别。某种程度上的需要使我认识到，用身体表达爱意没什么不妥。

经过长时间的考虑之后，我已经得出了结论，即同事之间的社交接吻是没问题的。事实是，接吻使我们很容易感受到同事之间真诚的热情，晚宴之后的接吻能表达彼此间的相互尊重。它表示：嘿，我们是伙伴，并不是百分之百的生意关系。但是，考虑到只有法国人才可能用任何形式的高贵完成社交接吻，我们应该记住一些规则，保证短暂的“吼哇”接吻不会变成长时间的“吼吼吼吼吼吼吼哇哇哇哇哇哇哇”式接吻。

第一，跳舞时为了尽可能减少尴尬、惹官司和头部碰撞，男士应当谨慎地让女士率先主动接吻。第二，如果你被接吻惊吓，尽量不要使自己看起来像是被蛇咬伤的受害者而突发疾病，毕竟，除了感染病毒性脑膜炎之外，还有什么更糟的事呢？第三，永远不要用舌头。第四，每天进出办公室时亲吻同事是过度骚扰。你会什么活儿也干不了。第五，问候时不要亲吻他人的手：在简·奥斯汀那个时代，人们会认为你是一个绅士，但是在当下，人们会别出心裁地认为你是一个彻头彻尾的怪人。

there's nothing wrong with physical displays of affection.

After lengthy consideration, I have concluded that the social kissing of colleagues is OK. The fact is that it is quite possible to feel genuine fondness for the people we work with and a kiss at the end of a dinner party can be an expression of mutual respect. It means: hey, we're mates; this isn't 100 per cent business. But given that only the French can pull off the social kiss with any sort of dignity, it is worth remembering a few rules to make sure "mwah" doesn't turn into "mwwwwwww aaaaaaa rrrrrr rrrggggh".

First, as with dancing, to minimize the risk of embarrassment, lawsuits and the clashing of heads, it is prudent① for the man to allow the lady to lead in kissing. Second, if you are surprised by a kiss, try not to look like a snakebite victim having a seizure-after all, apart from contracting bacterial meningitis, what's the worst that can happen? Third, no tongues: ever. Fourth, kissing colleagues when you enter and leave the office every day is excessive. You'll never get any work done. And finally, never ever kiss someone's hand in greeting: it may have classed you as a gentleman in Jane Austen's time, but today it will only single you out as a total and utter weirdo.

(925 words)

---

① prudent [ˈpruːdnt] *adj*. 审慎的

知识链接

Call center 呼叫中心。呼叫中心是在一个相对集中的场所，由一批服务人员组成的服务机构，通常利用计算机通信技术，处理来自企业、顾客的电话垂询，尤其具备同时处理大量来电的能力，还具备主叫号码显示，可将来电自动分配给具备相应技能的人员处理，并能记录和储存所有来电信息。一个典型的以客户服务为主的呼叫中心可以兼具呼入与呼出功能，当处理顾客的信息查询、咨询、投诉等业务的同时，可以进行顾客回访、满意度调查等呼出业务。

题 记

客户往往通过电话的方式留下对商家的第一印象，所以，电话在某种意义上是企业通向成功的生命线。无论企业在通往成功的道路上会遇到什么样的起伏跌宕，电话都会从不同的角度讲述不一样的故事：电话系统需要实时更新，保持这条生命线的完全开放；电话呼叫过程中的占线信号或忙音将可能导致客户的流失；任何时候都不要给客户留下他打扰了你或你急于挂断电话的印象；所有的电话都要在接收的当天回复；一定要让员工明白他们能做什么和不能做什么；把手机当做销售工具；确保微型企业的电话服务和电话礼仪。电话的使用极大地改变了企业的销售方式，它使企业的生命绚丽多彩，充满探索的欲望和好奇的动力，朝着通向成功的道路展开并延伸。

A Lifeline to Success

The first impression you leave with customers is often delivered over the phone, so make sure it's positive.

In any small business the telephone is a lifeline to success. Yet, for many small equipment rental businesses, the telephone is seen as a nuisance. It seems to ring at all the wrong times, and the incoming calls interrupt important work that "needs to be done." Or do they?

The truth is that most of your sales originate from a telephone call. Calls can be distracting, but without them you would be out of business. So, let's consider ways to use the telephone to your advantage. Follow these suggestions and you should see tangible benefits in your rental business.

Keep your telephone system up to date

Have you ever called a business and gotten a busy signal? Or maybe you've had the phone ring 15 times before it's answered. Is this happening in your shop? If it is, it's time for a new phone system. In keeping with the "your telephone is your lifeline" theory, it's vitally important that you keep that lifeline completely open. It will not be nearly as valuable if your phone system is out of date and can no longer handle the volume of calls coming in. Here are a few pointers regarding what your telephone system should and should not include:

通向成功的生命线

客户往往通过电话的方式留下对你的第一印象，所以，电话一定要传递正能量。

在任何小型企业里，电话都是通向成功的生命线。 然而，对于许多小型设备租赁企业，电话被看做一种骚扰。 它似乎总是在不恰当的时候响了起来，来电打断了“需要做的”重要工作，不是吗?

事实上，你的大部分销售来自电话。 虽然电话铃声分散了人们的注意力，但没有电话，你就没有生意可做。 所以，让我们考虑一下使用电话的方式，如何做到对你有利。 遵从下面的建议，你应该看到租赁电话可以给你带来实实在在的好处。

实时更新电话系统

你有没有遇到过打电话给公司时电话占线的情况? 或者是你在电话铃声响了 15 分钟之后才接电话。 这种事在你的店里发生过吗? 如果是这样，该是换一个新的电话系统的时候了。 为了符合“你的电话是你的生命线”这一理论，保持这条生命线完全开放是至关重要的。 如果你的电话系统已经过时，不再能够接通打进来的电话，那就相当于已经失去了价值。 以下是电话系统应该和不应该包括的几点：

* 如果可能的话，商店的每个人（包括销售人员和行政人员）

* Everybody in your shop (including salespeople and administrative employees) should have his/her own phone line if possible. If this is not feasible, at least install a system with multiple lines.

* Make sure you install a system that ensures no busy signals.

* Do not buy call waiting. You won't score any points with customers if you interrupt their call to take another one.

* Do not share telephone, fax and/or computer modem lines. You might save a few dollars by having only one telephone line, but the loss in productivity from performing only one function at a time will cost you dearly.

* Consider other options such as Caller ID, Voice Mail, Pager, Conference Calling, etc. based on the needs of your rental business.

* Don't let the cost deter you. Most phone systems can be leased with little or no money down. The monthly payment might seem daunting, but a good telephone system will more than pay for itself.

First impressions are critical

Many calls that come into your shop are from people you don't know at all or with whom you have infrequent contact. So, the first impression of the caller is critical. It's recommended that you have a central line that is answered by a salesperson or clerk first. Most people like to at least have the option of talking with a human.

If the designated person who answers the telephone is already on the phone or out, it is best to have the call automatically roll to another line. If this isn't possible because everyone is busy inside the shop, have a cordial message programmed into the system to automatically answer the call and explain that no one is available to take the call but that it will be returned

都应该有他/她自己的电话线。如果做不到这一点，至少安装一个多线电话系统。

* 务必安装一个没有忙音的电话系统。

* 不要购买呼叫等待。如果你中断客户的电话去接另外一个电话，你不会从他们那里获得好感。

* 切勿与人共用电话、传真和/或计算机的调制解调器线路。如果只有一条电话线路，你可能会节省几美元，但一次只有一个电话工作给交易带来的损失将会让你付出沉重的代价。

* 根据租赁业务的需求，考虑其他的选择，如来电显示、语音邮件、寻呼机以及电话会议等。

* 不要受成本的遏制。可以交很少或根本不用交预付费就可以租用大多数电话系统。月付费的方式似乎令人望而生畏，但良好的电话系统带来的收益远远高于付费本身。

第一印象至关重要

打到你店铺的许多电话来自你不认识的人或是很少与你联系的人，因此，访客留下的第一印象至关重要。建议你优先使用销售员或办事员回电的中央线路。大多数人至少愿意选择与人交谈。

如果指定的外接电话人已经在通话或外出，最好是将电话自动转接到另外的线路上。如果因为店里的每个人都很忙，这也行不通的话，可以编制一个语言亲切的信息程序，然后接入自动接听电话系统，向对方解释说没有人可以接听这个电话，但如果他们留下信息，就会迅速得到回复。如前所述，此时此刻电话呼叫过程中的占线信号或忙音将可能意味着客户流失，特别是设备租赁企业的紧急电话。

promptly if they will leave a message. As previously mentioned, a busy signal or no answer at this point in the telephone call process will likely mean a lost sale, particularly given the often urgent nature of calls in the equipment rental business.

Is the person who usually answers your phone pleasant? Try this. The next few times you call into your shop, pay close attention to the tone of voice and actual greeting used by the person answering. You might also want to check with some clients that you know well and ask them what they think of your telephone response system. They are likely to provide frank input as to whether the first impression left with your clients is positive or negative.

Be direct and honest

So, your assistant has routed a call to you or you're returning a voice mail message. What happens next? Well, if you aren't careful, you really can blow it. No matter how busy you might be, do not ever give the client the impression that he has interrupted you or that you are in a hurry to get off the phone. Be polite. Find out from the customer exactly what is needed in terms of equipment rental. Ask any questions that are pertinent and then give the customer the opportunity to ask you any questions. When it comes time to discuss the fee and availability of the equipment to be rented, try to under-promise and over-deliver. Following the opposite credo has tarnished① the reputation of many a rental equipment business.

Follow the sundown rule

This one is simple, but might be the most important one on the list.

---

① tarnish[ˈtɑːniʃ] *vt.* 败坏；玷污

接你电话的人通常感到愉快吗？尝试一下。你接下来可以打几次电话到你的商店，密切关注接电话的人使用的语调和实际问候。你可能还想要检查你非常熟悉的一些客户，征求他们对电话应答系统的看法。他们可能会坦率地告诉你，客户得到的第一印象是积极的还是消极的。

直截了当且诚实待人

因此，要么是你的助理给你打电话，要么是你自己用语音邮件回复资讯。接下来会发生什么？好吧，如果你不小心的话，真有可能把事情搞砸。无论你多么忙，任何时候都不要给客户留下他打扰了你或你急于挂断电话的印象。一定要有礼貌。根据设备租赁条款，查明客户到底需要什么。询问任何相关的问题，然后给客户留下向你提问的机会。讨论收费和有可能租用设备时，设法留有余地，然后出色完成公司的承诺。违背诚信已经损害了许多设备租赁公司的声誉。

遵循日落规则

这是个简单的问题，但可能是清单上最重要的问题。无论用什么系统收集电话信息，都应该竭尽全力（如果需要的话，带有点强迫性）迅速回复所有的电话。事实上，只要可能，任何时候都应该遵守日落原则。简言之，日落规则意味着所有的电话都要在接收的当天回复。虽然下午5点后的电话不太可能及时接听，也应该在当天尽可能回复打进来的电话。

培训员工

重要的是让员工了解下面两点：良好的电话礼仪是必不可少的；你究竟希望他们在电话里说什么。如果你已经有一份编辑好的

No matter what system you use to gather phone messages, you should be committed (a little bit obsessive if need be!) to returning all telephone calls promptly. In fact, the Sundown Rule should be followed whenever possible. The Sundown Rule simply means that all telephone calls are returned the same day on which they are received. While you might not get to the ones that come in after 5:00 p.m., you should be able to return most calls on the same day they are received.

Train your employees

It's important to let your employees know that good telephone manners are essential; and what exactly you expect them to say on the phone. If you have a scripted greeting that you would like to see used, share it with the appropriate employees. Likewise, make sure you have a plan for handling call transfers, message taking (if you have ever been given a message with a wrong return number, you know how important this is!), voice mail messages, etc. It's also important to let employees know what they are not to say on the phone. You may not want some employees quoting rental rates or availability. So, make sure all employees are aware of what they can and cannot discuss. Along the same lines of training employees, make sure you pay close attention to an applicant's potential telephone voice in making hiring decisions.

The cellular phone as a sales tool

Unless your name is Rip Van Winkle, you undoubtedly own a cellular phone or several by now. But have you checked with your cellular provider lately to see about updating your service? Many of the new services out there will help you increase your revenues by making you and your

问候稿，希望员工们能够使用，不妨与合适的员工分享。同样，一定要有计划地处理呼叫转移、信息接收（如果你收到过错误的返回号码信息，你就会知道这是多么重要！）以及语音邮件等。让员工了解他们在电话里不能说什么也是很重要的。你可能不希望员工说出租金率或可利用率。因此，一定要让所有的员工都明白，他们能讨论什么、不能讨论什么。在做租赁决定时，同样要考虑培训员工的理念，一定要密切关注申请人的潜在电话语音。

把手机当做销售工具

如果你的名字不是瑞普·凡·温克尔，毫无疑问，你到现在为止已经拥有一部或几部手机。但是，最近你是否与手机供应商核实过、考虑更新手机服务了呢？他们那儿有许多新的服务，能使你和你的员工更容易获得信息，从而帮助你提高收入。这些服务中的一部分包括欺诈防护、同一线路上的多部手机、步话机容量、寻呼、语音信箱、呼叫转移、无应答转移、数字服务和电话会议。还有一些改进过的硬件选项，它们使手机用起来更容易和更安全。带耳机和扬声器的手机现在也有售，它们使开车交谈更加安全。有关手机使用的其他建议包括：你所在地区的不同供应商的询价购物，外出时在语音邮件信息中提供你的手机号码，开车时始终保持手机畅通，以及确保你选择的手机服务从地理上涵盖整个服务区。

对微型企业的特殊要求

当然，有些设备租赁企业非常小，只雇用 5 名或 5 名以下的员工。就电话服务和礼仪而言，这带来了一系列完全不同的挑战。对微型设备租赁企业的老板来说，使用电话时要注意如下关键事项：

employees more accessible. Some of these services include fraud protection, multiple phones on the same line, walkie-talkie capability, paging, voice mail, call forwarding, no-answer transfer, digital service and conference calling. There also are improved hardware options that make cell phones easier and safer to use. Headsets and speaker cell phones are now sold that make talking in a vehicle much safer. Other suggestions regarding cell phone usage include price shopping different providers in your area, providing your cell phone number in your voice mail message when you're out, always keeping the cell phone on when you're in the car, and making sure the cell phone service you choose covers your whole geographical service area.

Special considerations for micro-sized businesses

Of course, some equipment rental businesses are very small and employ five or fewer employees. This presents a whole different set of challenges in terms of telephone service and etiquette. Here are some key considerations regarding telephone usage for the owner of a micro-sized equipment rental business:

* Separate telephone lines for phone, fax and computer are essential.

* Use voice mail or multiple lines, not an answering machine or an answering service. If you have an answering machine, throw it out immediately and replace it with voice mail!

* Make sure your outgoing voice message is kept very current to ensure the caller knows exactly when to expect a call back. Check your voice mail frequently to avoid lost sales.

* Look into other services, such as call forwarding, for your store phone and your cell phone, as well as voice mail for your cell phone and

* 有必要将电话、传真和电脑的电话线路分开。

* 使用语音邮件或复式电话线，不要用电话答录机或电话应答服务。如果你用的是电话答录机，立即把它扔掉，代之以语音邮件。

* 一定要实时更新外出留言信息，确保来电者准确了解何时可以等到回电。经常检查语音邮件，以避免销售损失。

* 查找其他服务，如为你的商店电话和手机服务提供的呼叫转移，以及为你的手机和传呼机服务的语音信箱。

* 确认你的电话系统可以处理占线时的来电或长时间未接的来电。

* 如果你拥有家庭企业，确保你的办公室与其余的房子分开。孩子们的尖叫声或狗叫声不会为客户营造良好的电话交谈背景。

有信心让你的电话系统和礼仪像本应该的那样既对客户友好又具有高效吗？如果不是，尝试使用这里提到的一些建议。如果你做到这些，你会发现设备租赁企业的销售额不断增加，并且发展得更好。

知识链接

VOIP 网络电话(Voice over Internet Phone)。网络电话是基于VoIP技术的语音通信软件，它与语音交换服务器、电话网关和接点交换服务器构成完整的语音通信平台。

Rip Van Winkle 瑞普·凡·温克尔。瑞普·凡·温克尔是美国作家华盛顿·欧文(Washington Irving，1783—1859)创作的著名短篇小说《瑞普·

beeper[①] service.

* Make sure your telephone system can handle the incoming call traffic with no busy signals or long unanswered rings.

* If you have a home business, make sure your office is separate from the rest of the house. Kids yelling or dogs barking will not make a good backdrop[②] for telephone conversations with clients.

Are you confident that your telephone system and etiquette are as client-friendly and as efficient as they should be? If not, try implementing some of the recommendations covered here. If you do, you are likely to see an increase in sales and a better bottom line in your equipment rental business.

(1,464 words)

① beeper [ˈbiːpə] *n.* 携带型的无线传呼机

② backdrop [ˈbækdrɔp] *n.* 背景

凡·温克尔》中的主人公。小说的背景是荷兰殖民地时期的美国乡村。瑞普为人热心，靠耕种一小块贫瘠的土地养家糊口。有一天，他为了躲避唠叨凶悍的妻子，独自到附近的赫德森河畔兹吉尔山上去打猎。他遇到了赫德森船长及其伙伴，在喝了他们的仙酒后，就睡了一觉。醒后下山回家，才发现时间已过了整整 20 年，人世沧桑，一切都十分陌生。瑞普终于知道，他现在已由英王的臣民变为“合众国的一个自由的公民”。欧文用轻快、幽默和带有浪漫色彩的笔调把朴实敦厚、知足常乐的民风展示给读者，含蓄地讽刺了殖民地时期的陈规陋习和唯利是图的商业气氛。